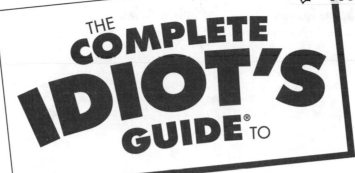

THE COMPLETE **IDIOT'S** GUIDE® TO

The Politics of Oil

by Lita Epstein, C.D. Jaco, and Julianne C. Iwersen-Niemann

ALPHA

A member of Penguin Group (USA) Inc.

Most Alpha books are available at special quantity discounts for bulk purchases for sales promotions, premiums, fund-raising, or educational use. Special books, or book excerpts, can also be created to fit specific needs.

For details, write: Special Markets, Alpha Books, 375 Hudson Street, New York, NY 10014.

Publisher: *Marie Butler-Knight*
Product Manager: *Phil Kitchel*
Senior Managing Editor: *Jennifer Chisholm*
Acquisitions Editor: *Gary Goldstein*
Development Editor: *Jennifer Moore*
Production Editors: *Megan Douglass, Billy Fields*
Copy Editor: *Jan Zoya*
Illustrator: *Jody Schaeffer*
Cover/Book Designer: *Trina Wurst*
Indexer: *Tonya Heard*
Layout/Proofreading: *Becky Harmon, Mary Hunt*

Contents at a Glance

Contents

Foreword

Like the Tin Woodsman in the *Wizard of Oz*, we need oil to move. Without it, we are as helpless as he was after a rainstorm. For those of us who experienced the energy crisis of the mid-1970s,

han we did then. And second, the real price of oil has actually declined to a point where it is almost the same price it was *before* the oil price shocks of the 1970s.

Today, that means wars in oil-rich regions in defense of vital U.S. interests. It's not really a matter of debate that the American way of life, and by extension, American security, rests on the free flow of oil from the rest of the world to the United States.

We live in a free-market economy. Higher prices prompt substitutes. In this case, higher oil prices should encourage efficiency and development of alternative energy resources, over the long term. So, in order to discourage that quest for efficiency and alternatives, the oil industry (producers, refiners, and retailers) has succeeded in moving the real price of oil to levels where conservation is economically illogical, and alternative energy sources are simply not cost competitive.

In a free market economy, conservation and increased efficiency follow higher fuel prices. The more expensive the gasoline, the more we focus on fuel efficiency. In the late 1970s and early 1980s, in the wake of that energy crisis, automobile marketers constantly extolled the miles per gallon (MPG) their cars could deliver. Today, almost no automobile marketing campaign focuses on fuel efficiency. Certainly not those campaigns that tout the virtues of SUVs, luxury sedans, and even the new Beetles. MPG simply doesn't sell today. Why? Because gas is cheap. To be sure, the price of gas seems higher lately, but real gas prices are still hovering around pre-energy crisis levels. Only when those real prices begin to climb will we start caring about MPG again. Until then, lifestyle and safety rule the auto marketing world.

And in case you were wondering, long-term low prices don't stop the oil industry from recording record profits in the short-run. Price spikes generate huge profit windfalls for the energy companies. Of course, these spikes eventually settle back to a lower level.

The debate over the politics of oil often devolves into a more hysterical discussion of "Big Oil" and its cozy relationship with the U.S. Government (indeed, with many governments). From the Teapot Dome scandal to the current Bush Administration's open ties to energy companies, we are wary of oil's ties to our leadership. There is no doubt that the oil lobby has quite effectively wielded its resources to optimal effect, in both the Executive and Legislative branches of the U.S. Government. However, this practice is certainly not limited to the energy lobby. It is fair to say that lobbying is an integral (if apparently distasteful) element in our way of governing.

Similarly, the practice of controlling (or at least encouraging) energy prices for long-term discouragement of alternative energy sources seems unfair, but is in fact a testament to the capitalist system in which we live. Pricing in energy may be manipulated, but it cannot be totally controlled. Good old-fashioned greed will ensure that over time energy prices will respond to the laws of supply and demand.

More intriguing is the eventuality that some day the lobbyists and oil industry will not be able to maintain that long-term price structure for oil. Supplies someday may become restricted to the point where prices will have to rise to the level where alternatives become cost effective. In fact, experts predict that oil production will peak in 2010 (it has already peaked in the United States, and is declining). One wonders what will become of the big oil companies then.

In many technology shifts of the past, dominant producers of the current technology didn't make the transformation to producing the new one. Only one carriage maker (Studebaker) made the transition to manufacturing automobiles. No vacuum tube makers made the transition to producing integrated circuits. The challenge facing the oil industry is no less acute. Optimizing on the efficient production, refining, distribution, and retailing of oil in order to satisfy current stakeholders may doom "Big Oil" from shifting into fuel cell technology, or whatever other technologies may spring from our eternal inventiveness.

If the economic impetus for developing alternative energy remains weak, given the low long-term price of oil, governments must create a regulatory impetus for developing these alternative sources. The tools are taxes, rebates, incentives, and rewards. Blunt tools, to be sure, but effective over the long-term that we are considering.

The challenge is how do governments accelerate the process of transition from non-renewable to renewable energy sources? The current oil lobby is effectively limiting governmental programs that would provide this artificial stimulus to develop alternative energy. The interplay of money and lobbying with presidents, cabinet secretaries, senators, and members of congress is the prime determinant of how soon and how effectively governmental programs can stimulate alternative energy sources.

One of the hurdles we face in our market-driven democracy is that we are not always presented with complete or even accurate information about oil, and the politics surrounding it. Becoming informed is the first step to becoming aware. At that point, the options are ours to determine how to deal with the future politics of oil. The challenges are two-fold: getting the right information, and then making sense of it. The authors of this book have helped us in these essential areas of information acquisition and understanding. In doing so, they have provided us a comprehensive, easy-to-understand resource. The politics of oil and its players are not welcoming to the common citizen, but this guide opens the door for our understanding this complex, yet vital issue.

—Joseph Tragert
Ipswich, Massachusetts
August 2003

Joseph Tragert is the author of *The Complete Idiot's Guide to Understanding Iraq* and *The Complete Idiot's Guide to Understanding Iran*. He is also co-author of *The Complete Idiot's Guide to Understanding North Korea*.

Introduction

Each day when you start your car, you probably *don't* think about what you would do if there wasn't enough easily attainable gas to keep it going. However, those of us who lived through the long gas lines during the 1973 oil crisis—when OPEC shut off the oil spigot—know how quickly oil scarcity can shatter our well-ordered lives.

And a severe oil shortage would have a far greater impact than long lines at the gas pumps. That's because in the past 100 years, petroleum or petroleum-based products have found their way into most of our kitchen products, our medicines and medical equipment, and a good deal of our consumer goods—essentially, if it's made out of plastic, it's made with oil. Oil also fuels our industry, and without it many of the products we buy would not be available today.

With its all-encompassing role in society, the oil industry has been able to use its power to control many of our political processes. Of course, they've paid for the privilege with corporate campaign contributions and even bribery in some countries.

In this book, we explain how oil has become one of the world's most important resources, point out what industry insiders have done to keep it that way, and consider whether oil will always be around to feed the world's addiction.

The Drama of Oil, in Five Parts

The story of oil is one of high drama. It is filled with intrigue, politics, money, ingenuity, greed, competition, and yes, even blood. We break that story down into five bloody parts, as follows:

Part 1, "Discovering the World's Blood: Oil's Early Years," recounts oil's more innocent days. For, although it's now hard to believe, there was a time when oil was considered more of a nuisance than a commodity—simply stinky black crud oozing from the ground. It didn't take people long to recognize the value of oil, however; soon enough, clever folks were building simple devices to pump oil from the ground and putting together crude pipelines to transport it. Even after the discovery that kerosene provided a relatively clean-burning source of light, oil didn't really provoke much controversy. These chapters tell the story of those early, more innocent times.

It wouldn't be long before those innocent days were gone for good. **Part 2, "Keeping the Blood Flowing: Petroleum Goes Global,"** recounts how the industry that grew up around oil developed into a powerful force that controls much of the world's machinery, heats our homes, and fuels our cars. And when any industry has a stranglehold on such a valuable commodity, you can bet that industry does whatever it takes to keep things just the way they are—just like John D. Rockefeller's Standard Oil Company did.

The actions that the oil industry will take to keep the oil flowing fast and furious is nothing compared to what national governments will do. **Part 3, "Bloody Wars: Fighting for Fuel,"** looks at the wars that have, at least in part, been fought to control access to oil. From World War I to the so-called War on Terror, don't be surprised to find oil as a spoil of war.

Part 4, "Clogging the Bloodlines: Policy, Politics, and Greed," takes the story of oil to Washington, D.C., to see how oil politics play out in our nation's capitol. It is in the White House and the halls of Congress that our nation's energy policy is set, and that policy has a tremendous impact on our economy and our environment. Many people question whether policymakers have Americans' best interests in mind when they set energy policy, or whether they are simply looking out for oil industry bigwigs, whose lobbyists dangle money in front of politicians' noses at every opportunity.

Part 5, "Looking to a Bloody Future," explores questions on everyone's minds, such as "Will our children and their children have enough oil to meet their needs and desires?" and "Is oil the cause global warming?" We'll explore critical issues facing the future of oil and look at the potential of energy alternatives.

Helpers

We've designed a few aides to guide you more easily through this book:

Petro-Facts

Facts and figures aren't everyone's favorite reading material. We've placed these helpers around the book for folks who like to read more about the details.

Drill Bits

The oil industry has a language of its own. We help traverse that geologic landscape with definitions of key words you might not use everyday.

Slick Sayings

It seems that everyone likes to talk about oil, and some of that talk can be pretty slippery. We've picked a few of the best quotes to help you better understand the issues.

Petroleum People

Wildcatters, oil men, politicians, and industry executives have all made critical contributions to the formation of today's huge oil industry. We've picked out a few of the more interesting players to give you a bit of background about them.

Acknowledgments

We'd liked to thank Jennifer Moore, whose talented editing really helped to make this book come alive. Without her dedication, the story of oil would not have been told as clearly or dramatically. We'd also like to thank Gary Goldstein for his efforts in getting this book on the shelves. Also, special thanks to Billy Fields and Megan Douglass, who kept the book moving through the production process, and to Jan Zoya, who helped to smooth out the rough spots.

Trademarks

All terms mentioned in this book that are known to be or are suspected of being trademarks or service marks have been appropriately capitalized. Alpha Books and Penguin Group (USA) Inc. cannot attest to the accuracy of this information. Use of a term in this book should not be regarded as affecting the validity of any trademark or service mark.

Part 1

Discovering the World's Blood: Oil's Early Years

From dinosaurs to flame throwers to wildcatters to oil gushers—the story of oil has never been boring. The following chapters trace the flow of oil back to its geological origins as decaying matter. They then move on to consider the first early uses of the black stuff that people found oozing out of the ground. Things start picking up pace at this point, as ingenious individuals started putting oil to use as pitch for their boats, fuel for their torches, and ammunition for their weapons.

Once oil started taking on value as a commodity, it wasn't long before the capitalists came on the scene to sell a product and turn a profit. The world would never be the same after that.

From Nuisance to World's Prized Commodity

In This Chapter

- ◆ How oil has shaped the modern world
- ◆ Cooperation and conflict among petroleum producers and consumers
- ◆ Where resource wars are likely to erupt
- ◆ Environmental consequences of oil

The twentieth century began the age of oil. Until around 100 years ago, petroleum had been a curiosity or a nuisance, oozing from the ground, creating what we call sinkholes. Throughout human history people have tried to find a use for the black crud. They slapped it on ships' hulls as pitch to make them waterproof, and squirted it in chariots' wheels to grease the axles. Even after the first modern oil well was sunk in 1859, petroleum was primarily valued for the distilled kerosene that replaced whale oil in the world's lamps.

Things turned around for oil in the 1890s, when engineers and tinkerers in the United States, France, and Germany almost simultaneously developed small internal combustion engines to power two and four-wheeled vehicles. In just 15 years, there were hundreds of thousands of automobiles and trucks in the United States, all of them powered by the black crud. It was a seismic technological shift that transformed the world.

In the twenty-first century, oil remains the most important commodity in the world. Without oil, industrial and technological society as we know it would not exist. Unfortunately, it is also responsible for death, war, political turmoil, and environmental damage. During the first Persian Gulf war, the world watched as flames engulfed hundreds of oil fields, having been set by Saddam Hussein's Iraqi troops as they retreated from Kuwait in 1991. In March 2003, Saddam Hussein again took center stage as the United States declared war on Iraq after 12 years of attempts by the United Nations to disarm Hussein. Although politicians and military strategists deny it, many people believe that oil is the primary reasons these wars were fought.

The Politics of Oil

Despite advances in computer and other "high" technology, oil remains the spine of modern life. Petroleum products power jets, cars, ships, and trucks, and are used to manufacture everything from furniture and telephones to computers and highways. Oil drives the modern industrial economy and will continue to do so for the foreseeable future, so exploring for oil, pumping oil, transporting oil, and using oil form the basis of many international political arrangements.

In terms of human history, this has happened overnight. Until the 1920s, for example, Kuwait was an oil consumer rather than an oil producer, importing American kerosene to light its lamps and American gasoline to power the few automobiles in the region.

Slick Sayings

Postwar development relied on cheap and abundant oil, kept that way largely by threat or use of force.

—Linguist and political activist Noam Chomsky, 1996

The world has been driven by the politics of oil for less than a century. Only since the start of World War II has it become the centerpiece of international policy.

Since oil is substitutable—that is, it crosses national borders with impunity and, with slight chemical variations, is the same in Indiana as it is in Indonesia—it's valuable anywhere it's found, as long as it can be transported to the industrial nations that need it.

For the rest of this century, the politics of oil will take several forms, including the following:

- ◆ Increased complaints from developing nations that they're being exploited to satisfy the oil needs of rich countries.

- ◆ Increased and more expensive efforts to explore for oil in both mature locations (the Middle East, the United States, Venezuela) and in previously unexplored or under-explored regions (West Africa, Russia, the Caspian Sea region, the Arctic).

- ◆ Increased concern about how the rise of Islamic radicalism might threaten Middle and Far-East oil supplies.

- ◆ Increased use of military force and economic leverage by the world's industrial powers to guarantee the continued flow of oil.

- ◆ Increased political battles between environmentalists and conservationists worried about pollution and political instability, and conservatives and pro-business groups worried about the continued flow of oil.

Will all this just be temporary and end when the world runs out of oil in the not-too-distant future? Despite popular wisdom, the answer is "no." A couple of examples illustrate why. By the end of the twenty-first century, oil reserves, at least oil reserves that can be explored at a reasonably low cost, will have largely been exhausted in Saudi Arabia. Offshore oil in West Africa and inland oil in the Caspian Sea region have barely been exploited.

It costs a good deal more money to drill in the Caspian mountains or the African seabed than it does to sink a well in the desert sands, so oil from these locations will probably, on average, cost more than oil drilled in Middle East desert sands today. Industrialized nations cut per capita energy use and have raised fuel conservation standards remarkably in the last two decades of the twentieth century. In addition, the low birth rates in industrialized Western Europe means that the number of people there will shrink, not expand, in the twenty-first century.

But the population of North America is growing robustly and will continue to grow. As China and India grow in technological prowess, their machines and the huge populations who operate them will need more and more energy.

Nobody doubts that one day, perhaps by the end of the twenty-second century, almost all fossil fuel reserves will have been sucked or gouged from the earth. By then, other fuels—hydrogen? Ethanol? Something currently unknown?—will have taken oil's place. Or maybe the power of the sun will be harnessed economically. Most likely, the world will have a combination of many energy alternatives.

But for the next dozen decades or so, oil will remain the fuel that fires many of the planet's worries. The fault lines will generally, but not exclusively, continue to split the world into two camps: the oil producers and the oil consumers.

The Oil Producers

The United States is the world's second largest oil producer. If the USSR still existed, it would top the list, but since the former Soviet Union split into numerous countries in the 1990s, Saudi Arabia has taken over the number-one spot. Here's a list of the world's leading oil producers in metric tons per year, ranked at the start of 2002 by the International Energy Agency:

World's Leading Oil Producers, 2002

Country	Metric Tons
Saudi Arabia	421
United States	354
Russia	347
Iran	186
Mexico	179
Venezuela	173
China	166
Norway	162
Canada	125
United Kingdom	118

Compare the list of the world's leading producers with the Agency's list of leading oil exporters from the same period, also expressed in metric tons of oil per year:

World's Leading Oil Exporters, 2002

Country	Metric Tons
Saudi Arabia	320
Norway	146
Russia	144
Iran	116
Venezuela	115

Country	Metric Tons
Nigeria	107
Iraq	102
United Kingdom	93
Mexico	92
United Arab Emirates	84

The difference is that in addition to *potentially* unstable countries like Russia, Iran, and Venezuela appearing in the first list, *actually* unstable countries like Iraq, Nigeria, and the United Arab Emirates show up in the second list. In fact, of all the nations on these lists, only the United States, Norway, the United Kingdom, Canada, and to a lesser extent, Mexico and China, have stable governments and societies that are not prone to either secular or Islamic revolutions.

Now the problem becomes clear: In general, stable developed nations depend upon potentially unstable developing countries for oil. That dependence is bound to grow in this century, as more countries from the former Soviet Union and Africa join the list of leading producers and exporters.

The biggest gap between oil-producing nations and oil-consuming nations, though, has nothing to do with geography nor ideology nor theology. It's a battle between the rich and the middle class, if not the rich and the poor.

Petro-Facts

In 2001, the Middle East was the largest oil-producing region on the planet, with almost 30 percent of total oil production. Asia, including China, and Latin America each produced about 10 percent of the world's total oil.

—Source: International Energy Agency, 2002

At the end of the twentieth century, average per-capita income in the United States was almost $32,000. In Western Europe and the industrial nations of Asia, the per-capita figure was between $22,000 and $23,000. The only non-European oil-producing nation to sneak onto this high-income list was Kuwait, with a per-capita income slightly greater than France's.

Arabian Peninsula oil producers Qatar and the United Arab Emirates each had per-capita incomes in the $13,000 range, a shade better than Spain. After that the difference between oil users and oil exporters becomes starker. Oil giants Saudi Arabia and Venezuela only have per-capita incomes around $9,000—less than a third that of the United States. Iran's is only $5,000, while African oil producers Nigeria and Angola have per-capita incomes around $1,000.

Drill Bits

Petrodollars is the term applied to money paid to oil-producing countries, which is usually deposited in Western banks. The primary currency for buying oil is the U.S. dollar.

Future security crises may very well be fueled by the failure of oil wealth to gurgle down to the average person in many of these nations. The irony is inescapable: The West often sees oil producers as gluttonous, greedy, and rolling in *petrodollars*; the oil producers often see the West as gluttonous, greedy, and wallowing in cheap oil ripped off from the Third World.

The Oil Consumers

The United States is the world's largest oil consumer, followed by industrialized Europe, Japan, and the emerging giants of China and India. As the latter two develop in this century, the calculations will change, but for now, the oil fields in troubled areas like the Middle East, Africa, and Latin America supply the energy to keep industrialized North America, Europe, and Asia running.

This makes the fight card of future energy disputes fairly clear—the world's industrial powers versus the earth's energy-producing heavyweights, a pattern that has endured for almost 100 years. At the end of World War I, the industrial powers of Europe and North America realized that their national security depended upon airplanes, ships, tanks, trucks, and armored cars—or in other words—on oil.

Oil's Role in WWII

The outbreak of World War II saw a direct emphasis on controlling oil supplies and energy sources. The primary internal justification the Japanese Imperial High Command used for the sneak attack at Pearl Harbor on December 7, 1941, was the oil embargo the United States had slapped on the Empire of Japan.

The Japanese theory was that if the U.S. Pacific Fleet were knocked out, the United States would be unable to oppose a Japanese push south toward the oil and rubber deposits of the Malay Peninsula, Indonesia, and Southeast Asia.

Half a world away, Hitler's invasion of the Soviet Union in 1941 was aimed not only at eliminating Bolshevism and the "subhuman" Slavs, but at controlling the oil fields in the USSR's Baku region along the Caspian Sea.

OPEC and OCED

The postwar world saw the rebuilding of Germany and Japan and a tremendous economic surge in the United States. Both oil consumers and oil producers formed their own organizations: *The Organization for Cooperation and Economic Development (OCED)*, made up of the industrial nations, and *the Organization of Petroleum Exporting Countries (OPEC)*, made up of most oil-producing nations.

The battle lines between the OCED members and other industrial powers, and the OPEC nations and other oil producers, remain drawn to this day. The OCED cartel is primarily interested in maintaining the free flow of oil, relatively cheaply if possible, but flowing nonetheless, regardless of price. The OPEC cartel is mainly interested in maintaining a relatively high price for oil and getting as much per barrel from the industrial nations as possible.

Drill Bits

The Organization for Cooperation and Economic Development (OCED) was formed among the Europeans and Americans in 1961 to maintain the free flow of oil.

The Organization of Petroleum Exporting Countries (OPEC), which held its first meeting in Baghdad in 1960, was started by oil-producing nations to maintain a high price for oil.

The two sides have managed to maintain an equilibrium of sorts, despite several OPEC boycotts and instability within several oil-producing countries. Ironically, the same oil wealth that's transformed places like Saudi Arabia and Kuwait has led to social instability because many countries spent money lavishly on modernization projects and on relatives of the ruling families, rushing former tribal, rural societies headlong into the modern era. This produced social dislocation and, in the case of the Saudis, demands from religious fundamentalists that their countries return to basic tenants of Islam.

Fundamentalists seized power in Iran in 1979, igniting a global crisis that we still face as adherents of fundamentalist Islam faced off with secular forces across the oil-producing Muslim world. At the same time, oil wealth has been used by countries like Iran, Iraq, and even Saudi Arabia, to funnel money to anti-Western terrorist organizations.

This quickly became another source of tension with the West, as anti-Israeli and anti-Western groups, both religious and secular, began terrorism campaigns in the 1970s. The struggle between oil producers and oil consumers has turned into something far more deadly than commercial disagreements about the price of oil. It has become a clash of civilizations, pitting the Middle Eastern and other terrorist/freedom fighters against Israel and its Western allics. We'll examine this entire issue in greater depth later in this book.

The Sole Superpower

At the end of the twentieth century, the United States found itself alone at the top of the international power pyramid. As the sole surviving superpower, the United States has said repeatedly that one of its primary national security objectives is to make sure oil keeps flowing to the oil consumers from the oil producers.

It's instructive to look at American power and how it protects its own oil supplies as well as the supplies of other nations. The Straits of Hormuz form a choke point at the mouth of the Arabian Gulf through which oil from Kuwait, Saudi Arabia, Iraq, Iran, and the United Arab Emirates travels to world markets. When people talk about "dependence on foreign oil," it's usually this region that comes to mind.

> **Slick Sayings**
>
> The free flow of oil became a vital national interest to the United States—witness the stand that the United States took during the Gulf War. The free flow of oil became of vital national interest not just to the United States, but to Europe and Japan as well.
>
> —Former U.S. Secretary of State James Baker, May 4, 1998

The United States tried to defuse the Iraq-Iran war by offering military protection to oil tankers in the 1980s. In 1991, of course, the United States went to war with Iraq to eject Iraqi troops from Kuwait and again in 2003 to overthrow the Iraqi regime. Even though the United States has remained active in protecting this region, it only gets a small percentage of its oil from the Persian Gulf. Just a little more than 13 percent of total oil sent through the Straits of Hormuz ends up in the United States, while Western Europe depends on the Arabian Gulf to supply more than 25 percent of its total oil needs, and Japan uses Persian Gulf oil for more than 75 percent of its total.

Even if oil exports from the entire Arabian Gulf ceased tomorrow, the United States' economy would continue rolling along, albeit at a slower pace and with more expensive oil. But a similar cut-off could cripple the Western Europeans' economies, and could come close to destroying Japan's economy. In an era when you may wear a shirt made in China, pants from Bangladesh, and shoes from Indonesia, use a computer from Japan with American software, and drive a car made in Canada or Mexico, there is no question that any curtailment of oil supplies will impact almost every country in the world. U.S. military and national security strategy concerning oil isn't so much about protecting American supplies as it is about protecting the supplies of our allies as well as preventing a global economic catastrophe.

Resource Wars

Resource wars have been with us ever since our early ancestors fought over who would control African hunting grounds. In the twenty-first century, resources ranging from diamonds to high-tech minerals like *coltan* have financed bloodthirsty rebels from Angola and the Congo to Afghanistan and Colombia.

But oil remains the resource with mass appeal, since it's used to power most aspects of everyday life in the developed world. As we noted earlier, and as we'll examine in much more detail later, conflicts over oil dotted the landscape of the twentieth century.

In this century, some oil supplies are relatively immune to disruption, given overall political and social stability in the countries where they're found. The United States, Norway, the United Kingdom, and Canada are all major oil producers and, outside of terrorist attacks, they don't face any immediate threats of disruption in supplies.

Drill Bits _____

Coltan is an ore found in the Congo. Its scientific name is columbite tantalite. In its refined form, it becomes a heat-resistant powder that holds a high electrical charge, making it perfect for capacitors in laptops, cell phones, and other electronic devices.

The situation is different in the rest of the oil-producing world. China will probably remain stable, but you never know how internal tensions in a Communist state dabbling with capitalism will play out, especially given the growing pains that go along with being an emerging global power.

Probable stability is also the outlook for Mexico and Venezuela, but both nations have a rich history of social disruption and violence, so, as with China, you never know. But after that, the forecast for possible disruption of oil supplies and possible wars over those supplies, becomes greater.

Outlook for the Persian Gulf

Reactionary monarchies in the explosive Persian Gulf region face the greatest threat. Saudi Arabia, Kuwait, Oman, Bahrain, Qatar, and the United Arab Emirates all have vast pools of oil wealth. They also all face the wrath of Islamic fundamentalists who want the monarchies toppled, Western influence curtailed, and Islamic governments established. Any or all of them could face coups in the coming years.

The Iranians have been there and done that. But the vast majority of Iran's population was born after the Ayatollah Khomeini overthrew the Shah in 1979, and secular opposition to the strict Islamic fundamentalist government is growing. Iran, a nation with

60 million people, nuclear capability, and a well-armed military, poses the biggest threat of oil disruption in the Gulf region. This disruption could take the form of anything from uprisings inside the country to military action by Western nations responding to Iran's continued support of terrorist organizations or development of nuclear capabilities.

Iraq, even after Saddam Hussein, doesn't exactly look like a model of stability. Neither does Libya, where the eccentric pan-Arabism of Mohmar Khadaffi seems on its last legs.

Future Oil Battles

While there are still many battles to be fought about known reserves, potential areas for future development may be even more controversial. The great unknowns of future oil supply and resource wars are the emerging oil producers.

Caspian Sea

Front and center is the Caspian Sea region, where oil and natural gas supplies are just beginning to be exploited. This area has the potential for wars and disruptions that could make the Persian Gulf look tame. Unstable countries rim the Caspian, including Russia, Kazakhstan, Turkmenistan, Uzbekistan, Iran, and Azerbaijan. Proposed pipelines to carry the oil run through hotspots, including Afghanistan, Pakistan, Turkey, Georgia, China, Russia, Ukraine, Romania, Bulgaria, Greece, and Kyrgyzstan.

The potential oil reserves below both the Caspian's caviar- and sturgeon-rich waters and the rugged mountain landscapes nearby make the prize worth the expense and the danger. With the exception of Greece, instability stalks all of the countries associated with Caspian oil, whether it's Islamic fundamentalism or breakaway ethnic nationalism.

Every proposed pipeline route out of the Caspian is a potential target for destruction and a potential cause of economic disruption and environmental disaster. Meanwhile, the region is isolated and unforgiving, so the cost of hauling in everything from drill bits to workers will be high. The expense associated with actually drilling in the region is also enormous, whether it's dealing with unforgiving rugged rock formations or bribe-demanding local officials and warlords.

South China Sea

The South China Sea is another potential site of twenty-first-century resource wars. Fabled in song and story for centuries, the South China Sea has seen Malay pirates, English frigates, Arab corsairs, Spanish galleons, Dutch sloops, Chinese junk fleets, and American carriers come and go. The Sea is hemmed in on all sides—on the north by China and Taiwan, on the south by Malaysia and Indonesia, on the east by the Philippines, and on the west by Vietnam.

Scattered throughout the South China Sea, spread out like random grains of rice on a tablecloth, is a series of coral outcroppings, islets, rocks, and shoals collectively called the Spratly Islands. The area under the Spratlys contains potentially enormous reserves of oil and natural gas. Parts of the islands are claimed by at least eight nations simultaneously.

This region could explode more easily than the Caspian region simply because no tentative agreements for any kind of organized exploration have been reached. While tentative pipelines have been mapped in the Caspian, rival navies and nations trade both verbal and artillery shots over the Spratly outcroppings. By the end of the twentieth century, China had established a rudimentary drilling platform on one island claimed by it, Vietnam, and the Philippines, and even drove off a Filipino gunboat with artillery.

Petro-Facts

The amount of oil underneath the South China Sea is the subject of some dispute. A 1995 Russian study estimated it contained reserves of 6 billion barrels, most of it natural gas. But the Chinese government has called the South China Sea "a second Persian Gulf" and has estimated its reserves at 150 billion barrels.

Unlike any other potential oil-producing region on Earth, the South China Sea fields are buried beneath one of the world's busiest shipping lanes in an area where rival nations with developed military capacities are glaring at each other. Several computer scenarios run by research institutes like the Rand Corporation have ended with World War III breaking out over the Spratlys.

Artic National Wildlife Refuge

But even in areas of relative peace and prosperity, like the United States, future oil exploration threatens to create major political problems. The prime example is a proposal to explore for oil in the Arctic National Wildlife Refuge, known as ANWR (pronounced "an-war").

The ANWR covers about 19 million acres along Alaska's north coast and is home to large populations of caribou and other wildlife. Environmentalists strongly object to any proposals for oil exploration in the region, citing concerns that the drilling operations and pipelines could permanently destroy areas where caribou come to mate and have calves, thus perhaps disrupting or even killing off the caribou species found in the ANWR.

They also note that pro-development arguments about "ending dependence on foreign oil" are false, since a good percentage of oil found in Alaska is not sent to the rest of the United States, but is immediately exported to Asia.

But pro-development forces say that anywhere from 5.5 billion to 16 billion barrels of crude oil and natural gas may be buried underneath the ANWR tundra and that new methods of drilling will ensure that only a tiny part of the entire ANWR would be disrupted. The battle between the two forces shapes up as one of the hottest political arguments over energy exploration in the developed world.

Black Gold, Blue Planet

Crude oil that spews out of the ground is just that—crude. It's loaded with chemicals and trace elements that make it unfit for most uses until it's refined into various products such as gasoline, heating oil, aviation fuel, lubricants, and so forth. So the trick is getting oil from point A (the oil well) to point B (the refinery) without spilling.

Like flying into space, it's more easily said than done. The task involves technological choreography that must coordinate oil fields, pipelines, and oil tankers, while dealing with bad weather, human error, technology failure, and conflict.

In fact, the two largest oil spills in history didn't result from tanker accidents or pipeline failure, but from war. According to Research Systems, Inc., a company that manufactures high-tech equipment to spot and track oil spills, the four largest spills in recorded history are as follows:

- An astounding 240 million gallons spilled during the 1991 Persian Gulf War, when Iraqi dictator Saddam Hussein ordered his retreating troops to torch Kuwaiti oil wells' open vent valves, allowing oil to rush into the Arabian Gulf.

- Nearly 150 million gallons spilled into the Persian Gulf in 1983 during the war between Iran and Iraq. This total includes oil leaking from bombed offshore oil platforms and from oil tankers that were attacked by both sides.

- Some 140 million gallons vented into the Gulf of Mexico in late 1979 and early 1980 due to a blowout in the Mexican-operated Ixtoc I offshore oil platform.

- Approximately 110 million gallons spilled into the Caribbean Sea in 1979 when the oil tankers *Atlantic Empress* and *Aegean Captain* collided off the coast of the island of Tobago.

Petro-Facts

The 1989 *Exxon Valdez* disaster, when the tanker ran aground off Alaska and spilled 11 million gallons, is the worst oil spill in U.S. history, but only the thirty-fifth-worst spill worldwide.

Environmentalists have long demanded that oil be shipped in *double-hulled tankers* to prevent, or at least lessen, shipping disasters like the collision between the *Atlantic Empress* and *Aegean Captain* in 1979. In 1990, a federal law required all oil tankers operating in U.S. waters to be double-hulled by 2015.

North America and Western Europe have responded aggressively with laws and technologies to fight oil spills. But the problem of this century will be the growing oil needs of emerging powers like India and China, where not much attention has been paid to environmental concerns. In addition, there's the problem of oil exploration in regions like West Africa and the Caspian and South China Seas, where environmental controls may take a back seat to pumping out as much oil as quickly as possible.

Later in this book, we'll take a much closer look at the balance between oil drilling and shipment and a clean environment. But what it adds up to is that oil is the most important commodity in the world and will remain just that through our grandchildren's lifetimes.

Drill Bits _____

Double-hulled tankers have a second hull built inside the outer hull, so that a collision or running aground will, in theory at least, not rupture both hulls. In addition, many double-hulled vessels have two engine rooms, two rudders, and twin propellers, all to make sure the vessel can maneuver should one system become crippled.

The Least You Need to Know

- The thirst for oil to run the world's economies is a fairly recent development.

- Tensions between oil producers and oil consumers, especially between emerging powers and emerging oil regions, threaten to create instability for the foreseeable future.

- New resource wars are likely to erupt as oil is discovered and exploited in politically unstable regions.

- Environmental dangers from exploration and shipping for oil could increase in the coming years.

The Making of Oil

In This Chapter

- Prehistoric conditions that set the stage for the age of oil
- How oil is formed
- Geology as the key to understanding oil
- The world's most bountiful sources of oil

Countless school kids were taught that oil was formed by dinosaurs' remains as they were compressed and eventually turned into oil. The Sinclair Oil Corporation even has a dinosaur for its logo—the company's ads once showed a smiling green brontosaurus sticking his head out of a car's gas tank. That's a great story and an even better ad campaign, but it's lousy geology. Oil is actually formed by the smallest of creatures, not the largest.

Or is it? Some think oil is the result of the roiling of *in*organic material near the earth's core. In this chapter, we'll explore the various theories about the formation of oil and where those formations are found today.

The Ancient Earth

The earth was formed as a boiling blob of gas and matter about 4.5 billion years ago. It took almost another billion years for the first rocks to form, along with the most rudimentary single-celled organisms. By 3.3 billion years ago, oxygen had formed and algae were blossoming, but it wasn't until another 300 million years later that sea-borne bacteria began to photosynthesize oxygen. Then it was another billion years for elementary plants to form, and a billion years after that for enough oxygen to collect to block harmful radiation and give life a kick-start.

Fast forward now another half-billion years to a mere 500 million years ago, when the first animals emerged in the form of primitive worms. The time from roughly 440 million to 400 million years ago, known as the Silurian Period, is when life began to take off in earnest and when—at least as far as we can tell—the first oil deposits began to form. The first insects, the first vertebrates with jaws, and the first life on land appeared.

The Devonian and Mississippian Periods ran from about 400 million years ago until 325 million years ago, launching the first plants with seeds. The planet at the time was composed of two massive continents. These periods were followed by the Pennsylvanian and Permian Periods, ending around 250 million years ago. The first reptiles, forests, ferns, and mammalian ancestors appeared. Plenty of organic material that died and rotted—at least conventional wisdom says—led to plenty of future oil deposits.

Petro-Facts

Here's when the percentage of oil you use today was first formed:

Period	Millions of Years Ago	Percent of Oil Formed
Silurian	400	9%
Devonian through Permian	400–250	16%
Jurassic	150	25%
Cretaceous	100	29%
Oligocene through Miocene	34–5	15%

Source: University of Wisconsin, 1999

Now we hit the Jurassic Period, which spans from about 200 million until 140 million years ago. During this era, when dinosaurs ruled the earth and small mammals began to scuttle about, around one fourth of the world's total oil deposits were laid down in the form of decaying material. The Jurassic was followed by the Cretaceous Period, when even more of the world's oil began to form. The Cretaceous ended when a huge asteroid collided with the earth about 65 million years ago, wiping out the dinosaurs and changing the biosphere almost completely. Now we're almost to modern times, with the Oligocene and Miocene Epochs, stretching from 34 million years ago to a mere 5 million years ago. This is the time when mammals ruled the earth, and when the last of our modern oil supplies began to be created.

Dinosaurs *No*, Tiny Critters *Sí*

As we mentioned at the beginning of this chapter, the old tale about dinosaurs forming oil is probably the biggest geological legend most of us grew up believing. Current conventional wisdom is that it wasn't the largest of the large, but the tiniest of the tiny, that died, rotted, and morphed into black gold. In a couple of pages, though, we'll look at a fascinating contrarian theory that nothing decomposed at all, that it was rather mammoth forces near the center of the earth that turned *in*organic matter into oil and pushed it up toward the surface.

But for now we'll concentrate on what the vast majority of scientists and researchers think happened. First off, look at the Petro-Facts box on when oil was formed and you'll see that a little over half of our oil deposits are thought to have formed in the Jurassic and Cretaceous Periods—the very time when dinosaurs ruled the ecosystem. This makes it easy to see how the decomposing dinosaur theory got started.

It's All About Carbon

The truth is probably less spectacular but more interesting. It starts with the plants at the bottom of the ancient food chain. Before animals came plants that respired and gave off oxygen, which enriched the atmosphere and took in carbon dioxide (CO_2), a sort of waste material floating in the air. Reacting to the sunlight, plants photosynthesized, oozing out oxygen, sucking in CO_2.

Slick Sayings

If there's something to eat, if there's a chemical reaction they can run at a reasonable temperature and pressure, you can almost guarantee there will be a life form that will be using that reaction.

—Professor Richard Kettler, Department of Geological Sciences, University of Nebraska, 1999

Inside the plant, the carbon dioxide bonded with several elements, including hydrogen, to become organic carbon. That became the pure scientific answer to the oldest philosophical riddle of all time: If the question is, "What is life?" then the answer is "Carbon." (You might have a more philosophic or religious explanation for the origins of life, but we won't go there—we're going to stick to science in this book.) The molecular carbon chain is the Mother Lode of Life, and without those prehistoric plants, we wouldn't have oil, or anything else.

The "Life Cycle" of Oil

Most life ends in this cycle: It dies, it rots, and it's eaten by bacteria. A large percentage of plants and tiny animals had a different fate tens of millions of years ago. They died and ended up, usually, sinking slowly to the bottom of some sort of body of water, generally a relatively protected one such as a swamp, a lake, or an ocean bottom along the continental shelves, protected from deep-sea currents.

Layers of silt, made up mostly of mud and sand, settled on top of the dead organisms. For a while, bacteria had their way with the dead material, but as layer upon layer of sediment accumulated, the oxygen supply for the bacteria was cut off. Since bacteria need elements like oxygen and sulfur to do their work, the decomposition slowly stopped.

By this time—at least according to the current rotting-plants-and-tiny-critters theory—just about all that would be left of the once-living material would be molecules of carbon and hydrogen. It was buried under millennia of sediment, grains of sand, and clouds of water-borne mud deposited year after year after year eventually burying the material deep under the surface.

Under increasing pressures and temperatures, the hydrocarbon soup, which was still over 80 percent carbon, sank deeper into the earth, seeping and oozing its way into underground voids and fissures in rock. The chemical composition slowly became crude oil and natural gas, and began to float to the top of underground water deposits, since both crude and gas are a good deal lighter than water.

Scientists break the transformation into three stages—diagenesis, catagenesis, and when things go too far, metagenesis:

- **Diagenesis** occurs between the surface and a little more than a mile down. Temperatures range between normal and 140 degrees Fahrenheit as the heat, pressure, and bacteria produce methane, carbon dioxide, and water.

- **Catagenesis** occurs at depths between 1 and 6 miles, with temperatures rising to 350 degrees Fahrenheit. The bacteria are gone, and heat and pressure transform the carbon molecules into petroleum.

♦ **Metagenesis** is the phase that needs to be avoided to form oil, because this combination of extreme heat and pressure, with temperatures above 390 degrees Fahrenheit, makes the carbon unstable and converts it not into oil, but into graphite and, eventually, pure carbon.

So, this is how oil was formed. Or was it?

Another Formation Theory ...

Mention the plant and animal origin of oil to some people, though, and you'll get a resounding *"Nyet!"* It started in 1951, when a group of scientists in the Soviet Union became convinced that oil had not formed by floating to the sea floor and slowly sinking into the earth. Instead, they proposed that the street ran the opposite way. Hydrogen and carbon needed to produce oil originated under great heat and pressure near the earth's core and bubbled its way upward.

The most striking part of the Russian theory holds that the original hydrocarbons did not come from living material at all, but instead resulted from a hellish soup made of water, iron oxide, and calcium carbonate crushed under astonishing pressure and cooked at searing temperatures far, far below the planet's surface.

It was the height of the Cold War in 1951 when the theory first came along, and almost no one outside of the U.S.S.R. paid any attention to it. But that changed in August 2002, when Dr. J.F. Kenney, an American geologist and oil company executive, published a scientific paper in the *Proceedings of the National Academy of Sciences.*

 **Slick Sayings**

It is absurd to believe that oil is formed from squashed fish and putrefied cabbages.

—Dr. J.F. Kenney, CEO, Gas Resources Corp., 2002

Kenney came up with a series of mathematical formulas that could predict how the complex molecular chains in the world of hydrocarbons will behave. He concluded that alkanes (the primary types of hydrocarbon molecules found in crude oil) could never have been formed by the relatively gentle and gradual decomposition of living material. Instead, he said that the basis for oil was formed when iron oxide, water, and calcium carbonate were cooked together some 60 miles below the earth's surface.

There they would have been heated to over 2,700 degrees Fahrenheit and smashed with a pressure 50,000 times as great as that on the surface of the earth. The result would be compounds like hexane and methane, the building blocks of crude petroleum.

"Ah ha!" say the supporters of the plants-and-animals origin, "Gotcha!" It's at this stage, they point out, that oil is more than hydrocarbons—that it contains some molecules that could only have originated with living things, including sterols. Sterols are found in plant pulp and have a chemical composition remarkably similar to cholesterol.

But the center-of-the-earth theorists respond that sterols are also found in many inorganic sources, including meteorite fragments. The inorganic deep-earth hypothesis, though, does have one serious and potentially fatal flaw. If oil were, indeed, formed under intense heat and pressure dozens of miles down, it would tend to fall apart chemically as it rose from regions of high temperature and pressure to the benign, cooler, low-pressure world closer to the earth's surface.

The only way to avoid disintegration of the crude oil molecules would be for them to be cooled down rapidly as they traveled upward. And the only way this cooling could have happened fast enough would have been for the crude to spurt almost all at once from the planet's core into rocks and cavities relatively close to the earth's crust.

As we said, the vast majority of scientists and petroleum experts still favor the rotted-plants-and-animals theory. But a growing number of researchers now question that origin and think that the stuff that drives modern civilization originated near the center of the earth.

Rocks Tell the Story

The history of the earth rushes by your window every time you drive through a part of the country where a highway has been cut through rock. Layer by sedimentary layer, you can see where tides have ebbed and flowed, where oceans receded, where millions of years of time left its thumbprint. Next time you zip by, consider for a moment what those layers tell you about the gasoline in your tank and the oil in your engine.

The petroleum, whether from rotting plants or the planet's core, exists someplace inside rocks much like those. We say "inside" because, like water in a sponge, oil permeates many kinds of rock. That's how it exists, and that's how it has to be sucked from the ground.

There Are No Underground Oil "Lakes"

We've all seen simplified drawings of how oil wells work, and somewhere in the picture there's always a black line representing the drill shaft sinking down until it hits a small underground pond of oil. Maybe it's because areas of rock rich in petroleum are known as "oil reservoirs" that we think they look like small subterranean lakes.

Actually, they look much like any other rock nearby except that drops of oil pack the microscopic openings (called pores) in the oil-rich rock. The oil droplets cling tenaciously to the rock, and the trick, of course, is to get them to leave.

If the rock is fairly permeable and the oil can flow through the "sponge" relatively easily, the driller's job is a good deal less complicated than if the rock is impermeable and the oil doesn't want to move from Point A (the ground) to point B (the drill shaft). Oil that has seeped into odd fractures in rock can also present a problem. So can pockets of water, underground salt domes, and dozens of other factors.

The first thing oil explorers search for is the kind of rock that probably contains petroleum. Like a laminated board or a parfait dessert, the rock beneath our feet is made up of the accumulated layers of material deposited over hundreds of millions of years. One of the most important things to look for is some sort of barrier that prevents any petroleum from migrating. This most often takes the form of layers of extremely hard and dense rock, like shale, that oil can't penetrate. That means the oil will accumulate beneath these *stratigraphic traps* and form oil reservoirs.

> **Drill Bits**
>
> A **stratigraphic trap** is any layer of impenetrable rock that traps oil or natural gas underneath it, acting as a sort of dam and forcing the petroleum to accumulate.

Things to Think About Before You Sink a Well

But first things first. If you're looking for oil, you need to take five things into account before taking the time and expense of actually sinking an exploratory well:

- **Source:** Are there any indications where any petroleum in these rocks might have come from?

- **Migration pathway:** How does any oil move through the rocks?

- **Trap:** Is there a layer of rock sealing in any oil deposits?

- **Seal:** If there is a trap, is it sealed tight, or does it leak?

- **Timing:** How long have oil deposits been laid down in these rocks? That helps determine the potential size of any oil reservoir.

Let's take a closer look at each of these variables.

To determine the source, the geologist first looks to see if any oil or natural gas has been discovered in the area, and whether any underground basins may fit the overall types where oil may be found. Taking a look at rocks nearby can help determine the source. Oil formed in different types of rock has different characteristics.

Using sonar waves bounced into the rock, oil explorers try to determine the migration pathway—how the oil might have slowly been squeezed from one rock into another. Tracing this pathway back to its beginning helps determine the potential size of an oil strike.

The trap, as we've previously mentioned, is most important, and is also found through sonar imaging. If there's a solid trap with an impermeable seal, there's a good chance you'll find more, not less, petroleum underneath. But in oil as in life, timing may be everything.

Drill Bits

Lacustrine is anything having to do with a lake. Remember that it was in shallow lakes and basins where the tiny critters died to form oil.

Time in this case refers to geologic time and to how long and when the suspected oil deposited was laid down. One classic example of what to look for is some sort of rift running along the earth's crust where the giant tectonic plates that slowly crawl across the planet's surface meet. Along these rifts, geologists look for one specific kind of rock— *lacustrine* rock.

So if the timing of the geology was right, the lacustrine rock stands a very good chance of containing some sort of petroleum deposits. But the difference between these deposits and other oil reservoirs is that the oil here was formed over a fairly narrow range of temperatures. Because of that, the trap holding in the oil would have to have been formed at almost precisely the same time as the petroleum deposits in order to hold in the oil reservoirs. So the geological timing of the entire deposit is vitally important to how much oil might be discovered.

If sonar readings look promising, geologists will send low-level electric currents through the rock. If the microscopic pores in the rock contain water, the current will zip right through, but if the tiny imperfections hold oil, the current will move more slowly. As a final fail-safe, a test well will be drilled into the rock, with small rock samples hauled to the surface for microscopic examination. If oil is found squeezed inside the rocks, and all the other trends look promising, then it's time to sink the actual oil wells.

Moving Oil from Point A (the Ground) to Point B (the Surface)

But how does the oil flow into the drill shaft and then on to the surface? If the oil is contained inside rocks, won't it just stay where it is? On the earth's surface, that's exactly what would happen. But deep down, remember, temperatures and pressures are higher, sometimes a great deal higher, than here on the earth's crust.

Because of that pressure, the oil is almost literally straining to escape, and all it takes is the right shaft sunk in the right place at the right depth and angle to relieve the pressure and send the oil gurgling toward the surface. Of course, that pressure won't last forever. It may only last hours, it may go on for days, or it may even last for months, but eventually the underground pressure will drop so that pumps have to be used to suck the oil to the surface.

This formation interests politicians and power brokers as well as geologists, since patterns of ancient geology help draw the modern political map. Take a look at where conditions are ripe for oil, and you'll find an area that's bound to become vitally important to the world's industrial nations.

Quest for Oil

Oil is found across the planet, from Australia and Algeria to Yemen and Zaire. But geology has conspired with time to produce a few hot spots—regions where there are billions of barrels of recoverable oil beneath the surface. Almost all of them have the potential to produce both huge amounts of oil and a fair amount of political turmoil at least through this century.

So where is most oil still hidden? According to the United States Geological Survey, the two largest oil regions with more than 100 billion barrels of oil beneath the surface are as follows:

- **The Arabian Peninsula/Persian Gulf/Middle East Region.** This includes the entire eastern third of the Arabian Peninsula, including the Persian Gulf itself and all the countries bordering it. It covers all of Iraq and a surprisingly large chunk of both Syria and Jordan, as well as a hefty coastal area of Iran.

- **The Tundra of North-Central Russia.** This is an area just west of the Ural Mountains and stretches from the semi-permanent icecaps of Nova Zemlya Island, sticks out into the Kara Sea off Russia's north coast, and runs over a thousand miles to the south, stretching west to embrace most of Siberia's frozen wastes.

This next group of eight is thought to have between 20 and 100 billion barrels of oil ready to be taken:

♦ **The Caspian Sea Region.** In the previous chapter, we touched on the Caspian Sea area and how it has the potential to become a major flash-point in the twenty-first century. The Caspian is bordered by Russia, Iran, Kazakhstan, Turkmenistan, and other nations where at the least, corruption, and at the worst, wholesale slaughter, are possible.

♦ **The North Slope of Alaska.** This area poses a domestic political problem in the United States, as environmentalists and oil companies, liberals and conservatives square off in the decades to come about how much oil exploration there should be done here.

♦ **The Gulf of Mexico.** A huge crescent sweeping outward from the southern tip of Texas and arcing north until it intersects with the coast at the Alabama-Florida border. Even after decades of exploration and exploitation there is still plenty of oil left in this region.

♦ **The Bay of Campeche.** This slice of oil riches is sandwiched between the Mexican mainland and the Yucatan Peninsula. We've already discussed a major oil spill that happened here because of an offshore-well blowout.

♦ **Venezuela inland and offshore.** This usually prosperous country on South America's northeast coast still has between 20 and 100 billion barrels of oil. But as always in most of Latin America, a volatile mix of concentrated pockets of poverty, nationalism, simmering anti-Americanism, and political instability could disrupt supplies.

♦ **Libya.** A great oil field stretches under the Sahara Desert and spreads toward the Mediterranean coast, underlying most of Libya. The question here is whether Mohmar Khadaffi's mixture of Islamism, nationalism, and pan-Arabism will survive him, or whether Libya will evolve into a more stable source of crude.

♦ **Nigeria.** The Niger River Delta spills out into the Gulf of Guinea, a broad arm of the Atlantic that covers Africa's "armpit," where the continent's West Coast veers almost due east and then makes a sharp turn almost due south. Offshore are some of the world's largest deposits of oil and natural gas. The factors likely to turn Nigeria into a hot spot are nationalism and Islamic fundamentalism, since the northern half of Nigeria is Muslim and in many places is ruled according to strict Islamic law.

♦ **The North Sea.** The Vikings navigated these stormy waters between Scotland and Norway a thousand years ago. Now the plunder, shared by Norway and the United Kingdom, is below the waves. Two of the world's most prosperous and peaceful countries mine the sea floor for black gold here, so the question is not one of political unrest but of weather, overcoming technical obstacles, and possible terrorism problems.

These are the 10 richest oil fields on the planet in terms of the amount of *recoverable oil* that still lies beneath the surface. Now we come to the secondary fields, areas with estimated recoverable oil in the 10 to 20 billion-barrel range. These, too, could be vital in the coming decades, especially if the price of crude oil rises permanently and makes exploitation of these areas more profitable. They are listed here in the order of their potential to be the focus of unrest:

> **Drill Bits**
>
> **Recoverable oil** includes oil that can be found, developed, and produced from a reservoir for use within the country the oil was found or exported for sale at a reasonable cost. Some oil is **technically recoverable,** which means we have the technology needed to get it out of the ground, but the costs to do so may be higher than the price at which it could be sold.

- **The Southern Caspian/Iran.** This field butts up against the richer Caspian Sea oil fields to the north, and spreads into Iran, Turkey, Syria, and Kazakhstan. Needless to say, two things make this a potential hot spot: its proximity to the incredible riches of the north Caspian Sea region, and the chance of political and military instability brought about by a combination of resurgent nationalism and Islamic extremism.

- **Kashmir/Pakistan/Afghanistan.** This potential oil field spreads across some of the wildest and most violent terrain, geographically and politically, on the earth. For centuries, warring religions, tribes, and empires have collided in this area, and there's no reason to think that's about to change. Kashmir is claimed by India and Pakistan, two nuclear powers that despise one another. Northern Pakistan, under which this field runs, is ground zero for support of various fundamentalist religious movements. And despite the U.S. invasion in 2001, Afghanistan seems no closer to stability than it was a century and a half ago.

- **Central China.** There are a pair of oil fields of untapped potential that almost join to form one huge oil reservoir in central China. These fields could actually go a long way toward preventing instability, in that they could provide the emerging Chinese superpower with much of the oil it will need for the twenty-first century.

- **The Russian Siberian Tundra.** This huge field sits right next to one of the 10 largest fields, the one in North-Central Russia, and sprawls from Russia's North Coast almost all the way to the Chinese border. The problem with this reservoir, as well as with its richer next-door neighbor, is that it covers such a huge area, making it unlikely that any one set of oil wells will produce much of a bonanza.

- **Algeria.** This field covers much of the country's interior, which is a major problem, since this is the region where radical Islamic fundamentalists have been gunning down government officials, foreigners, and suspected heretics for years. The crisis here accelerated in the 1990s, when fundamentalists won a majority of seats in Algeria's parliament. The election results were nullified by the military, sparking violence and sometimes wholesale slaughter by the fundamentalists. This oil reservoir will remain under-utilized until the government and the Algerian people rid themselves of the ultra-violence of the Islamic fundamentalists.

- **Western Canada.** This giant field runs from where the provinces of Alberta and Saskatchewan meet the United States, all the way up to the semi-Arctic North Coast. The problem here is the same as in the Russian tundra—the oil field covers such a mammoth stretch of real estate that any one site for exploration probably won't produce all that much oil.

- **Western Texas.** This last one may be a bit of a surprise to some people, since Texas oil has been sucked out of the ground for the better part of a century now. But from the Rio Grande border with Mexico all the way up toward Oklahoma, there are still tens of billions of barrels of oil beneath the surface.

So now we've listed the 17 regions with the potential to produce the most oil, many of which are also political hotbeds. These, of course, are not the only areas where political problems may emerge in the next century. Oil in the South China Sea, for example, is not nearly as plentiful as in any of these other areas, but its location among several contending nations and near one of the world's busiest shipping lanes makes it a potential flash point.

Now that we know how oil was formed and where to find it, let's take a look at what the world was like B.P.—Before Petroleum.

The Least You Need to Know

- The oil we use now was formed millions of years ago, probably from decomposing plants and animals.

- Oil doesn't exist in stagnant underground lakes. It is found clinging to microscopic pores inside the rocks themselves.

- Complex geological analysis is needed to figure out where oil is most likely to be found.

- Some of the world's richest supplies of oil sit underneath some of the earth's most politically volatile areas.

The World B.P.–
Before Petroleum

In This Chapter

- How ancient people used petroleum
- The Chinese sink the first wells
- Oil becomes a fierce weapon
- Petroleum's early medicinal uses

Ancient and not-so-ancient people used animal fat for many of the same things that modern petroleum is used for today, including cooking, soap, lubrication, paint, and to treat animal hides. The disadvantages, of course, were obvious. The chemical composition of animal fat would change over time, and with exposure to the air it would become rancid and attract disease-bearing animals and insects. It wasn't much good at waterproofing either, since some animal fats tend to be soluble in water.

But then there was the matter of a dark, smelly substance that either oozed up from the ground or was found collecting in tar pools near some ancient settlements. For most, the stuff was merely a nuisance, although there are legends in almost all civilizations of some nameless ancient ruler from the dawn of time who discovered that the material was good for everything from greasing chariot wheels to polishing swords.

No one is sure when the first human took it into his or her head to put petroleum to use. But there are some early citations that indicate black gold was being used in various ways thousands of years ago. In this chapter, we glance at the civilizations of the past and see how they regarded petroleum, or whether they even knew about it at all.

Stinking Rocks

Probably the first use of oil was in the form of *asphalt*, or bitumen, that would seep to the surface from oil deposits in the rock below. Some asphalt deposits, like the famous La Brea Tar Pits near Los Angeles, have formed small lakes where prehistoric animals became trapped and died.

Some of the earliest writings about the use of pitch or bitumen can be found in biblical stories. There is mention of the use of pitch to waterproof Noah's Ark. Bitumen is mentioned in a story about the birth of a legendary king of Assyria, Sargon:

> Sargon, the powerful king, King of Akkad am I.
> My mother was a princess, my father I did not know.
> She placed me in an ark of rushes,
> With bitumen my exit she sealed up.
> She launched me in the river, which did not drown me.

This is sometimes compared to the account in Exodus about Moses:

> And when she could no longer hide him
> She placed him in an ark of bulrushes
> And daubed it with slime and with pitch
> And put the child therein.

Drill Bits

Asphalt is also known as pitch or bitumen and is formed naturally when petroleum bubbles to the surface and the gases trapped inside evaporate. In modern times, asphalt is one of the products left behind after crude oil is distilled for various uses.

The three key words in these accounts—bitumen, slime, and pitch—mean roughly the same thing. In fact, the translation of the word "bitumen" from the Sumerian and the word "pitch" from the Hebrew mean *exactly* the same thing. Both refer to a thick semi-liquid that was used for everything from caulking the chinks in a wooden ship's hull to mortar that held together large stone buildings. "Slime" is an oilier, more diluted form of pitch and was brushed over surfaces, much like paint, to make them waterproof.

We know, then, that petroleum was used by civilizations at least 5,000 years ago, including the ancient Mesopotamians, Sumerians, and Babylonians, to provide bitumen or pitch that was used to seal stonework in cities and towns, and waterproof a round river craft called a *guffa*. The Biblical Tower of Babel and almost every other large stone structure of the period were held together by mortar made of pitch mixed with clay. The earliest civilizations were able to trade with one another because pitch and slime waterproofed their boats. And one of the earliest large bridges in human history was a 370-foot span across the Euphrates River, built in Babylon during King Nebuchadnezzar's reign. The wooden piers they sunk into the river were first sealed in asphalt to prevent rotting.

> **Petro-Facts**
>
> The earliest historical oil field we know of is near the modern city of Hit, in Iraq, about 150 miles northeast of modern Baghdad and ancient Babylon. Here asphalt bubbles to the surface as it did five millennia ago. Relatively nearby, on the banks of the Tigris River, are a few tiny asphalt springs near the ancient city of Asshur.

Several thousand miles away, at roughly the same time—3000 to 2500 B.C.E. (Before the Common Era)—the civilization springing to life in the Indus River valley of what's now India also found a use for natural asphalt. At a site called Mohenjo-Daro, as in Mesopotamia, the material was used to hold buildings together and to seal small boats used to navigate up and down the river.

About this time, Egyptians still had yet to discover the wheel as a method of transportation, although they did use potter's wheels to manufacture vases and bowls. But they did take to the water. Around 2500 B.C.E., Egyptian ships sealed with pitch and coated with slime began humankind's first voyages of discovery. Within 500 years, humans took to the open oceans in earnest, propelled by the wind in their sails and saved from sinking by the pitch caulk and slime outercoat on their hulls.

Around 2000 B.C.E., a people known as the Beakers (so named for the sharp prows of their boats) launched from the Iberian Peninsula and traveled from what is now Spain and Portugal to Germany and Britain. At almost the same time, the precursors of the modern Malay landed on the Malay Peninsula from China, and the residents of what is now Turkey—possibly the Trojans—established a seafaring culture that spread throughout the Aegean Sea.

About 200 years later, vessels from modern Ireland, England, and Norway intermingled with craft from present-day Greece, Turkey, and Egypt on the ocean. The Bronze Age was underway. It was made possible by stinking black lakes and springs scattered across the earth.

The Bamboo Pipeline

No one's sure exactly when the first crude oil was distilled, but it seems to have happened at least as early as 2000 B.C.E. The Chinese are thought to have been the first to refine raw asphalt and the oil tars that came with it, separating the various elements by trial-and-error, heating and creating the first distilled petroleum product. They also grew weary of hauling the more liquid forms of the seeping petroleum in jars on their backs and devised a series of crude bamboo pipelines, allowing the liquid to run to where it was needed. About the same time, Egyptians began a rudimentary form of refining, and by 1500 B.C.E., oil lamps had come into widespread use in Egypt, China, and Mesopotamia. This was a significant and fairly sophisticated breakthrough because it allowed smoky, noxious torches slathered in pitch to be discarded in favor of a relatively clear oil that burned slowly and posed no danger of explosion. History doesn't mention how many people had to lose their lives before just the right mixture was found for oil lamps.

Petro-Facts

The word *mummy* comes from the ancient Persian word *mumiai*, which means "asphalt, pitch, or bitumen."

Egyptians are credited with taking petroleum from this world into the next, inventing a complex embalming process that used herbs, cinnabar, camphor, alcohol, resin, and pitch to preserve the bodies of the ruling classes for their trip into the afterlife. Petroleum is a key ingredient in the composition of the ancient Egyptian mummy.

By this time, civilizations across the globe were in full swing, to one extent or another. Less technologically advanced cultures, such as the Native Americans and the Inuit of Alaska, used seeping petroleum for ceremonial fires and for painting their bodies, and they utilized oil-soaked porous rocks as fuel.

But those who had advanced beyond using petroleum simply as it came from the ground used it to light and heat their homes, to grease the wheels of their carts and chariots, to waterproof their buildings and ships, and generally to make life better and easier than it had been previously. All one had to do was distill the petroleum into various products without dying in the process.

Going Underground

Leaping ahead 900 years or so, we arrive at around 600 B.C.E. Classical Greek city-states were in full flower. The Assyrians built the world's first great national library, recording 3,000 years of Mesopotamian culture. Zoroaster and his theology based on fire first appeared, and his followers revered the oozing oil pits and blazing natural gas springs along the Caspian Sea as sacred. A Pharaoh of Egypt ordered a team of Phoenicians to sail all the way around Africa, and they succeeded within three years. Jerusalem fell to the Babylonians. And each and every one of those civilizations knew about, and used, petroleum.

In China, a civilization equal to any was thriving. General Sun Tzu had just written *The Art of War.* And the Chinese were doing something no other culture had yet fathomed—they were drilling for oil. Other civilizations dug pits near natural oil seeps, and these hand-dug holes were the first attempt to go beneath the surface, but they were dug merely as catch basins.

Using sharpened bamboo poles, the Chinese first punched out a small hole and then put weights and a rope on the bamboo, dropping it into the shaft to eat out more earth, a few centimeters at a time. This was the first example of *percussive drilling*, and the process enabled the Chinese to bore wells as deep as 1,500 feet. The spew of crude up the bamboo pipe would be directed into the bamboo pipelines, and the earth's first distribution system for crude oil was in operation.

Drill Bits

Percussive drilling, as the name implies, probes the earth by pounding down and digging in. The system invented by the Chinese around 600 B.C.E. was in use until the nineteenth century, when the first rotary drills were developed.

It would be centuries before other parts of the world caught on and began bringing the oil to them rather than the other way around.

Sooner or later, of course, the innovative material was bound to be used for war. Unfortunately, it was sooner.

The Fires of War

In about 450 B.C.E., with the splendor of the Greek cities at their height, the historian Herodotus first wrote about petroleum, describing not only the oil pits and fountains near Babylon, but the springs on the Greek island of Zante that bubbled up pure pitch.

Around 325 B.C.E., Alexander the Great marched out of Greece and conquered the known world to the East, including chunks of India. One of Alexander's strategies for defeating an opponent who was using elephants as cavalry was to use flaming torches made with a liquid petroleum product to spook the giant creatures so that swordsmen could get behind them and slice the beast's hamstrings.

Three hundred years later, the Romans used giant cauldrons filled with flaming oil and launched by catapults to terrify opponents from Gaul to Germania. The favor was returned a few times, such as at the Battle of Samasota in 69 B.C.E. along the Euphrates River, when a Roman legion was attacked with what was described as "a flaming mud" that not only stuck to skin and clothing, but burned "even more fiercely" when doused with water. Scientists now believe this crude napalm was probably made of sulfur, ground corrosive limestone, and petroleum.

It took several hundred years before chemists in Arabia and Persia were able to recreate this cocktail, known thereafter as "Greek fire." But it was the Romans who gave the primary ingredient a name that stuck: petroleum, from *petra*—meaning "rock"—and *oleum*—"oil." Around 70 C.E., the Roman historian and naturalist, Pliny the Elder, described oil seeps in Sicily and how the residents of Agrigentum used refined oil in lamps—an innovation already long used in Persia, China, and Egypt. Just a few years later, the Roman writer Plutarch traveled into Babylon and wrote about the petroleum to be found bubbling from the ground near what is now the city of Kirkuk in Iraq.

Slick Sayings

And the asphalt and the salts are made solid forthwith and the oil—the Persians call that rhadinace—is then black and a furnisher from itself of an unpleasant smell.

—Herodotus, *Inquiries*, Book 6, roughly 450 B.C.E.

When the Roman Empire collapsed in the sixth century, Europe fell into the Dark Ages and promptly forgot most of what the ancients had learned about crude oil and its uses. It was a different story in Asia, though, starting with the Eastern Roman Empire and its gilded capital of Constantinople, whose walls were protected by soldiers manning cauldrons of boiling pitch and by catapults that could toss clay jars of Greek fire down onto the heads of any army besieging the city.

In China, they were still sinking crude pipelines to transport the thick black liquid, while in Japan, crude oil was being distilled for use in lamps. By this time, almost every culture—except those in Europe—was using roughly refined oil for lighting, and boiling oil and flaming pitch as weapons. China was even using oil for home heating by sending the oil through their bamboo pipelines.

Dividing Wall

But there, history hits a kind of wall. For the next several hundred years, the technologies of China were kept from the outside world, Islam was sweeping across the Middle East and Africa, and Europe was mired in a period of literal and figurative darkness. New technology was hard to come by and, when it was developed, it didn't tend to travel very far.

So the uses of petroleum remained pretty much the same as they had been for the ancient Greeks, Romans, and Persians—weapons, lubrication, crude lighting, and some dubious medicines. The real advances were being made in the new world of the Islamic conquest.

Around 850 C.E., the Abbasid faction took control of the Islamic Empire from the Umayyad faction. One of the Abbasid's major weapons was their own form of Greek fire, which had terrorized their enemies and which the Abbasids called "naptha." In fact, the Abbasids established a special military unit—the Naptha Troops—to use petroleum-based fire weapons.

> **Drill Bits**
>
> **Naphtha** is no longer used as a weapon, but instead describes a component of petroleum used to make gasoline. Naphtha also is used in the production of solvents and feedstocks for the petrochemical industry.

Before Guns, There Was Oil

Military researchers began years of experiments on how to refine the oily weapons and developed the first large-scale oil refining operations, heating the crude to various temperatures to see what products might be distilled from the black sludge. This distillation process produced a new kind of lamp oil—what we now know as kerosene—and enabled the homes, public buildings, and mosques of the Middle East to be lit with kerosene lamps almost 1,000 years before the innovation came to Europe.

Proof of the deadly power of oil-based weapons and the widespread use of distillation and refining in the Islamic world came in 1167. The First Crusade had resulted in the occupation of Jerusalem by European Christian armies. The Crusaders anointed nobility from what is modern-day France as Kings of Jerusalem. Amalric I became King of Jerusalem in 1162 and immediately realized that the best defense was a good offense.

The Christian enclave in what is now Israel, Lebanon, and Syria was being chipped away by a series of Muslim military victories. Indeed, it would only be 20 more years until Jerusalem was recaptured by Islamic armies in 1187—a victory that lasted to modern times. But in 1167, Amalric thought that the best way to protect the Christian borders was to invade neighboring Muslim kingdoms and shove Islam back into the deep desert, so he mounted several unsuccessful attempts to conquer Egypt.

Amalric got close, fighting his way into what now are the northern suburbs of Cairo. But he had no idea that the Muslims, skilled in working with petroleum, had several major distilling operations in the city where military storehouses were filled with jars of naphtha and kerosene. The Islamic caliph vowed that rather than let Cairo fall to Amalric, he would torch the city. He did just that, using the huge stores of petroleum. Two hundred years later, Egyptian historian Taqi al-Din al Maqrizi wrote this account:

The caliph ordered that Cairo be evacuated and forced residents to leave everything behind and flee with only their families. In the wholesale panic, the fleeing mob looked like an army of ghosts …. Some sought refuge in mosques or public baths, resigned to die at the hands of the Crusaders. The caliph ordered 20,000 pots of naphtha and 10,000 fuses with which to ignite them to be distributed throughout the very city he ruled. Flames and smoke engulfed the city in a truly horrible spectacle. The fire burned for 54 days.

Europeans Start Catching Up

Less than 100 years after Cairo was burned, Europeans got their first chance to learn how to distill petroleum, thanks to a book and a conquest. The book was written by a Syrian cavalry officer and titled *The Book of Horsemanship and the Art of War.* Written in Arabic in 1285, it included descriptions and diagrams of how to distill crude oil into various products like kerosene and naphtha. Included in the drawings is a rocket powered by a crude form of gunpowder carrying a flaming naphtha pot as a payload. No physical evidence has ever been found of such a weapon, so it may have only been an idea sketched by the author.

But thanks to the Muslim conquest of most of modern-day Spain and Portugal, a copy of the book found its way into medieval Europe. Europeans began their first crude and cautious experiments to find new uses for the crude tar and oil that they found every so often bubbling from foul-smelling seeps or springs.

Petroleum People

Najm al-Din Ahdab was an officer in a cavalry unit that had recaptured Damascus from the Crusaders. Little is known of him except that he must have had extensive experience in using petroleum weapons, since he wrote detailed instructions for refining oil in his book written in 1285, *The Book of Horsemanship and the Art of War.*

By the mid-1300s, what may have been the world's first flamethrowers were in use by the Persian armies. Paintings from the era show the Persian "Iron Cavalry" at work. The unit was made up of metal weapons on wheels forged to look like knights charging atop their steeds. Flames would spout from the ends of the lances and from the iron horse's nostrils, powered by reservoirs of naphtha inside the devices. The machines probably didn't kill or wound too many enemy soldiers by themselves, but did probably win several battles by sending opposing troops into a wholesale panic.

Used for Medicine, Too

Many cultures also took to using the slick stuff as medicine, both internally and externally. Plutarch told of how Alexander the Great's army used petroleum derivatives to treat scalp disorders and stomach upsets. Around 200 C.E., the Roman physician Galen described the use of petroleum poultices to reduce the swelling from infections. Aztecs in Mesoamerica used oil products to treat skin conditions ranging from rashes to lesions, and in Europe, monks of the Dark Ages made all sorts of medicinal potions from petroleum.

Desert nomads used a petroleum concoction to treat their camels for mange. Holy Roman Emperor Charles V is believed to have used oil to treat his gout. Ancient Persians and Sumatrans also thought that petroleum had medical value.

These ancient cultures took just a peek at how valuable petroleum could be in helping people treat their illnesses and disorders. In the United States, the first uses of oil for medicine were carried out by the American Indians to treat colds, coughs, burns, and cuts. In fact, some of these Indian concoctions were later sold as "snake oil" to "cure what ails you." You can bet that didn't taste or smell very good.

> **Petro-Facts**
>
> Today petroleum plays a major role in our medical industry. Hundreds of medications are derived from petroleum. It is also used in the manufacturing of hearing aids, bandages, artificial limbs, heart valves, and contact lenses.

Here Comes the Sun

As we've seen, the Dark Ages were pretty much limited to European civilization, since the Chinese, Japanese, and Arab peoples were utilizing everything from distilled oil to mathematics and technology while Europe was mired in the centuries-long funk that followed the collapse of the Roman Empire. But night always turns into day, and the bright light of the Renaissance—a rebirth of culture and learning in Europe and a new dawn for European art and technology—burned the Dark Ages away.

Most historians pick the year 1400 C.E. as an arbitrary start for the Renaissance, and the century between 1400 and 1500 saw some of Western, Islamic, and Asian civilization's most important developments. The fifteenth century began with the Black Plague devastating most of Europe, while Islam entrenched itself throughout the Middle East and North Africa. In 1405, the Chinese emperor Yung-lo authorized the first of seven voyages in a huge fleet of over 300 ships, some the size of modern aircraft carriers.

The 37,000 men aboard the huge flotilla may have explored most of the world for trade, and, according to some historians, even landed in North America in 1421, 71 years before Columbus.

Throughout this century, innovation flourished. Leonardo da Vinci painted and designed flying machines in Italy. Johannes Gutenberg invented the printing press in Germany. The Christian holy city of Constantinople finally fell to Muslim troops in what is now Turkey. At the other end of Europe, Islamic occupiers were driven out after over 600 years in Spain.

In 1492, Columbus set sail from Spain, and on his third voyage in 1498, landed on the island of Trinidad. His crew noticed a foul smell in the air but never investigated, so it took another 100 years for Europeans to discover the Great Pitch Lake in Trinidad, oozing and bubbling raw petroleum to its 60-acre surface. Sir Walter Raleigh stumbled upon Trinidad's Great Pitch Lake in the 1590s. At the time, petroleum was still just a lubricant, a fuel for crude lamps, and a caulking and sealing material for the world's great ocean-going ships.

Despite a dizzying century of innovation and invention, the uses of petroleum remained essentially the same as they had for the Egyptians and Romans. But slowly, the technological tide was turning, preparing the way, as we'll see in the next chapter, for an industrial world that would eventually need petroleum in huge quantities.

Slick Sayings

In the Venetians' arsenal as boils
Through wintry months, tenacious pitch, to smear
Their unsound vessels, for the inclement time
Seafaring men restrains ...
Boil'd there a glutinous thick mass, that round
Limed all the shore beneath.

—Dante, *The Inferno, Canto XXI*, circa 1300, comparing the boiling tar pits of Hell to the pitch used by Venetian sailors to seal their ships.

For example, by the early 1600s in Great Britain, most of the island's trees had long since been cut for fuel, so a gradual change was underway, substituting coal for wood. The ability to gouge large amounts of coal out of the ground eventually made it possible to power many of the inventions coming down the road in the next 200 years.

About this time, the first commercial whaling operations began, hoping to find a new source of oil for the world's lamps (whale oil). In the oil-rich areas along the Caspian Sea, petroleum products were being gathered from surface sumps to be used in lamps. But petroleum's main value continued to be the way it enabled huge ship's hulls to be waterproofed for long sea voyages.

Dutch, English, Spanish, Portuguese, Italian, and French ships crossed one another's wakes from the Baltic and Mediterranean to the Indian Ocean and the South China Sea. Trade in grain, gold, spices, slaves, textiles, and timber began to link the earth in a truly global economy, as worldwide empires were built thanks to ships that traversed the farthest oceans.

Human history never moves in a straight line, but jumps in fits and starts with spasms of creative energy. As we'll see in the next chapter, that's precisely what happened when the Industrial Revolution came around. What began with the destruction of old forests led to new methods of agriculture and eventually produced machines that needed petroleum to drive them.

The Least You Need to Know

- ◆ Almost every ancient culture was aware of petroleum.
- ◆ The Chinese developed the first crude drilling equipment and pipeline system.
- ◆ Petroleum weapons were widely used throughout the Islamic world.
- ◆ The uses of petroleum changed very little between the time of the ancient Egyptians and the time of Columbus.

Chapter 4

Dawning of the Modern Age

In This Chapter

- Oil's energy-providing predecessors: wood and coal
- Steam drives major industrial changes
- Industry brings about social upheavals
- The stage is set for oil

The face of the world changed when inventions created a greater need for oil. This increasing reliance on oil resulted in new fault lines of international oil politics. Great powers suddenly collapsed and others rose to take their place. Mass manufacturing was developed. Cities and technology grew rapidly. Politics was forever changed. In this chapter, we trace the fault lines of our modern oil-based economy back to their beginnings, to see why they shaped up the way they did.

The Ages of Wood and Coal

In the beginning, there was wood. As this became scarce in some areas, coal replaced wood. Then oil replaced coal. That's the short version of how we ended up where we are today. Let's take a deeper look at this progression to oil and how the destruction of forests in Europe led directly to modern oil wars in the Middle East and elsewhere.

Even by the time of the Dark Ages, wood was becoming scarce in many parts of Europe, as forests were hacked down for buildings and waterwheels, as well as for fuel. By the late 1200s, it was becoming apparent that, at least in some parts of Europe, wood was far too precious to burn up in a fireplace. The Italian adventurer Marco Polo traveled to China in the thirteenth century and remarked upon how surprised he was to find the Chinese were using coal as a fuel. He brought the first samples of coal back to Europe, where some Europeans noticed that a similar substance was to be found near their own homes.

> **Slick Sayings**
>
> … there is found a sort of black stone which they dig out of the mountains where it runs in veins. When lighted, it burns like charcoal. These stones do not flame, except a little when first lighted.
>
> –Marco Polo, *The Travels of Marco Polo*, 1295, describing Chinese coal.

Metal smelting and refining a crude form of steel from iron were already growing cottage industries across medieval Europe, but they required huge amounts of charcoal to keep the fires stoked. Charcoal, like the trees it's made from, was becoming scarce all around Europe.

The situation was worst on the islands of Ireland and Great Britain, where the towering oak forest of King Arthur and Robin Hood legends was gone by the late 1600s. Some coal had been used for a couple of centuries, the so-called sea coal that appeared along the surface, especially near the coasts. The city of Newcastle had been exporting the easily obtained but filthy-burning sea coal since the 1300s, shipping it to London and even to France.

Now the rush was on to find new sources of fuel. Ireland and Britain had imported wood from the dense forests of Germany, and for awhile, even had raw timber sent via ship from colonies in North America. But the wood ended up being as valuable as precious metals because of the shipping costs. So exploration for more coal began, and veins of the burnable black rock were soon found in the north of England, the middle of the country, and in Wales.

This, remember, was before railways began to link centers throughout Europe. Small individual industrial operations for refining iron ore into steel began to spring up near the coal mines so the fuel wouldn't have far to travel. People began to move from farms into towns to either mine coal or work in small industries that used coal. At the same time, an agricultural revolution made it possible to grow more food to feed more people, and ship the food across some distance to be sold. That meant a new, steady supply of food for the concentrations of people now working in industries.

We're getting ahead of ourselves, since we'll cover the social and political upheavals resulting from this in a later chapter. But by 1700, the rough outlines of our modern petroleum economy began to take shape. Goods were increasingly made not by hand but by machine, which resulted in growing industrial towns near coal mines. That, in turn, resulted in new methods of farming to feed more people using less space. The American Revolution was still 70 years in the future when an invention that changed everything came along.

The Age of Steam

Whether coal mines in Wales or tin mines in Cornwall, mines in the early eighteenth century were among the most dangerous places on earth. One of the biggest problems was water seepage, which could weaken support timbers, flood the mines, and cause cave-ins. Miners had to pump water out of the mines continually, using hand-pushed pumps. In 1705, an English engineer named Thomas Newcomen invented a device that consisted of a normal pump handle connected to a vertical piston and cylinder. Newcomen pumped steam into the cylinder and then sprayed in cold water to condense it. That allowed normal atmospheric pressure to force the piston down and created a steam-driven pump that was a good deal more powerful than hand-pushed pumps.

This wasn't exactly a new idea. Around the year 300, a tinkerer known as Hero of Alexandria wrote a treatise called *The Pneumatics*, in which he described a crude steam engine. In 1543, a Spanish naval officer named Blasco de Garay designed and built a steam boiler to power a pair of paddle wheels. On June 17, 1543, his device moved the 200-ton ship *The Trinity* around the harbor of Barcelona. But de Garay, a secretive man, would never reveal details of how the device worked, and the Spanish King Charles V was too busy with a series of wars against Italy and France to pursue the idea much further.

Around 1759, a Glasgow University professor named James Watt began tinkering with the idea of the steam engine. He wasn't so much thinking about improving Newcomen's device as he was mulling over new uses for it— steam-driven ships, locomotives, even carriages might be possible, Watt mused, with some minor modifications to the vertical piston-cylinder design. It took years of tinkering and frustration, but by 1765, Watt had perfected a design for a powerful steam-driven *reciprocating engine*, much more powerful than anything Newcomen had come up with because Watt's device used steam at an astonishingly

Drill Bits

James Watt's engines, and the internal combustion engines that followed 125 years later, are called **reciprocating engines**. A reciprocating engine uses a piston to compress air (or a mixture of air and fuel) until that compressed material is either ignited (like in an automobile engine) or the compressed steam expands (like in Watt's engine). In both cases, the piston is forced down in the cylinder.

high pressure. It made the engine work exceptionally hard and efficiently, but it also meant anyone working near the high-pressure boiler and steam lines was at an extra risk—if the boiler or lines blew, nearby workers would be scalded with piping hot steam or water.

Watt added a flywheel, and suddenly the vertical pump could work on a horizontal surface, propelling everything from large wheels to giant machines. The American Revolution was about to boil over in 1774 when the British industrialist Michael Boulton formed a partnership with Watt, and every three days, week in and week out for the next 25 years, their company built and delivered a steam engine.

Does a piston inside a cylinder capable of doing a tremendous amount of work sound familiar? It's the great-grandfather of the internal combustion engine, the single invention that led to the modern age of oil. Watt's engine began to power everything from giant textile weaving looms to automatic forges used to hammer out refined steel, and everything in between.

Suddenly, it became necessary to find huge amounts of fuel to heat the water to make the high-pressure steam to drive the engines to make the various goods. The fuel was coal, and as industries popped up around the coal fields, the population followed. We'll see shortly how this transformed the entire social landscape and paved the way for inventions a hundred years later that demanded not coal, but petroleum as fuel.

This was arguably the biggest upheaval in Europe since the fall of the Roman Empire. And it was the birth of our modern world, where things used by people were made possible by machines, and finding the fuel to run those machines became necessary to keep society running.

The Soul of the New Machines

In the twentieth century, Chinese dictator Mao Tse Tung, said "Political power grows out of the barrel of a gun." In the late eighteenth century, it was becoming clear that political power grew out of the cylinder of Watt's engine. Around 1700, industrialization meant using water wheels for power; by 1800, it was the steam engine that did all the work.

New inventions for creating yarn and weaving cloth made manufactured clothing available for the first time. Mass-manufactured pottery meant that people could purchase containers that were safer to use than in the past, because the price of pottery dropped and manufactured plates and bowls held less disease-bearing bacteria than wooden ones.

We'll look at the huge changes in people's lives next chapter, and how society was evolving rapidly into the industrial, urbanized society we recognize today. But the monumental changes powered by fossil fuels—coal—had started, and there was no turning back.

Across the Atlantic Ocean, the leaders of the bubbling American independence movement looked at the growing industrialization of the mother country, and more and more of Europe, and disliked what they saw. Polar opposites like the flinty New Englander, John Adams, and the aristocratic Virginian, Thomas Jefferson, agreed on one thing—the peace, virtue, and prosperity of America would depend not on belching machines, but on the character and grit of individual farmers. The idea was a strong one that the factories and cities of England were morally corrupt when compared to the farms and villages of America.

There are echoes of this, of course, in the twenty-first century, as people urge society to wean itself from petroleum and revert to more "natural" fuels, whether wind or solar power. The agrarian tradition that tries to wean itself from a technological society is an old one.

> **Slick Sayings**
>
> There is not, in that state [humanity's natural agrarian state] any of those spectacles of human misery which poverty and want present to our eyes in all the towns and streets of Europe. Poverty, therefore, is a thing created by that which is called civilized life.
>
> —Thomas Paine, *Agrarian Justice*, 1797

But turning back the fossil-fuel-fired technology of the eighteenth century proved to be impossible. From the mid-1770s until 1800, Watt and Boulton's factories cranked out 500 steam-powered engines, shipping them across Great Britain and all of Europe. They revolutionized the entire continent, but there were so few of them because the sole legal manufacturers were Watt and Boulton. Then, in the last year of the eighteenth century, 1800, something happened that changed everything again—Watt's patent on the steam engine expired.

Once Watt was no longer the sole source of steam engines, technology and transportation took off. Tinkerers and inventors across Europe began to try to figure out how to use the steam engine to move either a boat or a carriage. A 5-foot 4-inch engineer from Pennsylvania had traveled in Europe during the late eighteenth century and had seen some of the prototypes. Fascinated with water and hydraulic engineering, he soon came to the attention of the wealthy U.S. ambassador to France, Robert Livingstone.

The young engineer was named Robert Fulton, and in 1794, he drafted a letter to the Boulton and Watt firm, inquiring about purchasing a steam engine. Thirteen years later, in 1807, Fulton had used Livingstone's political connections and fortune to get exclusive rights to run a steam-boat service between the metropolis of New York—population 84,000—and the city of Albany, up the Hudson River. The only hitch was that there was no such thing as a steam boat, and the New York legislature gave Fulton the contract based only on his idea. On August 17, 1807, the ungainly *Clermont*, 142 feet long, only 14 feet across, with a rounded bow and a deck barely above the waterline, chugged off from a pier in New York. Smoke billowed from its 15-foot-tall smokestack, and the hiss, roar, and clatter of the pistons, rods, and boiler of the steam engine in the boat's center echoed off Manhattan's buildings, convincing most onlookers that the entire contraption was bound to explode. The *Clermont* made 5-miles-an-hour progress upstream against the Hudson River current and forever changed the world.

Within four years, the first huge steamship to ply the waters of the Mississippi and Ohio Rivers was launched in Pittsburgh. Within 40 years, steam-powered vessels were regularly chugging across the Atlantic, plowing ahead regardless of the wind. It was coal and steam that made it possible, and suddenly agrarian America found that it had manufacturing cities springing up near coal deposits, imitating the despised Europeans.

The steamboat now made it possible to carry goods—including coal—long distances, so that almost any city could become an industrial center as long, that is, as it was on the water. Meanwhile, back at the mines, mine operators for years had laid down flat-topped metal bars and put wheeled carts on top, to better move the coal from the mine to a furnace, or wherever else it needed to go. The same sorts of tracks were set up in industrial or port cities like London and Munich, to better move goods off ships. But the carts were either pushed by hand or pulled by horse.

Petro-Facts

The first steam-powered locomotive fired by coal took to the tracks in 1801. It wasn't until 1896 that the first locomotive boiler heated by petroleum was introduced.

In 1801, an engineer named Richard Trevithick had a small coal-powered steam engine mounted in front of a line of tracked cars, carrying tin around the mine where he worked in Cornwall, in southwest England. In fewer than 20 years, tracks had been laid between the industrial cities of Liverpool and Manchester, and a coal-fired locomotive named *The Rocket* pulled a train of loaded cars with a top speed of 14 miles an hour.

In 1825, an American inventor named John Stevens constructed what was essentially the world's largest model railroad in the huge yard of his home in New Jersey. This was the first coal-fired locomotive in the United States, and Stevens got a charter to establish the Pennsylvania Railroad in 1823. In 1827, the first track was laid for the

Baltimore and Ohio Railroad, and by 1829, the B and O—total track length 14 miles—was up and running, while by 1834, the Pennsylvania—total track length 70 miles—was in operation.

The railroad sent more tremors throughout Europe and America. It was now possible to have prosperous industrial cities exist nowhere near navigable water. They could instead ride twin ribbons of steel to prosperity. But more than transportation was changing due to fossil fuels. A Scots inventor named Walter Murdock figured out early in the nineteenth century how to light an entire factory using "coal gas," the vapor given off when coal was heated.

But it was then discovered that you could get a liquid version of exactly the same thing if you heated coal almost to, but not quite at, the burning point. This produced *coal oil*, and by 1807, the streets of London were illuminated at night by the glow of coal oil lamps.

These lamps used coal oil, or *kerosene*, and were the first direct application of a modern product of refining oil. As we'll see in the next section, kerosene was the only valuable distillate obtained from crude oil for almost half a century. We'll also look at various claims of where and when the world's first modern oil well was drilled, although it's known that several small wells were sunk in area rich in pitch and tar around the world in the early nineteenth century. But let's catch our breath for a second. In the 150 years between 1700 and 1850, the world changed forever. Steel mills, iron foundries, coal mines, shipyards, textile mills, railroads, steamships, and big cities suddenly dotted the landscape that human beings inhabited. Almost all of it was due to the availability of the fossil fuel that ruled the earth before oil took over—coal. And it formed the world we know today, allowing petroleum to take over from coal almost seamlessly.

> **Drill Bits**
>
> Coal oil and **kerosene** are the same thing. Coal oil is extracted from coal by heating the coal to just below the burning point, and condensing the gas that's emitted. Kerosene is extracted from petroleum by condensing the vapor that boils off between 300 and 525 degrees Fahrenheit.

This was more than technology. It was people. And the world inhabited by our great-great-great grandfathers and grandmothers was changing, quickly and forever. The new machines gave rise to a new kind of human being—urbanized and industrialized, a human who no longer made nor grew what was needed for the family, but traded, bought, and bartered goods from all over the world. Where the machines led, modern capitalism, revolution, and what we now call the middle class followed.

The Social Earthquake

At the start of the eighteenth century, the vast majority of Europe's people lived on farms, and by the end of the nineteenth century, the vast majority lived in cities. Modern capitalism and modern revolutionary ideas fought for control over people's minds. The American and French revolutions destroyed the old idea of two classes—the rulers and the ruled—and replaced it with a middle class that, in theory at least, ruled itself. Work was done by machines and machines were powered by fossil fuels, and the availability of those fossil fuels determined how advanced any given country would become.

Factories, cities, shipping lines, and railroads slowly came into being, as did the modern concept of time, since you had to have accurate clocks to measure everything from scientific experiments to commercial timetables. The agrarian rhythm—up at sunrise, to bed at sundown, and measuring time by the passage of the moon's phases—was as old as humankind itself, and was now replaced by having to be at work by a certain arbitrary time determined by a clock.

Jethro Tull and His Revolutionary Turnips

And it all began with Jethro Tull and turnips. Mention Jethro Tull and most people think of the English rock band popular in the 1970s. But the real Tull was born in 1674, and revolutionized agriculture at a time when it was needed the most. He invented the seed drill, which allowed more seeds to germinate by placing them below the surface, out of the reach of wind, rain, and birds, and also developed the horse hoe, a device pulled by horses that enabled large areas of ground to be chopped up and prepared for cultivation.

Tull came along just as the traditional English system of wide-open unfenced fields was dying, being replaced with enclosed, smaller farm plots. Prior to the early 1700s, a third to a half of the land was left fallow each season, to give the earth time to recharge its nutrients. But Tull and others preached the value of root crops like turnips, used in a four-year cycle of crops, that not only fixed nitrogen, thus not depleting the soil, but offered a variety of foods ranging from cereals to potatoes.

This agricultural revolution came along just as the supply of wood was being replaced by coal. As we've seen, that meant new cities and factories of all kinds were springing up across Great Britain. And that meant tens of thousands of people were flocking to those areas to find work. And that meant some sort of reliable method had to be found to feed them all. Soon, far more food was being grown on far less land. So farms that could get food to the new working classes in the new cities in a reasonable period of time could prosper.

Better Sheep Means Better Meat and Wool

Around the time of the American Revolution, an English farmer and breeder named Robert Bakewell was involved in some highly successful experiments in breeding sheep. His sheep were larger, healthier, and more disease resistant, and gave far more wool than other varieties. This meant the growing, grimy industrial city populations now had access to more protein from mutton at lower prices and also had more access to clothing made from wool.

The Middleman and the Middle Class

Prior to the Industrial Revolution, you largely grew, made, or killed what your family used, and somehow bartered for other goods. But now, men worked in factories and stopped prowling the forest primeval. Women often worked in front of clattering rows of textile machinery rather than living on the farm. And that meant that their food and clothing and just about everything else had to be purchased from someone else. A new class, the prosperous mercantile class, sprang up, making its living either selling goods retail to the customers, or selling them wholesale to the shopkeepers.

And for the first time in history, a broad heterogeneous mass, called the middle class, came into existence. It ranged from the shop-keepers and lower management at factories on through the senior executives and the owners themselves, all different but all sharing one thing in common for their livelihoods—economic expansion driven by machines and the fuel that powered them. This was a death blow to aristocracy because the middle class was propelled by a belief that hard work, not inherited title, was the measure of human beings.

> **Slick Sayings**
>
> To found a great empire for the sole purpose of raising up a people of customers may at first sight appear a project altogether unfit for a nation of shopkeepers, but extremely fit for a nation that is governed by shopkeepers.
>
> –Adam Smith, *The Wealth of Nations*, 1776

The anti-aristocratic feeling became politically potent, driven by technology and commerce. New scientific ideas, from understanding the blood's circulation and discovering carbon dioxide to the steam engine and the cotton gin gave humans a growing feeling that they could not only understand the elementary forces of nature, but master them. The spirit of the age became upbeat, and progress—humanity's mastery of nature and their use of knowledge to make life better—became an end unto itself.

Science bred rationalism, which bred skepticism of the old, which bred enthusiasm for the new, which led to the Declaration of Independence, the French Revolution, the humanism of Adam Smith, Thomas Jefferson, Voltaire, and Benjamin Franklin, all built on Jethro Tull's turnips and James Watt's steam engine.

Europe had a middle class of sorts as early as the 1300s. But coal and machines resulted in a totally new class—the working class—men and women who owned nothing except the ability to rent out their sweat in the new factories. As the Industrial Revolution ripened in the years before the American Civil War, radical thinkers like Karl Marx divided this new industrial world into three basic parts—the working class, which produced the wealth, the bourgeois or middle class, and the ruling class, which owned the means of production.

Marx wanted to replace the profit motive with a social revolution that would transfer ownership of the means of production to a government run by the working classes. It took more than a century and a half for Marx's ideas to be proven insightful socially but disastrous economically. In the meantime, everything was in place for the coming age of petroleum. All that was needed were the oil and the machines, and they were both on the way.

Thar She Blows

The first verifiable account of killing whales for their oil comes from northern Spain around the year 700, but whale oil didn't become a popular source of fuel until the 1600s when it was needed to help light the cities at night. All through the 1600s, fleets of English and Dutch whalers searched northern Atlantic and Arctic waters for the bowhead whale. These English whaling men were recruited to settle the Massachusetts island of Nantucket in 1672, and began hunting the close-in coastal waters for whales which, at the time, were plentiful.

The whales were hunted for their blubber, which, when stripped from the carcass and cooked down, made oil used for lamps and tallow used for candles. The slowly growing Industrial Revolution made the market for whale oil illumination all the more valuable, since more light meant more hours could be spent working. In 1712, one Nantucket whaler was blown off course and encountered, for the first time, a sperm whale, which was promptly killed, skinned, and cooked down for oil.

To everyone's surprise, the sperm whale oil burned much cleaner and brighter than other whale oil and even coal oil, and it had no unpleasant odor or smoke. By the time James Watt's steam engine patent expired in 1800, Nantucket was home to a fleet of several hundred ships that plied the world's waters in search of sperm whales and whale oil.

Whale oil lamps lit homes across the world. The small glass spheres with flat bottoms and cheerful names like The Little Sunbeam and Star Lamp were manufactured cheaply and sold almost as cheaply, all to light the homes of the growing middle class. It was something their parents could only have imagined—clean, bright, and relatively inexpensive fuel available to the masses.

Whale oil was used for more than just lighting homes and businesses. It was a staple in cosmetics and lubricants, and was even used as a photographic glaze to help preserve the earliest photographic prints.

Petro-Facts

The most prized whale oil of all didn't come from the cooked down blubber of whales, or even that of the valued sperm whale. Instead, it came from a waxy oil inside a mammoth gland near the whale's head called the spermaceti. To this day, no one's quite sure exactly what function the organ performs, although it's thought to either be a device to help the whale rise and sink to tremendous depths in the ocean, or a giant gland that helps the whale focus sound waves for guidance and a form of speech.

In the decade before the Civil War, whaling was at its peak. Unlike the modern petroleum barrel, which holds 42 gallons, the barrel of whale oil held closer to 100 gallons. But by converting them into today's standard 42-gallon models—the same as used for modern oil—we can calculate at its height that the whaling industry produced around 20 million barrels of oil a year.

In 1856, oil from the sperm whale sold in New York for $1.77 a gallon. Forty years later, that same gallon cost only 40¢ due to an almost complete lack of demand. What happened? Kerosene happened, and a clean-burning odorless lamp invented by Michael Dietz that came on the market in 1857.

The kerosene, in this case, was distilled from coal. But a different source of kerosene was ready to appear. The year before Dietz marketed his lamp, in 1856, the first oil well in North America was sunk in Ontario, Canada. Two years after the Dietz lamp came to store shelves, in 1859, an oil well was drilled in an obscure Pennsylvania town, and our modern world was born.

Petro-Facts

The clean-burning kerosene lamp patented and sold by Michael Dietz starting in 1857 had an astonishing effect. Within two years, the lamp had single-handedly increased the market for kerosene (coal oil) and had forced most whale oil lamps off the market.

Everything was now in place—the mines, the factories, the railroads, the cities, the middle and working classes, and the machines that did the work of people. All that was needed was a new fuel and new machines—ones that could be owned by individuals.

The fuel was at hand. The machines would take a little more time.

The Least You Need to Know

- After the forests of Europe were largely destroyed, coal became the major source of heat and light.

- The steam engine became the driving force behind major changes across the world.

- The basis for modern industrial society and the coming age of oil was established.

- The whale oil business had a brief but glorious history before being sunk by petroleum.

Chapter 5

Up from the Ground

In This Chapter

- ◆ Titusville—America's first commercial oil well
- ◆ Science and business take an interest in petroleum
- ◆ Getting the oil out of the ground
- ◆ Birthing our modern petroleum age

In August of 1859, financial speculators played midwives to the birth of the modern world. They had leased dozens of acres of land around the inelegantly named Oil Creek in northwestern Pennsylvania, hoping to find petroleum that could be used to lubricate the Industrial Revolution's machines and to be distilled into kerosene to light the nation's homes and businesses.

In this chapter, we'll focus a close-up lens on the area and the characters involved. They all became microcosms of Industrial America in the nineteenth century—brash technical innovators buoyed by the optimism of the age, backed by finance capitalists whose only concern was making a profit and who didn't have time to worry about niceties like business ethics.

A Town Called Titusville

Canadohta Lake sits in northwest Pennsylvania, about 30 miles southeast of the Lake Erie shoreline and about 20 miles south of the border with New York. Go there today and you'll find fishing—with a 10-horsepower limit on outboard motors—hunting, miniature golf, a skating rink, and a scattering of mom-and-pop vacation cabins scattered around the rim of the 168-acre lake.

The half-mile-by-mile-and-a-quarter lake was originally named Washington Lake in 1798, but has gone through several name changes, probably because the name that kept sticking was one that residents didn't care for—Oil Lake. Canadohta Lake is the headwater for a 13.5-mile stream whose name has never been changed. It's been known for centuries as Oil Creek. Today, Oil Creek is a pleasant meandering stream, running swift and limpid, stocked with brown trout and surrounded by a state park.

In the time around the Civil War, though, Oil Creek was a little slice of hell on earth. The stream was fouled with mud and petroleum runoff. Every tree for miles had been chopped down. Great pools of oil sloshed along the banks and trickled into the stream. This all happened because oil had been discovered and humans were in a rush to get it to the surface, regardless of the consequences.

American history is full of myths that attribute momentous changes to what might be called the eureka theory—Henry Ford invents the automobile, the Wright Brothers invent the airplane, Edwin Drake drills the first modern oil well in the United States. But Ford, the Wrights, and Drake did no such thing. Each of them, like every inventor and innovator in human history, refined and developed ideas and concepts that had been around for years. Some, like Ford, develop not a thing but a process, like mass manufacturing. Some, like the Wrights, successfully test a design that has been knocking around for years. And some, like Drake, happen to be in the right place at the right time.

That place was the town of Titusville, or more properly, land in the edge of Titusville. Visit the bucolic town in northwest Pennsylvania today and you'll find streets lined with stately homes that testify to the nineteenth-century oil wealth that flooded the area. The town was founded in 1796 by pioneers opening up what was then the gateway to the Northwest Territories of Ohio, Indiana, Michigan, and Illinois.

Oil Creek runs into the Allegheny River about 20 miles downstream from Titusville. The Allegheny merges with the Monogohela to form the Ohio, the Ohio runs into the Mississippi, the Mississippi runs from the frigid north to the Gulf of Mexico and is fed by the Missouri, the Missouri snakes into the far west, and therein lies the history of the United States, beginning with small eastern towns like Titusville on small eastern streams like Oil Creek.

The Native Americans had known about surface oil deposits and small springs for centuries, and the first white settlers learned to use the stuff for lubrication and even for quack medicines. One use was for skin balm, which might have been effective, given that modern shampoos for dandruff have the same petroleum base. Another was as a purgative, which would seem logical, since a few teaspoons of crude oil taken internally would clean out the system one way or another.

How the unlikely town of Titusville gave birth to the modern oil industry and the modern oil economy is a story of missed opportunities, greedy exploitation, farsighted speculation, and blind dumb luck; in other words, it's the story of human progress itself.

The Early Oil Seeps

As we noted earlier, oil had been leaking from underground around Titusville for thousands of years. In the early nineteenth century, a local sawmill was using the gooey globs of crude to lubricate the mill's machinery, but not much else was going on with it. At least one local farmer tried to corral the seep oil by building a wooden barricade around the oil pool on his property, but it was still mainly used as a skin balm and lubricant. About 75 miles south of Titusville, though, at least one man in the river city of Pittsburgh had different ideas.

Samuel Kier was a druggist in Pittsburgh, a town where Watt's steam engine, iron ore deposits nearby, and the booming river traffic combined to create a growing industrial monolith. Kier was heir to a salt business owned by his father, who ran a series of small salt mines near Pittsburgh. At the time, salt was valued primarily as a preservative, and only secondarily as a spice. Meat, game, and fish could be safely shipped to the booming western frontier, cured and packed in the salt the Pittsburgh-area mines provided.

But Kier's father's business had a problem. Along with salt and salt brine, sticky oozing crude oil was also being sucked up from the salt wells. In early 1850, an English engineer named James Young patented a process for refining various by-products from surface oil and from oil shale, a process that became the basis for refining as we know it. We don't know if Samuel Kier was aware of Young's breakthrough, or if he simply used his own ingenuity.

> **Petroleum People**
>
> Samuel Kier was born in Tarantum, Pennsylvania, in 1806, the son of an Irish immigrant. Using a whiskey still, he developed the first modern distillation of petroleum products in the United States.

We do know that at some point—and the year is variously given as 1849, 1850, 1851, or 1853—Kier came up with an idea to try and get rid of the oil that was causing so much trouble in his father's salt-mining operations. Kier cobbled together pieces from an old whiskey still in his Pittsburgh apothecary shop, and began to heat the oil to various temperatures to see what came out of it.

If Kier knew of James Young's refining innovation, he was certainly unaware of its primary use. Young thought that refined seep oil could be distilled into kerosene, providing a cleaner way to light lamps than using coal oil. Kier, on the other hand, concentrated on using petroleum as a patent medicine.

Trying to get rid of the oily byproduct from salt (and make a buck or two on the side) Kier began to peddle a concoction advertised as "Samuel M. Kier's Petroleum or Rock Oil, Celebrated for its Wonderful Curative Powers." He had colorful advertising posters printed, showing the derricks and pumping machinery used to suck the oil-bearing salt brine out of the Pennsylvania salt wells.

Through happy coincidence, that poster, not the patent medicine, made Kier a wealthy man and ensured his place in history, and all because of a man named George H. Bissell. If you had to choose an unlikely prototype for the first American oil tycoon, it would be Bissell. He was a Latin scholar and attorney who had worked his way through the Ivy League's Dartmouth College, and went on to a career as a journalist and a school superintendent in New Orleans.

The story goes that as he traveled upriver from New Orleans to Pittsburgh, and then over land to New York, he became intrigued by bottles being sold—not by Kier—as "Pennsylvania Rock Oil." About now is when a series of coincidences began, coincidences that would seem outlandish if they were scripted in Hollywood. But these were real, and led directly to the world we live in today.

At roughly the same time that Bissell was knocking about the country, another Dartmouth alumnus named Dr. Francis Brewer arrived in Titusville and became a partner in the local sawmill, the same sawmill that was using the *seep oil* to lubricate its machinery. Dr. Brewer, intrigued by the oil, carried several bottles of it back east with him, where they came to the attention of some Dartmouth professors.

Drill Bits

Seep oil is the term applied to any form of crude oil that seeps to the surface from underground "springs," from eroding rocks rich in hydrocarbons and fissures leading to oil deposits.

In an 1853 trip to New Hampshire, Bissell happened to be visiting a Dartmouth chemistry professor who had a bottle of the rock oil and knew of Young's research in England that had produced kerosene. This stuff, the professor told Bissell, might someday provide a cheap and clean-burning fuel to use in lamps.

Like many people, Bissell had plenty of ideas but almost no money. By this time, he was a very junior partner in a New York City law firm, where one of the attorneys, Johnathan Eveleth, had a fair amount of cash on hand. With money from Eveleth and some Connecticut speculators, the two attorneys formed the first oil company in the United States, The Pennsylvania Rock Oil Company, and purchased 100 acres of land near Oil Creek, just outside of Titusville. At about the same time, they gathered three barrels of the stinking crude from the Titusville oil seeps and had it shipped to them in New York City, intending to have the goo analyzed chemically. Then the comedy of errors began.

The three barrels of oil made it to New York well enough, but were deposited on the street in front of the building housing the Eveleth and Bissell law offices. Their offices were on the second floor, while the street level was taken up by a series of elegant retail establishments. The attorneys were unaware that their oil had arrived, but passers-by and shop owners on Lower Broadway couldn't escape the pungent, tarry oil fumes that wafted up from the barrels.

Finally, the shopkeepers contacted a cartage company and had the barrels hauled away. Finally discovering what had happened, Bissell and Eveleth went into a panic, and scoured Manhattan until they found the missing oil. Under cover of night, they hauled the three reeking barrels up to their offices for safekeeping until they could contact Dr. Benjamin Silliman, chemistry professor at Yale University.

Silliman began a series of experiments on the oil in his laboratory. Several times, the crude oil was overheated during the experiments, causing several small fires and at least one explosion that destroyed much of Silliman's lab equipment. Finally, in the spring of 1855, he finished his work and produced a sheaf of papers titled "Reports on the Rock Oil, or Petroleum, from Venango County, Pennsylvania." He refused to release the report until he was paid the $525 he was owed for his work, plus the university's destroyed laboratory equipment. This was the first scientific analysis of crude oil and its possible uses, and confirmed that the black glop in northwestern Pennsylvania was potentially valuable stuff.

In the two years that Bissell and Eveleth had owned the 100 acres near Titusville, they had not made a penny in profit, but instead had poured so much money into the enterprise that they were almost flat broke. The only way they had managed to extract any oil from the seeps was to have a series of trenches hand dug, and channel the crude into barrels.

Slick Sayings

In short, your company has in its possession a raw material, from which, by simple and not expensive processes, they may manufacture very valuable products.

—Dr. Benjamin Silliman, in a cover letter to George Bissell and Johnathan Eveleth, 1855

Which brings us back to Samuel Kier and his patent medicine made from the oil he was trying to peddle from his father's salt mines. As Bissell strolled down a New York City street one day in 1855, he came upon one of the garish advertising posters for Kier's oil in a druggist's window. The poster showed pumps, drills, and derricks at work pumping salt brine and the oil residue up from the salt wells in Pennsylvania. Bissell concluded on the spot that the same drilling and pumping method could be used to bring the oil itself to the surface.

It was Bissell's idea, but it would be left to others to put it into use.

The Seneca Oil Company

The East Coast investors in the Pennsylvania Rock Oil Company had, by this time, grown fairly impatient. Chief among them was a man named Robert Townsend, president of the City Savings Bank in New Haven, Connecticut. Located in the same town as Yale, Townsend had seen Silliman's original report on the value of the Titusville oil, and listened as Bissell told him of his plan to use the same kinds of derricks currently used to pump salt brine to pump oil to the surface.

Townsend, though, had grander ideas. He sent a team of fellow New Haven investors to Titusville to see for themselves, and they reported back that oil was oozing up all over the place and that simple drilling mechanisms could turn the gurgle into a steady stream without too much trouble. By this time, the Wall Street Panic of 1857 had washed over many fledgling businesses, including the Bissell company, so Bissell, Eveleth, and their partners found themselves unable to make payments.

Townsend, on the other hand, was flush with cash, and took advantage of the crisis to gobble up the Titusville leases. Townsend also decided to reorganize the Pennsylvania Rock Oil Company, and removed both Bissell and Eveleth from executive positions. This is not to say the two attorneys were shut out—far from it. While they no longer drew salaries or had official positions, both Bissell and Eveleth became quite wealthy from the royalties on oil production.

One of Townsend's first moves was to rename the company. For years, locals around Titusville had called the "medicine" made from seep oil "Seneca Oil," in dubious honor of the Seneca Nation, part of the Iroquois Confederacy of Indian nations. The Seneca had populated the land stretching from Lake Erie down to modern-day Pittsburgh until a "treaty" in 1794 removed them. So Townsend rebranded the "Pennsylvania Rock Oil Company" as the "Seneca Oil Company," over the objections of both Bissell and Eveleth.

The Seneca Oil Company came into being with $300,000 in capital—a huge sum in those days—on March 23, 1858. But the company still needed someone to oversee the actual drilling in the gooey muck of Pennsylvania, something neither Townsend nor his syndicate of Connecticut millionaires wanted to bother themselves with. Through another series of coincidences, they found exactly the right man at the right time.

Mister Drake

Given the financial panics of the late 1850s, hard-luck stories abounded in the United States, but few were as heart-wrenching as that of Edwin Laurentine Drake. Drake was charming and talkative, making friends easily wherever he went. His outgoing disposition was at odds with his turbulent personal life. A railroad conductor by trade, he had been forced to retire in his mid-thirties because of ill health. He was also a widower, responsible for raising a young son alone on a meager railroad pension.

In late 1857, Drake happened to be visiting a friend at New Haven's Tontine Hotel where, as it happened, Townsend lived in a palatial suite of rooms. The two men struck up a conversation, and Townsend was attracted not only by Drake's winning personality, but also by the fact that, as a railroad retiree, Drake was allowed to keep his rail pass, which enabled him to travel for free. Townsend dispatched Drake—at no cost to the company—to Titusville in late 1857, and Drake reported back that up to 5 gallons of oil per day could be had merely by skimming the surface of the company's marshy leased ground, and that many times that amount was probably beneath the surface, waiting to be pumped up.

> **Petroleum People**
>
> Edwin L. Drake was born in 1818, and is credited with starting the modern oil industry in much the same way Henry Ford is credited with beginning the automobile industry. In August, 1859, "Colonel" Drake struck oil in Titusville. Drake never became rich from his strike, and lived mostly on his railroad pension until his death in 1880.

Townsend decided to impress the residents of Titusville—population 125—by adding just a shade more cachet to his agent, so he drafted letters referring to Drake as "Colonel" Drake, a title that stuck. So, the "Colonel" relocated to Titusville in May of 1858, hauling his second wife and (by now) two children along for the ride.

Townsend told Drake he wanted oil in large amounts and wanted it as soon as possible. Buoyed by his native optimism and precious little else, Drake began hiring drillers who worked at nearby salt wells. By the end of the summer, all that the "Colonel" had accumulated were bent and broken drill bits, a hole that kept gurgling up salty brine and then filling quickly with gravel and rock, and bills owed to the workers. Drake then attempted to improve the operation by building an enclosed "drill house" and a wooden derrick that looked more like a chimney.

The locals began calling the entire operation "Drake's Folly," and worse. Drake even found he had difficulty hiring workers, but he did manage to hire one experienced blacksmith who forged tools and drills for the salt wells. Despite being not quite 50 years old, the blacksmith—named William Smith—had a shock of white hair and a white Santa-Claus-type beard and was universally known as "Uncle Billy."

Colonel Drake and Uncle Billy slogged on through the spring and early summer without success, although Drake did come up with one invention that solved the problem of the bore hole filling with gravel and dirt—he merely inserted a pipe into the hole and operated the drill inside the pipe. But by August of 1859, Townsend and the eastern investors had run out of patience, and ordered Drake to cut their losses, shut down the entire operation, and take his free railroad ride back to New Haven.

Drake ignored the letter from his bosses, and was sorry he had, until Saturday, August 27, 1859.

Sixty-Nine-and-a-Half Feet

By that sultry summer afternoon, the drill bit and pipe had sunk 69 feet into the bedrock when it hit an underground pocket, suddenly sank another 6 inches, and stopped. Sweaty and exhausted, Drake ordered Uncle Billy to shut the operation down for the weekend. The next day, Sunday, Smith dropped by the derrick house to check the pipe and found a black substance had floated to the top of the salt brine.

The white-haired blacksmith immediately ran to Drake's house with the news that they had finally struck oil. Drake, by this time almost crippled with a debilitating nerve disorder, decided not to get over to the well immediately, but waited until the Sabbath ended before painfully making his way to the drill site. On Monday, August 29, he and Smith attached a hand pump to the pipe, the kind usually reserved for bringing water to the surface. It was primed, and pumped, and instead of clear drinkable water pumped out thick foul-smelling petroleum, 10 barrels of the stuff in just one day.

Drake and Smith soon attached a steam-driven pump to the pipe, and the first commercial oil well in the United States was bringing oil to the surface in quantities only dreamed of previously. Ten years earlier, in 1849, gold had been discovered in California, triggering a gold rush that drew thousands of miners to the Golden State and despoiled entire valleys and hillsides in the frantic search for gold. This small rural town's population increased by thousands within nine months.

Men, mules, horses, and machines began to stumble over one another in their rush to get to this remote, mountainous part of Pennsylvania. Previously barren hardscrabble patches of oily farm land were sold for several hundred times the $5,000 Drake and Townsend had paid for their 100-acre exploration site.

Within days, holes were gouged in the ground anywhere near Oil Creek, the sides lined with cement or rough-hewn boards. Every tree for miles was felled and used to build pumphouses and derricks. Within three months, the tiny settlement of Pitsville went from containing a half-dozen shacks to 3,000 brawling oil men. Within a year and a half, almost a hundred oil wells sprouted within a few miles of the Drake well. The fumes, spilled oil, barren hillsides, and streams clotted with crude turned the bucolic area into a Bruegel-esque vision of Hades within a few years.

 Slick Sayings

The excitement attendant on the discovery of this vast source of oil was fully equal to what I ever saw in California when a large lump of gold was accidentally turned out.

—*New York Daily Tribune,* September 13, 1859

A tiny hamlet where Oil Creek met the Allegheny River changed its named from Corn Planter to Oil City. In 1865, a reporter for a Cleveland newspaper described the scene there:

> Oil City, with its one long, crooked bottomless street. Oil City with its dirty houses, greasy plank sidewalks, and fathomless mud. Oil City, where horsemen ford the street in from four to five feet of liquid filth [el] Oil City is worthy of its name. The air reeks of oil. The mud is oily. The rocks hugged by the narrow street perspire with oil. The water shines with the rainbow hues of oil. Oil boats loaded with oil throng the oily stream, and oil men with oily hands fasten oily ropes around oily hitching posts. Oily derricks stand among the houses … and the citizens are busy boring in their back yards, in waste lots, or wherever a derrick can be erected.

Stories circulated about one Pennsylvania man—probably a composite of several people—named "Coal Oil Johnnie." According to the tales, he sold his family's failing farm for hundreds of thousands of dollars, built an opera house in Cincinnati, lined his shirt with studs made of diamonds, and carried fists full of $10 and $20 bills to hand out to total strangers on the street. The various stories disagree on almost all the details except one—Coal Oil Johnnie died penniless.

Changing the World

By the end of 1859, the area around Titusville resembled a pillaged war zone. But the gurgle of oil, the shouts of the drillers, and the creaking of timbers and wagon wheels were the sounds of more than just men scrambling to become rich. They were the sounds of the petroleum era being born.

But at the same time, the first wildcatters were staking claims in Pennsylvania. Other changes were at work that would shape the modern world and the modern politics of oil. The world was changing in 1859, in ways that lead directly to where we are today:

♦ The underpinnings of the slave-based, agricultural, antebellum economy of the southern half of the country were starting to creak, groan, and collapse. In 1859, the ship *Clothilde* sailed into Mobile Bay, Alabama, off-loaded its cargo, and was promptly burned to the waterline to prevent it falling into the hands of federal authorities. The ship carried the last load of African slaves ever brought into the United States. Because the slave trade with Africa had been illegal since 1820, the ship's owners and its crew were federal criminals. Also that year, abolitionist John Brown raided the federal arsenal in Harper's Ferry, Virginia, hoping to incite a slave rebellion. Brown failed, and just before his execution handed his jailers a note that read, "I, John Brown, am now quite certain that the crimes of this guilty land will never be purged away but by blood." The stage was set for the Civil War, the end of slavery, the dominance of urban, industrial society, and eventually, the age of petroleum.

♦ Charles Darwin published *The Origins of Species*, and John Stuart Mill wrote his essay *On Liberty*. Both publications firmly cemented the world into a new age. Darwin examined how humans could have evolved over time, putting forth the idea of the "survival of the fittest." Mill wrote that, in a new age when control of governments had passed from monarchies to the people, the biggest threat to liberty was the "tyranny of the majority." Darwin wrote that humans came to exist not by Divine intervention, but by natural processes, while Mill wrote that humans should govern themselves not by Divine laws, but by human institutions aimed at the greatest good for the greatest number. If humans were the result of natural selection, and if humans governed themselves, then maybe humans could govern nature through their machines. And those machines, sooner or later, would require the stuff Drake found.

♦ Gold was discovered in 1859, not in California, but in Colorado. At almost the same time, huge veins of silver were discovered in the Nevada Territory. The Far West was opening up—a process that would lead to a transcontinental rail-road within a decade. The trans-Atlantic telegraph cable had entered its first full year of operation, making almost instant communication across the ocean possible for the first time. Half a world away from Titusville, French engineers were beginning to dig the Suez Canal, so that ships from the West could get to the East without having to sail all the way around Africa. It was a foretaste of global communication and the global economy—still powered by coal, but soon to be fueled by oil.

◆ And it was on February 11, 1859, that Illinois lawyer Abraham Lincoln delivered a speech in Jacksonville, Illinois on the new industrial age, the age of innovation, the age of invention: "We have all heard of Young America ... some think him conceited and arrogant, but has he not reason to entertain a rather extensive opinion of himself? Is he not the inventor and owner of the present, and the sole hope of the future? ... The iron horse is panting, and impatient, to carry him everywhere in no time, and the lightening stands ready harnessed to take and bring his tidings in a trifle less than no time."

All of these loose threads—communication, invention, machinery, industry—merely needed to be melded together. And the glue that would do it into the twenty-first century was just beginning to burble from the ground around Titusville.

The Least You Need to Know

◆ The first oil produced in the United States was found and developed partly by design, partly by coincidence.

◆ Crude oil's value as a replacement for coal oil was verified by experiments at Yale, and exploited by businessmen from Connecticut.

◆ Within months of oil first being discovered in Pennsylvania, an oil rush was on, much like the Gold Rush of a decade earlier.

◆ As the United States stood on the threshold of the Civil War, the world stood on the brink of an accelerated industrial revolution—this one global in scope.

Part 2

Keeping the Blood Flowing: Petroleum Goes Global

Money might not grow on trees, but it does ooze from the ground. They called oil "black gold," and it became the lifeblood of one of the world's most powerful industries. The following chapters recount the story of the oil industry's growing dominance—an era when a little shop that sold seashells and trinkets would become one of the world's largest oil companies, and a high-school dropout named John D. Rockefeller would amass one of the world's biggest fortunes.

And just as the oil industry got used to filling its coffers with oil money, consumers got used to filling their needs and desires with petroleum products. Our growing dependence on—dare we call it an addiction to?—oil has put us at the mercy of a single industry. Is there any way to kick the habit?

Chapter 6

Oil Spreads Around the Globe

In This Chapter

- ◆ The world's first oil well
- ◆ Oil exploration in Europe
- ◆ Digging for oil by hand
- ◆ Harnessing natural gas to provide lighting

Titusville may have captured the world's attention because of its location in the densely populated eastern United States. The news of an oil strike spread quickly by railroads, telegraph wires, and (relatively) short distances between major cities.

But Drake's well wasn't the world's first. Other adventurers and technicians around the world had been working on similar problems and had come up with similar solutions. The problem was that they were working in technologically backward countries with sparse populations and governments that were often less than interested in oil exploration.

As we've seen in previous chapters, the world was just about ready for the coming age of oil. Urban, industrial centers were growing, global trade and communication were entering the semi-modern era, and coal oil/kerosene was the primary means of providing light for most of the industrial world's homes and businesses. But as always, the politics of oil would affect the future as much as the oil itself.

The Russians Drill First

The Baku Peninsula juts like a hitchhiker's thumb into the oil-rich Caspian Sea. The mountain tribesmen of what's now called Azerbaijan had converted to Islam centuries before the Tsar of All the Russias, Alexander I, conquered the area in 1806. As we've noted previously, the area was rich with petroleum seeps and fissures through which natural gas rose to the surface and ignited, creating natural towers of flame worshiped by the cult of Zoroaster.

As early as the tenth century, hand-dug wells proliferated in the region. By the thirteenth century, Marco Polo noted the Azerbaijani oil in his journals, noting that traders traveled for miles to procure the oil, used as both a salve for skin ailments and, in some areas, to light lamps. By 1821, there were at least 120 hand-dug oil wells and trenches in the area. About the same time, a crude distilling operation that refined kerosene from oil was in use in the city of Baku. It was, at best, a cottage industry, with the refined product only shipped a few miles from where it was made.

But an enterprising Russian engineer named V.N. Semyonov was about to change all that. In 1844, 15 years before the Drake well in Titusville, he suggested that a drilling mechanism be used to sink a shaft instead of digging the holes by hand. A hole was drilled about 70 feet deep in an area called Bibi-Heybat just south of the town of Baku, and oil was pumped to the surface.

Petro-Facts

Bibi-Heybat is a marshy area just south of the modern city of Baku in Azerbaijan. The oil field there was first explored with a drilled well in 1844. The field continues to produce oil today.

Unfortunately for Semyonov, his report on the success of the drilling operation didn't come to the attention of his superiors in Moscow for two years, and even then, they showed little interest in the development. Had Russia and its conquered territories had the same industrial and political infrastructure as the United States, they would have beaten the Americans by a decade and a half, and could have become world leaders in the production and refining of the new product.

As it was, only the name of the new product for lamps was credited to the region. In the local dialect, "kir" referred to the tarry crude oil that had seeped to the surface for centuries. So, it was only natural that the word for the refined product that could light homes and factories should include the original word for the tarry oil and become what we today call kerosene.

Exploration in Romania

When the Roman legions first marched into what's now Romania about the time of the birth of Christ, they noted the foul-smelling oil seeps that dotted the landscape between the Carpathian Mountains and the Black Sea. Those seeps would become the basis of what may be the world's first commercial refining operations.

While there were plenty of raw materials, the other ingredients to develop a thriving petroleum industry—infrastructure, population, stable government—were all missing. The country that eventually became Romania was, in the mid-nineteenth century, a collection of Christian principalities under the control of the Islamic Ottoman Empire. But because the Ottomans kept losing militarily and politically to the European powers, what became Romania was, in the 1850s, technically controlled by Turkey, but was partly administered by a coalition of European powers that included France, Britain, Prussia, Russia, and Austria. This created not only a political mess but a government bureaucracy that responded slowly, if at all, to innovation.

So when oil began to be pumped successfully from the fields, and the world's first successful commercial refinery was established in 1857, Romania was in no shape to take advantage of the advances in technology. Two years before Drake's well was pumping up Pennsylvania crude, the Romanians were producing almost 300 metric tons of crude a year. And by the time the Titusville well came on line in 1859, the Romanian city of Ploiesti was largely lit by the kerosene that was both pumped and refined nearby.

But Romania was far from the only country in Europe—or even in eastern Europe—to develop a petroleum industry before the Titusville discovery.

> **Slick Sayings**
>
> Romania was a country very rich in oil and natural gas. I don't know if you know the history of oil but exploration of oil around the world started here in Romania in 1857, even two years before the United States.
>
> —Aureliu Leca, President, Romanian Electricity Authority, 2001

The Wells of Poland

Seep oil had been a resource and a nuisance since ancient times in Poland. Oil skimmed by hand from the surface seeps had been used in lamps in the Polish town of Krosno as early as the sixteenth century. But the stuff wasn't refined, and burned with a stench and smoke that almost made it unusable.

Druggists in the nineteenth century were more than mere pill-pushers and prescription-fillers; they were scientific tinkerers, on the front lines of practical scientific innovation.

Petroleum People

Abraham Gesner was born in Nova Scotia, Canada, in 1797. A geologist by avocation and a physician by training, he developed what seems to have been the world's first practical method for distilling kerosene from crude oil in 1849. A monument to him in Nova Scotia reads, in part, "He first refined kerosene and promoted its manufacture in New York." Dr. Gesner died in 1864.

Remember Samuel Kier from Pittsburgh, the druggist who developed a way of distilling petroleum that came up from his father's salt mines? His Eastern European counterpart was Ignacy Lukasiewicz, a Polish druggist who had also been experimenting with seep oil and what to do with the stuff.

Lukasiewicz was looking for a better alternative to the whale oil that burned in European lamps. He had read about some preliminary work done in Canada by Dr. Abraham Gesner to produce clear-burning kerosene from seeping crude oil, and began fiddling with the process, trying to improve it so that he might be able to produce relatively clean-burning energy in large quantities.

Lukasiewicz got a chance to try out his development in the real world in July of 1853, when a nighttime emergency operation at a local hospital was made possible because the pharmacist provided illumination courtesy of one of his experimental lamps. The hospital, more than slightly grateful, ordered dozens of the lamps and hundreds of barrels of the new clean-burning fuel. Lukasiewicz, in turn, went to Vienna and secured a patent for his process good for Poland and the rest of the Austro-Hungarian Empire.

Remember, we're still six years away from the Drake well in Titusville. The Polish druggist was now able to secure financial backers for his project and began to extract sluggish crude from hand-dug wells in southeastern Poland. But these wells were relatively shallow, producing a thick, clotted oil that, in turn, produced a low-grade form of kerosene. Lukasiewicz began to wonder if lighter, more suitable oil could be found further below the surface.

The Poles began to dig deeper, but did it by hand, not machine. In fact, the earliest deep wells were simply called "petroleum mines," because they were wide shafts gouged out by pick and shovel, the same way salt mines in Pennsylvania and coal mines in Poland had been dug.

Starting in 1854, these mines were sunk to depths of 150 feet, then 200 feet, then 250 feet, each producing a slightly better grade of crude oil than the one before. By 1856, mines as deep as 500 feet had been sunk in the foothills of the Polish Carpathians, and were producing a lighter, cleaner-burning product than ever before. For the deeper wells, mere hand-digging alone wasn't doing the trick, so an unusual, somewhat ridiculous, and ultimately effective technology was developed.

A metal drill bit would be attached by cables to the end of a strong yet limber wooden pole. The pole would be inserted in a pre-dug hole, and a man—chosen for both bravery and sheer weight—would climb the pole and literally hug it near the top, secured by a safety belt, his feet resting in a pair of stirrups. The man would bounce up and down, forcing the pole and the drill bit up and down, slowly but surely digging into dirt and rock. Before long, scores of men were jumping on wooden poles in the ground, creating oil mines across an entire section of what's now Poland.

In a country like the United States, fired with the fuel of entrepreneurial capitalism, many of these enterprising Poles on poles would have become rich men. But in the turmoil of the Austro-Hungarian Empire, where Poland didn't exist as a country at all and where the aristocratic government was embroiled in disputes with its more powerful neighbors, the hard work and zeal of the early oil explorers didn't, in the end, amount to much.

The same year Drake struck oil, the Empire went to war with the Kingdoms of Italy and Napoleon III of France. The Austro-Hungarians lost, and lost another war five years later with Prussia. In this case, as in so many others, the international politics didn't lead to exploration and exploitation of oil, but did just the opposite—they delayed the use and development of what would soon become the world's most important industry.

Hand Digging in California

The decade before Drake dug in Pennsylvania was a turbulent one on the other side of the North American continent. In 1846, the United States went to war with Mexico. One of the largest prizes was California, which had been ripped apart by fighting between independence-minded settlers and the Mexican government for years. Finally, in 1847, a truce was signed between American Colonel John Fremont and Mexican General Andreas Pico, a truce that gave the United States control of California and gave General Pico generous surrender terms.

Andreas Pico gave up his military career and became a land baron and businessman. Intrigued by stories of gold that might be found near the settlement of Los Angeles— population 3,500—Pico hired laborers and began scouring the surrounding hillsides. Pico also began coveting land, and when California was finally legally ceded to the United States, Pico went before the United States Supreme Court with a claim that he had been given a grant to some 44,000 square miles of land. The document turned out to be a forgery.

Pico never did discover much gold, but another sort of wealth was at his feet. Oil seeps covered parts of California, and Native American tribes like the Maidu and

Yokut had used the oozing crude oil for centuries to waterproof boats and to decorate baskets and pottery. Anglo settlers bringing their wagons into California following the gold discoveries of 1849 had used the stuff to grease the axles of their wagons. Some had even scraped up enough to lay down crude pavement in some settlements.

In 1850, Pico used his miners to start excavating the crude in larger quantities. Using much the same distilling methods as those in England, Poland, and Pennsylvania, he began to refine kerosene from the crude—the first refining operation of any kind in California.

Lighting Up Stockton

Stockton, California, was the first city in the Golden State to have a non-Hispanic, non-Native American name, having been christened in honor of Commodore Robert Stockton, the military commander who captured San Francisco and San Diego during the war with Mexico. Stockton was preferable to one of the original names for the settlement—Gas City. Plopped in the middle of the agricultural San Fernando Valley, Stockton had a problem: It sat atop old marshes and oil seeps, and the water was undrinkable because it either tasted of petroleum tar or sulfur.

A number of small rivers came together near Stockton, and the rotting material that produced the oil seeps also produced natural gas. In the late 1850s, Stockton harnessed the gas output and became one of the first cities in the world to be lit by natural gas, not coal tar gas. The streets, shops, several homes, and the entire Stockton Courthouse were illuminated with the natural gas, a by-product of the petroleum that lurked beneath the surface.

Combined with the mineral water heated by natural gas burners—unfit to drink but dandy for curative baths—the use of natural gas for illumination turned Stockton into something of a tourist resort. But by and large, the natural gas and the oil pockets containing it remained something of a sideshow. Even the coming Civil War wouldn't change that a great deal, as we'll see in the next chapter. But other events were taking place as the world slowly but surely staggered its way toward the age of oil.

Oil by Water

The Schuylkill River empties into the Delaware River 102 miles from the Atlantic Ocean. Today, the port of Philadelphia that surrounds the confluence is still a major shipping hub, but in the eighteenth and nineteenth centuries, it was one of the world's largest ports, a vital part of one of America's oldest cities.

The oil being produced in northwestern Pennsylvania had an easy enough time reaching the new inland empire of the United States, since the barrels of both crude and distilled kerosene could just be shipped down the Ohio and then either upriver to St. Louis or downriver to New Orleans. But shipping oil to the populated and profitable east required either trips by rudimentary railroad or grueling journeys overland. It didn't take long for businessmen in Philadelphia to realize that an even larger profit might be realized by shipping the oil to Europe.

The 224 ton *Elizabeth Watts* was a two-masted brig, square-sailed and sturdy, a veteran of several trans-Atlantic crossings. In November, 1861, she rode low in the water at her Delaware River dock, her hold packed with more than 1,000 barrels of crude oil from the fields of western Pennsylvania. She would soon be bound for London, if only Captain Charles Bryant could find a crew.

> **Petro-Facts**
>
> The sailing ship *Elizabeth Watts* is often described as the mother of all oil tankers. She left the port of Philadelphia on November 19, 1861, carrying a cargo of 1,329 barrels of crude oil, and docked in London on January 9, 1862. It was the first time oil was transported from one country to another by ship.

Word had spread along the docks for weeks that the ship would be carrying oil, and almost none of the sailors wanted anything to do with her. The fumes from the reeking barrels of crude could be smelled blocks away on the docks, and the hold below decks was filled with a miasma of choking and potentially explosive oil vapors.

Captain Bryant turned to one of the most time-honored traditions of the sea—he shanghied a crew. Bryant sent his agents prowling the docks the night of November 18, 1861, exploring the waterfront taverns for the most able-bodied and drunkest sailors. By the time they awoke the next day, dazed and hung over, they found themselves in the widest part of the Delaware River, heading out to sea with their noxious cargo. None of them died, although several probably wished they would have as they suffered both the stormy North Atlantic winter and the putrid reek of their cargo. Six weeks later, the *Elizabeth Watts* docked safely in London, and the oil tanker industry had been born.

Les Carriages sans Chevaux

We've noted before that the age of petroleum couldn't really begin until there was an internal combustion engine that needed oil products for fuel. Humans had been working on the problem for centuries, and the very earliest successes in horseless carriages came from France.

In 1769, the first self-propelled wheeled vehicle in history was put on the road by a French engineer named Nicolas Cugnot. Operating under a contract from the French army, Cugnot cobbled together a steam-powered three-wheeled tractor at the Paris Arsenal. It could pull artillery pieces at a speed of almost three miles an hour, but had to stop every 15 minutes or so for a new head of steam to build up in its boiler. The French military eventually decided that horses were a more reliable means of hauling field pieces.

> **Petroleum People**
>
> Nicolas Joseph Cugnot was born in France in 1725, and is recognized by both the Automobile Club de France and the British Royal Automobile Club as being the inventor of the automobile in 1769. His experiments ended when funding was cut off before the French Revolution. Cugnot died in 1804.

But Cugnot decided that if his steam vehicle could pull cargo, it could also haul people, so, in 1770, he designed a massive three-wheeled steam carriage that could transport up to four people. The vehicles were powered by reciprocating engines, using the steam to push a piston down a cylinder, and using the resulting power to turn the wheels. As we've noted in previous chapters, this is essentially the same design used in modern automobile engines.

Before Cugnot was forced to abandon his steam experiments with horseless carriages, he recorded another first. In 1771, one of his vehicles lost control and slammed into a stone wall near Paris. It was the world's first motor vehicle accident.

Progress marched ahead. A few years later, French engineer Onesiphore Pecqueur invented the differential gear, which allowed power to be transferred more efficiently to the wheels of Cugnot's vehicle. In 1789, an American inventor named Oliver Evans was given a patent for a steam-powered land vehicle. In 1801, the first British version was perfected by English inventor Richard Trevithick. Steam-powered stagecoaches rattled across British roads starting in 1820, but were banned because of the noise and danger. All of these early vehicles used steam.

That changed around the time of the American Civil War. In 1858, a Belgian immigrant to France named Jean Joseph Lenoir took the steam-powered reciprocating engine and substituted a mixture of coal gas and air for the steam. He ignited the mixture using an electric spark, and patented the device in 1860. He kept tinkering, and by 1863, had developed a version of his horseless carriage that ran, not on coal gas, but on refined petroleum.

Lenoir needed to find a way to inject the petroleum-air mixture into the cylinder, so he invented the great-granddaddy of today's automobile carburetor. Would the contraption work? Lenoir answered the question by attaching the engine and carburetor to a three-wheeled farm wagon, and taking it on a 50-mile trip through the French countryside.

A year earlier, in 1862, another French engineer—Alphonse de Rochas—patented what would have become the world's first four-stroke engine. He submitted detailed drawings and diagrams, but never built the device. Had he done so, he would have constructed what amounted to the world's first modern automobile engine. As we'll see in the next chapter, it was left to German engineers two decades later to perfect the design and usher in the age of internal combustion.

Why was de Rochas's design, theoretical as it was, a breakthrough? Because most modern engines work on the basic four-stroke (or four-step) principle he devised:

◆ **Stroke (or step) One:** A piston goes down the cylinder and a valve at the top of the cylinder called the "intake valve" opens, allowing a mixture of air and fuel to be sucked into the cylinder. When the piston reaches the bottom of the cylinder, the valve closes.

◆ **Stroke Two:** A turning crankshaft pushes the piston toward the top of the cylinder. This compresses the fuel and air mixture. When the piston is close to the top of the cylinder, the fuel-air mixture is compressed to the point where it becomes explosive.

◆ **Stroke Three:** There is a spark plug at the top of the cylinder. When the fuel-air mixture is compressed, the spark plug is turned on by the position of the crank shaft, which closes an electric circuit, which causes a spark that ignites the fuel and air to cause a small explosion. This shoves the piston down to the bottom of the cylinder.

◆ **Stroke Four:** Another valve at the top of the cylinder, called the "outlet valve," opens as the piston rises in the cylinder. This allows the smoke and waste products from the explosion to be expelled. As the piston reaches the top of the cylinder, the outlet valve closes, the inlet valve opens, and the process repeats itself.

Inventors, tinkerers, and engineers throughout Europe were working on roughly the same ideas at roughly the same time. Another breakthrough came in 1864, courtesy of an engineer from Austria named Siegfried Marcus. Marcus was fiddling about in his Vienna workshop with a one-cylinder horseless carriage and decided to use a different kind of fuel—he called it benzene. We call it gasoline.

The crude distilleries in Europe were producing kerosene for lighting lamps, and it was this product that had been used so far to power the early experimental petroleum-driven horseless carriages. In 1864, the 33-year-old Marcus had lost three fingers of his right hand, blown off in his experiments. Those experiments were not focused on creating an automobile, but were instead trying to generate electricity by means of a petroleum-powered motor.

Drill Bits

Gasoline boils off of crude oil at temperatures between 99 and 356 degrees Fahrenheit. Kerosene boils off at temperatures between 302 and 482 degrees Fahrenheit. So gasoline is distilled from crude at lower temperatures, followed by kerosene.

Marcus discovered that if you used the product distilled from crude oil at a lower temperature, you got what we call *gasoline*, and that it exploded with a good deal more power inside a cylinder than kerosene. So he began using the lower-temperature distillate in his engines with a fairly spectacular increase in efficiency.

Marcus created an electric generator that consisted of a 4-foot-tall cylinder-and-piston arrangement. He later mounted the device on two wagon wheels so that it could be portable, and then came up with the idea of trying to power a vehicle using essentially the same setup.

In 1864, Marcus rigged his cylinder and piston arrangement to a wagon, with two large wheels in the rear used for propulsion and two smaller wheels in the front used to (more or less) steer the contraption. He fired it up, and the motor vehicle crossed over 500 yards of rocky, unpaved ground.

Siegfried Marcus doesn't get much credit in modern histories of internal combustion and petroleum, for a pair of reasons, one of which is connected to the darker chapters of the politics of oil. On a simple bureaucratic level, Marcus received patents for many of his inventions—a form of carburetor, an electric magneto, and a "thermal column," one of the earliest generators designed to convert heat from a piston and cylinder arrangement into electricity. But Marcus never applied for a patent on his horseless carriage *per se*, which allowed other inventors in the following decades to use his research and patent the thing themselves.

Marcus had one other problem: He was a Jew. Despite anti-Semitism in the nineteenth century's Austro-Hungarian Empire, this didn't prove to be much of an impediment during his lifetime. Indeed, Marcus was continually honored by various academies and scientific societies, and received a glowing multi-page write-up in an 1867 publication called *Distinguished Personalities of Imperial Austria*.

But after his death, Marcus's contributions to modern life and automotive engineering were almost obliterated when another Austrian, Adolf Hitler, came to power in Germany, determined to eliminate almost all references of Jewish achievement from the history books.

When Nazi forces rolled into Austria in 1938, Hitler ordered them to erase all traces of Marcus's inventions and innovations, including destroying the original Marcus vehicle then on display at a museum in Vienna. But officials from the Viennese Museum for Trade and Industry not only risked their lives to hide Marcus's research papers, they made off with the car and bricked it up behind a wall in the museum's basement.

But Hitler's ploy worked well enough that even today, the Germans Daimler and Benz are given almost total credit for inventing the internal combustion engine. In the next chapter, we'll show how they, along with Henry Ford, did indeed usher in the age of mass transportation and mass consumption of petroleum products. But none of their work would have been possible without Marcus. And his work couldn't have happened without Alphonse de Rochas. And de Rochas's breakthrough depended on the work done by Jean Lenoir. Any one of those links missing from the chain of human enterprise would mean we would not be living in the type of modern world we live in today.

The Least You Need to Know

- Early oil wells were drilled and dug in Russia, Poland, and Romania.

- The early nineteenth century exploration and conquest of California resulted in the discovery and exploitation of pockets of natural gas and crude oil.

- The first shipment of oil by sea from one country to another took place just as the American Civil War was beginning.

- Innovators in France and Austria paved the way for the modern automobile and the age of petroleum.

Chapter 7

The Crude New World

In This Chapter

- ◆ The American Civil War slows petroleum's progress
- ◆ Rockefeller builds an empire based on kerosene
- ◆ Edison's light replaces the need for kerosene
- ◆ Oil finds a new future in the automobile

Looking back from the twenty-first century, we can't seem to recognize much of our modern world in the early nineteenth century. Things begin to look familiar, however, once we get past the Civil War and start to move into the era of mechanization, manufacturing, and mass production.

In the second half of the nineteenth century, we see the emergence of not only a world we recognize, but of the giant corporations that, for better or worse, are such an integral part of our modern planet. Names like Rockefeller, Edison, Daimler, Benz, and Ford appear on the landscape, creating a new era of mammoth business enterprises that control everything from raw materials to final manufactured products.

In this chapter, we'll see how the politics of oil began to play out in the United States and in the world, as the nineteenth century headed toward the twentieth century.

Blue, Gray, and Black

When the first Confederate shots were fired at Fort Sumter to ignite the American Civil War in April, 1861, one natural resource from the Middle East suddenly became amazingly valuable. Nope, it wasn't oil. It was cotton.

The United States Navy slapped a blockade on most Confederate ports, which meant that cotton from the American South suddenly had a very hard time finding its way into markets in Europe.

Cotton from Egypt became vitally important for European, and especially English, textile mills. While the American Navy choked off commerce to the South, the Confederate Navy took to the high seas and began to hunt down Yankee whaling ships. One of the most successful rebel raiders was the *CSS Shenandoah*. This lone Confederate vessel circumnavigated the globe and sank a number of American whaling vessels in the Arctic Ocean after the Civil War had technically ended.

The Confederate raids helped destroy the American whaling industry, but even more damage was done by skyrocketing insurance premiums. Also, many of the Union vessels used to blockade Southern ports were whaling vessels that had been purchased by the U.S. government. Suddenly, it became less and less profitable and more and more hazardous to go to sea and look for the whale oil that had previously lit the world's lamps (a turn of events that probably kept whales from extinction).

At almost precisely the same time that the whale oil industry fell on hard times, the new petroleum industry took off in Pennsylvania with new oil discoveries being made in places ranging from Indiana and Ohio to California. The distilling process was becoming more and more sophisticated, meaning that kerosene to light the world's lamps could be made more cheaply and more quickly than ever before.

The modern oil industry was about to be born, and the midwife was a bookkeeper from Cleveland named Rockefeller.

> **Slick Sayings**
>
> We went through the Bering Strait into the Arctic Ocean, until the ice again prevented us from going further, so we turned, passing again through the Aleutian Islands into the Pacific Ocean. By this time we had absolutely destroyed or broken up the Federal whaling fleets.
>
> —Capt. W.C. Whittle, *CSS Shenandoah*, Confederate Veteran Magazine, October, 1904

A Fellow Named Rockefeller

John Davison Rockefeller was the second of six children, born to a laborer's family in the town of Richford, New York, in 1839. In 1853, when John was 14, the family moved to a farm near Cleveland, Ohio. The father, William Rockefeller, insisted he be called "Doctor" Rockefeller, since he had a business making and selling dubious home remedies and patent medicines.

By age 16, the young John D. had dropped out of high school and was working as an assistant bookkeeper for $4 a week. The teenager put in long hours at the firm, and by age 20, in 1859, he was made a partner in the firm of Clark and Rockefeller, "Produce and Commission Merchants, and Dealers in Salt, Fish, and Water Lime," with offices near where the Cuyahoga River dumped into Lake Erie.

When the Civil War broke out in 1861, Clark and Rockefeller quickly landed contracts to provide salted meat and fish, as well as other provisions, to the Union Army. It was an exceptionally profitable business, netting the firm a profit of $17,000 in the first year of the war.

Ever since oil had been discovered in Titusville, Rockefeller had his eye on the burgeoning kerosene lighting industry as a way to make even larger profits. But his sense of order was offended by the rough-and-tumble ways of the Pennsylvania oil men, and he realized that the way to profit from the budding business was to try and control it from top to bottom. At the same time, he saw that railroads would soon become the preferred means of shipping products, and that the growing grain and rail center of Chicago would soon eclipse Cleveland when it came to shipping foodstuffs.

John D. Enters the Oil Business

Starting in 1862, Rockefeller and his partner, Maurice Clark, began to inquire seriously about going into the oil business. Clark said he knew a young chemist from England named Sam Andrews who had experience in the fledgling kerosene business and who was convinced that distilling the crude oil into usable products was where the money was to be made.

The men decided to scrimp and pool their money to set up a refining operation on the banks of the Cuyahoga, where the refined crude could easily be transported by ship to the growing markets for kerosene across the United States. But the taciturn Rockefeller first had to avoid going off to war. One exemption had been written into the government law requiring a military draft, an exemption that allowed men of means to purchase a "substitute" to fight for them, providing they could pay the then princely sum of $600.

In July, 1863, after the battle of Gettysburg and about the same time anti-draft riots were ripping New York City apart, Rockefeller paid the money and avoided being drafted into the Union Army. That same year, with chemist Sam Andrews and commissary partner Maurice Clark, he founded the oil refining firm of Andrews, Clark, and Company of Cleveland.

Slick Sayings

The only time I ever saw John Rockefeller enthusiastic was when a report came in from the creek that his buyer had secured a cargo of oil at a figure much below the market price. He bounded from his chair with a shout of joy, danced up and down, hugged me, threw up his hat, and acted so like a mad man that I have never forgotten it.

—Maurice Clark quoted in *Titan: The Life of John D. Rockefeller*, by Ron Chernow, Random House, 1998

While Maurice Clark and his brothers—whom he had brought into the business—saw a handsome profit to be made refining small amounts of oil, Rockefeller saw something grander. He had long since decided that the best way to make a profit in business was to watch every expense, and to control almost every aspect of any particular industry. He started out by buying up huge tracts of white oak trees in northern Ohio—the kind used for making oil barrels. He then decided that it cost too much to ship the timber to cooperages to be made into barrels, so he set up wood-drying kilns on the timber tracts to dry the wood, so it weighed less, so more of it could be transported at a lower cost.

He then purchased the wagons and horses to transport the timber to the barrel makers, and then bought out the barrel-making shops themselves. The cost to Rockefeller of each barrel to carry his refined oil was cut in half—from $3 down to a $1.50. But the ever-cautious Clark brothers refused to expand the business fast enough to suit Rockefeller, so in 1865, at the age of 26, he bought out his former partners for what was then the astronomical sum of $72,500.

The Civil War was over, the agrarian life of the South was in ruins, and the industrial machine of the North was moving at full throttle. Rockefeller decided to expand the business, and took on Henry Flagler as a partner. Flagler had gone into business during the Civil War mining salt in Pennsylvania, and went broke doing it. He managed to recover, and by the end of the war, was running a successful business making oil barrels in Cleveland.

The Beginnings of a Monopoly

Instead of buying out Flagler as he had the other barrel-makers, Rockefeller took him on as a partner. Three years after the end of the war, in 1868, the men and their company were the largest refiners of crude oil products in the world. Notice that we said *products*. The use of the plural is vital here because at this point, kerosene was the only thing most distillers bothered to remove from the crude oil, since it was the only product used for lamp fuel. Rockefeller and Flagler quickly decided that there was too much waste from the crude oil—gasoline, for example, was dumped into the Cuyahoga by many other refiners as a waste product. But the Rockefeller operation refined it. In all, they refined the following products from crude oil:

- **Kerosene,** which was used for lamp fuel.

- **Lubricating oil,** made from the sludge left over after the refining process was complete.

- **Gasoline,** which they discovered could be used as fuel, although not for burning in lamps.

- **Benzine,** used as a solvent and cleaning fluid.

- **Paraffin,** used to make candles, waterproofing, preservatives, and so forth.

- **Petrolatum,** a whiteish inert grease used for medical dressings and often taken internally for constipation. This product later became famous under the trademarked name of Vaseline.

- **Naphtha,** used as everything from a cleaning product for clothing to making paints.

In addition, the partners owned the forests the oil barrels were made from, the kilns used to dry the barrel wood, the barrel-making operations themselves, the horses and wagons used to transport various products, the warehouses in other cities where the oil was stored, the huge containers next to the refineries where the crude oil was held, the specially designed railroad cars fitted with giant tubs to transport the oil, and even their own plants to make the sulfuric acid used in the refining process.

The two men didn't own the railroads—at least not yet—but they had the next best thing. Unlike most cities where rail service was a monopoly, Cleveland was served by two competing railroads, the Erie and the New York Central. The Rockefeller oil operation was able to keep its costs well below those of any other refinery by negotiating deals with the rail companies. The Rockefeller refiners called them "rebates," while their competitors called them "payoffs." But whatever you called them, Flagler and Rockefeller were able to ship their products by rail at far lower rates than anyone else.

The advantage in cost soon started to drive other companies out of business. There were hardly any regulations on fair trade or competition at the time, so the fledgling company was able to bankrupt its competition and then buy them out at a fraction of their value.

Rockefeller and Flagler Build an Empire

By the time that Rockefeller, one of his brothers, Flagler, Andrews, and others formed the Standard Oil Company of Ohio in 1870, the pattern had been established for the future operations of the Rockefeller empire. The strategy had four basic components:

- **The creation of a monopoly.** While making sure that his company owned almost every part of a business necessary to refine crude oil, Rockefeller was able to deny his competitors everything from oil barrels to storage facilities for their oil.

- **The use of rebates.** We'll look more closely at this shortly. Railroads that transported oil were forced to acquiesce to Standard's demands for reduced rates, thus enabling Standard to ship its oil far more cheaply than competitors were able to. This crossed the line from cutthroat business practice to illegal operations when Standard began receiving kickbacks from the railroads for oil its competitors shipped.

- **The use of price cuts.** Because of its mammoth size, Standard was able to survive cutting its prices drastically for short periods of time, thus driving smaller competitors out of business.

- **The use of strong-arm tactics.** When all else failed, Standard would hire men to sabotage competitor's operations and intimidate employees.

Because the Standard behemoth was so large, it was able to leverage its position with lawmakers and other industries to deal in what today would be clearly illegal business practices. The Standard deal with some railroads was one prime example.

Petro-Facts

The Standard Oil Company of Ohio was incorporated by John D. Rockefeller in Cleveland in 1870. It grew as the original company in the Standard Oil trust until it was broken up by federal regulators in 1892. In the early twentieth century, Standard of Ohio became Sohio, marketing gasoline in neighboring states under the trademark of Boron until it "merged" with British Petroleum and sold gas under the BP trademark, which it continues to do today. Other Standard Oil companies were broken up in 1911 when the Supreme Court found Standard Oil to be in violation of the 1890 Sherman Antitrust Act. This breakup spawned the babies that are now two of today's largest oil companies—Exxon Mobil and Chevron.

In 1870, the same year created a corporation called the South Improvement Company. This was nothing more than a legalized series of interlocking monopolies, based on a deal cut some years earlier among five railroads and two coal companies. That earlier arrangement enabled the rail and coal companies to create virtual monopolies on the shipment of and exploration for coal.

The idea behind South Improvement was to set prices for both the railroads and co-operating oil companies at a high-enough level to ensure large profits for both parties. The deal was much deeper than that. Oil refiners that were part of the company got significant "rebates," enabling them to ship oil much more cheaply than their competitors. But the oil refiners that were not part of the arrangement were charged extra to ship their oil, and that extra charge was funneled by the railroads directly to the refiners who were part of South Improvement.

This meant that the noncooperating refiners were, in effect, *paying their competitors* for the ability to ship oil. Rockefeller and Standard were an integral part of the scheme, which collapsed when the oil drillers themselves demanded a cut of the action. When the background of South Improvement became public, it was a black eye for Rockefeller. It wouldn't be the last.

Undeterred, Rockefeller and Flagler became determined to forge a monopoly, and by 1872 had managed to buy out just about every other refining operation in the Cleveland area. That was just the start, and as the 1870s progressed, Standard bought out as many other companies as it could, keeping the transactions so quiet that senior officers of the targeted oil operations often weren't aware that they were being bought out until the deed was done.

A good deal of this was made possible by the Great Collapse of 1873, a financial crash that had echoes in the stock market disaster of 1929. Rockefeller and Flagler used the depressed economy and enormous sums of money at their disposal to secretly buy up controlling interests in refining operations from Cleveland to Pittsburgh. They bought out the entire refining capacity of the state of West Virginia in less than a year.

Slick Sayings

The impression was gaining ground with me that it was a good thing to let the money be my servant and not make myself a slave to the money.
—John D. Rockefeller, 1904

By 1878, Rockefeller was one of the 20 wealthiest men in America, and tightened his stranglehold on oil refining and oil shipping. By the end of the year, Standard Oil was able to ship oil by rail from refineries in Titusville, Cleveland, and Pittsburgh for a mere 80¢ a barrel while competitors were charged $1.45 for the same amount.

John D. Rockefeller now controlled 90 percent of the oil refined in the United States, and 70 percent of the oil being exported from the United States to overseas ports. His wealth, in twenty-first century dollars, was in excess of $100 billion, and he was determined that Standard Oil would soon control the lion's share of every refinery, oil pipeline, and retail outlet selling kerosene and lubricating products.

His dreams were dashed by Edison, whose success with electricity made Rockefeller's kerosene almost worthless except in rural areas.

Edison's Invention

Maybe there was something in the Ohio water that led to committed and often mercenary men. Thomas Alva Edison was born in February, 1847, to a middle-class family in the Lake Erie port town of Milan, Ohio. Edison's story, like Rockefeller's, is the stuff of American myth and legend.

Mechanically minded since his earliest years, Edison mastered the telegraph and was determined to improve on it so that it could actually be used to transmit a human voice. Building a series of workshops and labs in Menlo Park, New Jersey, with the money he had been paid for inventing an improved stock ticker, Edison toiled away at the device, only to be beaten to the punch—and the patent—by Alexander Graham Bell.

Edison got over his disappointment and aimed for a new quest. He wanted to invent a way to use electricity to create light. In 1879, he went through hundreds of combinations, trying to find just the right filament that would provide light inside a vacuum bulb without bursting into flame. He finally managed to find a combination that worked—cotton fibers coated with carbon. First they burned for a few hours, then for a few more, then finally for dozens of hours, then finally for days.

Edison's electric lamp received U.S. patent number 223,898, one of over a thousand patents Edison was to be granted in his lifetime. The problem, though, was that while the thing worked, there was nowhere it could be used, since it required something that didn't yet exist: commercially generated electricity.

> **Slick Sayings**
>
> Object: Edison to effect imitation of all done by gas, so as to replace lighting by gas with lighting by electricity.
>
> —Thomas Edison, Volume 134 (out of 3,400) of his diaries

His supporters call it research, his detractors call it theft. But whichever way you look at it, Edison was cobbling together his dream of an empire of commercially generated electricity based on research and work done by others, from the brilliant theoretician Nicolai Tesla to the British researcher Joseph Hopkinson. Edison convinced people with even deeper pockets than his own, notably the banker J. Pierpont Morgan, to help underwrite his venture.

Edison soon built a giant power-generating station in lower Manhattan. He dreamed of electrifying New York City by putting wires on poles above the city streets to carry current to every house. He hit a major barrier. Energy was lost in those wires and he often couldn't send electricity two city blocks without the power sputtering and fading out.

His first plan to correct the problem was to build an electric power generator in every neighborhood so that wires would never be more than a few blocks long. Imagine what our country would look like if that plan was implemented.

This is when a talented engineer from Russia named Nicholai Tesla entered the scene. He later quit his job with Edison because he claimed Edison had patented his ideas and didn't give him the monetary rewards promised.

Tesla pushed the idea of alternating current, or AC for short. Edison's design was DC or direct current. Unlike DC, AC allows the voltage and the current to oscillate between positive and negative 60 times every second. AC starts with a low voltage current and, when put through a transformer, becomes high voltage AC. This means that very little power is lost in the wires and allows electricity to be sent for longer distances. When electricity gets closer to a home, it is converted back to low-voltage AC. A small transformer is placed on electrical poles near homes, which enables electricity to be transported without the need for power plants in every neighborhood.

Edison rejected AC as too dangerous, and Tesla got support from George Westinghouse to develop the system we actually use today. Edison didn't give up the fight easily. He actually put on a number of demonstrations to show the public how dangerous the Westinghouse/Tesla high-voltage system could be by electrocuting puppies and other small animals. When these didn't have the desired effect, Edison got desperate and even electrocuted a horse. Imagine what the animal-rights people would have done today during these demonstrations. When these electrocutions didn't work, Edison agreed to electrocute an elephant named Topsy. Interestingly, the Society for the Prevention of Cruelty to Animals approved of this execution because the animal had killed three men. The only alternative was to hang Topsy.

Even after this dramatic demonstration, Edison's DC lost to Tesla/Westinghouse's AC. We can all be grateful he did, or our neighborhoods would be filled with electric power plants.

What Next for Rockefeller?

While Rockefeller saw the market for his most lucrative product fall, he also got lucky. A new invention hit the market to preserve his fortune—the automobile and its internal-combustion engine.

The first internal-combustion engine was developed over a 20-year period by Alfred Drake of Philadelphia. Stuart Perry patented two improved designs in 1844 and 1846. Perry's design is very close to today's internal-combustion engines with a piston and cylinder, camshaft, water pump, throttle valve, igniter, and a lubrication system. Two inventors are thought to have built the first gasoline-powered cars—Charles Duryea and Elwood Haynes.

Petroleum People

Charles Duryea collaborated with his younger brother J. Frank Duryea to build their first automobile by converting a buggy. Frank drove the first Duryea on the streets of Springfield, Illinois, on September 21, 1893. This car was given to the Smithsonian Institution.

Elwood Haynes of Portland, Indiana, purchased a gasoline-powered engine in 1893 and designed a "horseless carriage." He is also credited with inventing the muffler and certain metal alloys.

Petroleum People

Henry Ford was born on a farm near Detroit, Michigan. He drove his first home-built automobile in 1896 and founded the Ford Motor Company in 1903. He developed the Model T by 1908. Ford perfected the idea of the assembly line and amassed a fortune of billions of dollars.

Petro-Facts

Before the automobile, gasoline was a byproduct that sold for only about 2¢ a gallon. By 1912, there were already more than 900,000 car registrations filed in the United States. By 1949, Gasoline costs had jumped to more than $1.50 per gallon.

German engineer Nicolaus August Otto is commonly given credit for perfecting the gasoline-powered internal-combustion engine and making mass production possible. He patented his four-stroke design on August 14, 1877. It was Henry Ford who took this design and developed the mass-production of automobiles. He designed the production line and created the need for many new industries, such as specialized tools, heavy-duty machinery, plant construction, and related raw materials. Communities that won these plants saw major increases in jobs not only in the automobile industry, but also in businesses that supported the new workers. Even jobs for school teachers increased as new communities developed.

Henry Ford's Model T quickly became an indispensable part of American life. The timing of the automobile development couldn't have been better for Rockefeller. The auto's need for gasoline saved Rockefeller's company.

But Rockefeller's monopoly wouldn't last. Independent oil companies in Europe and the United States found new sources of oil, developed new shipping techniques, and opened new markets in their efforts to undercut the giant.

The Least You Need to Know

- The Civil War slowed the development of the U.S. oil industry, but not for long.

- Rockefeller built a monopoly that is the foundation of much of the U.S. oil industry in existence today.

- Edison threatened Rockefeller's fortune, but the automobile saved it.

- Ford's mass production of the internal combustion engine was a major boost for Rockefeller and his monopoly.

Chapter 8

The Industry Grows

In This Chapter

- ◆ Wildcatters move to Texas
- ◆ Spindletop's big gusher
- ◆ Companies that got their start in Beaumont
- ◆ Fueling the fires of competition

While Rockefeller was busy building Standard Oil on the east coast and starting to look at possibilities on the west coast, another major oil boom was exploding onto the scene in the Southwest. Some of the east coast oil-men who bristled at Rockefeller's growing monopoly had started looking for other sources of oil in Texas—and they found it.

These east-coast independent types and some far-sighted Texan speculators developed an oil field on a hill in southeastern Texas that birthed some of today's largest oil companies. That hill was called Spindletop, and the oil boom of Texas started there.

The Story of Texas Oil

Spindletop was formed by a dome of salt that heaved toward the earth's surface in the distant geological past. The American Indians recognized the importance of the area around Spindletop as a source of oil and used the black tar they found there for treating a number of different ailments. Spanish explorers used the black, sticky stuff that washed up on the beaches along the Texas coast to water-proof their boots. But it wasn't until the late 1800s that drillers realized the potential for Texas.

Texas's first oil field was in the central town of Corsicana, about 250 miles northwest of Spindletop. When local businessmen started drilling in this area, they were looking for water, not oil. In fact, oil was considered a nuisance because water was usually found below the oil.

Two Texans, H. G. Damon and Ralph Beaton, saw dollar signs where others only saw a problem. They formed the Corsicana Oil Development Company and brought on board Pennsylvania *wildcatter* John Galey and his partner James Guffy to decide where to drill the wells. As part of their payment, Galey and Guffy usually took a part ownership in a drilling project.

John Galey was a geologist famous for his ability to find oil. In the 1890s he worked with James Guffy to develop his first major oil field in Kansas, which the pair sold to Rockefeller's Standard Oil. He was thought by associates to be able to smell oil and was dubbed "Dr. Drill." James Guffy was Galey's promoter and ran the business side of the operation. Guffy was active in Democratic politics and had even served for a while as chairman of the party.

Drill Bits

Wildcatters are speculators who mine for minerals or drill oil wells in areas that are not known to be productive. These are the people or companies who take the initial risks to figure out whether an area might hide a potential gold mine or oil rich reservoir.

Dr. Drill must have had a stuffy nose in Corsicana because he didn't sniff out a very productive well. Even at its most productive, the Corsicana oil field generated only 25 barrels a day. Galey and Guffy got frustrated with the potential, sold their interest in the well, and left Texas.

Searching for Oil at Spindletop

Three years later, however, Galey was back in Texas sniffing for oil. Captain Anthony F. Lucas had been hired by Texan Patillo Higgins to drill for oil at Spindletop. Higgins was a self-taught geologist who believed that there was lots of oil to be found underneath the salt dome at Spindletop. Most of the people in the petroleum and geologic communities in Texas thought he was a fool.

Higgins advertised for an engineer to drill the wells in the late 1890s. Captain Lucas, who had served as a Captain in the Austrian Navy and had experience as both engineer and salt miner, answered the ad. He drilled a few wells for Higgins, but all were failures. Then Higgins ran out of money.

Lucas still believed that there was good oil at the salt dome and wanted to pursue exploration, but no one in Texas thought that he had a chance of finding oil at the salt dome, so he had a hard time finding Texan backers. He then turned to Guffy and Galey for backing. In 1900, John Galey decided to take another stab at finding oil in Texas and accepted Lucas's request to come to Beaumont. Dr. Drill definitely smelled oil this time. Drilling began at the site Galey selected on October 27, 1900.

Coastal Texas presented different challenges than what oilmen encountered out east. In Pennsylvania and Ohio, drillers had to grind through yards of rock. They used water to wash out the cuttings and clear the newly formed hole. But in Texas, sand stood between the men and the oil, and that innocuous-seeming sand got the best of many an oilman. Holes in sand have a tendency to cave in, and adding water to the mix only made matters worse.

Petro-Facts

To make the mud that he used when drilling through the Texas quicksand, Curt Hamill drove a herd of cattle around a slush pit (essentially a hole in the ground filled with dirt and water). Mud-based drilling fluid is still used for drilling oil today.

One of Lucas' drillers, Curt Hamill, found a way around the problem. Instead of sending water down the drilled hole, he used mud. Mud not only helped to clear out the hole, but it also helped to fortify the sides of the hole, thereby preventing cave-ins.

The task of drilling still wasn't easy, but they made steady progress. After two months of work, when the exhausted crew took off a week for the Christmas holiday, they had reached a depth of 880 feet. They returned to the job after New Year's Day rejuvenated, and drilled down to 1,020 feet in just one week.

On January 10, 1901, they took the equipment out of the hole for maintenance. As they lowered the equipment back into the hole, mud started bubbling back up. Within seconds, the drill pipe shot out of the ground, followed only by silence. Drillers waited to see what would happen next. When nothing happened, they started to clean up the muddy mess so they could see what equipment could be salvaged. But then they heard a loud noise, and mud shot out of the ground like a rocket, followed by natural gas and then, finally, oil. The oil "gusher" shot to a height of more than 150 feet. This first well turned out to be the most productive of any in the United States, with an initial production rate of almost 100,000 barrels per day. That was more oil per day than the combined production of all of the other wells in the United States at the time.

Oil Rush Was On

News of the success at Spindletop spread around the globe. Just like the gold rush of California, thousands of people headed to Beaumont, Texas. More than a hundred small companies set up shop and tried to get a piece of the action at Spindletop.

> **Slick Sayings**
>
> The mad scramble for leases began immediately, with some plots traded again and again for even more astounding prices. A woman garbage collector was thrilled to get $35,000 for a pig pasture. But, soon, land that had only two years ago sold for less than $10 an acre now went for as much as $900,000 an acre … The town swelled with sightseers, fortune seekers, deal-makers, and oil-field workers; each train disgorged new hordes drawn by the dream of instant wealth embodied in the dark gusher … Upwards of 16,000 people were said to be living in tents on the hill. Beaumont's population ballooned in a matter of months from 10,000 to 50,000.
>
> —From *The Prize,* by Daniel Yergen

Fortunes were quickly made while others were just as quickly lost. Indeed, so many people lost their money in fraudulent transactions that some started calling the salt mound Swindletop. Estimates are that $50 million was made at Spindletop, but investments totaled $80 million. There were far more losers than winners.

Within a year, more than 200 wells were belching crude oil out of the ground at Spindletop. By 1902, the combined wells had produced 17.5 million barrels of oil. The rapid extraction, however, hurt production, and by 1902 the production rate had dropped to 10,000 barrels per day.

Production continued to slow for more than two decades until another speculator decided to drill deeper. On November 13, 1925, a well drilled to 5,400 feet proved that Spindletop was still sitting on a lot of oil. This time, production was more carefully controlled, and in 1927, Spindletop production reached its all time high of 21 million barrels in a year.

Spindletop's Legacy

At its peak, more than 100 companies were operating in Beaumont. Most of the companies didn't survive or were gobbled up by the majors. Some of these tiny operations grew into global corporations—among them Texaco, Gulf, and Exxon. The founder of Shell also dabbled at Spindletop. Let's see how these companies got their start.

Texaco

Texaco started as Texas Fuel Company under the leadership of former Standard Oil employee Joseph "Buckskin Joe" Cullinan. He was involved in oil drilling at Corsicana when he heard about Lucas's gusher, and within 24 hours had scurried to Spindletop to check out the situation. The savvy oilman knew a good thing when he saw it.

Petroleum People

Joseph "Buckskin Joe" Cullinan was a native of Pennsylvania who began working in the oil fields at age 14 and was active in the industry until his death at age 77. His early duties in the oil business included messenger boy, oil wagon teamster, pipeline laborer, and drilling crew member. He literally learned the business from the bottom up. He worked at Standard Oil until 1885 when he left to form his own company, Petroleum Iron Works, which specialized in fabrication and erecting steel storage tanks and steam boilers. In 1897, he was asked by the town fathers of Corsicana to advise them on their new oil fields and decided to stay in Texas. By 1901, he had formed the Texas Fuel Company.

Cullinan moved to Beaumont in 1901 and enticed a number of investors, led by former Texas governor, James S. Hogg, to help create the Texas Fuel Company, which would purchase, store, and transfer oil from the Spindletop field. By March 1902, when more money was needed, Cullinan and his partners formed the Texas Company, which ended up buying the Texas Fuel Company and absorbing it. The Texas Company began marketing its petroleum products under the brand name of Texaco.

Cullinan created many subsidiaries for his petroleum products including refineries and an international marketing program. In 1908, he relocated the Texas Company headquarters to Houston, seeing that as the critical new oil town. In 1913, he was ousted from the Texas Company by major stockholders after complaints about his management style. After his ouster, he continued to work in oil exploration and production, but stayed out of the refining and marketing sides of the business.

Gulf

James Guffy had been a key investor in the first gusher at Spindletop. That success spurred him to found his own company to suck up Spindletop's oil—Guffy Petroleum and Gulf Refining—which Pennsylvania bankers Andrew and Richard Mellon financed. The Mellons invested $300,000 for exploration and, once oil was struck, contributed several million dollars more to the business. As production slowed at Spindletop, the Mellons got nervous about their investment and sent their younger brother, William, to investigate.

William, who had been in the oil business since he was 19, was the ideal person to send. With family money financing the project, he had started a successful oil refining company in Pennsylvania. This company had its own pipeline and sold oil in the United States and Europe. By 1903, the Mellon's company had about a million barrels in storage and was responsible for about 10 percent of U.S. oil exports. However, it couldn't defend itself against Rockefeller's voracious appetite for oil, and Standard Oil gobbled it up—most likely in a deal that gave Mellon more of Standard's banking business (Mellon became a major stockholder in Rockefeller's companies).

It didn't take William Mellon long to determine that Guffy was a terrible manager. He told his brothers that if the Mellons wanted to protect their investment, then Guffy needed to be replaced. Fortunately, William had the perfect replacement in mind: himself. The younger Mellon took over the management, eventually reorganized the company as Gulf Oil Corporation, and pushed Guffy out. The Mellons also bought out Captain Anthony Lucas's share, which gave them full control of the company. Andrew Mellon became president, Richard Mellon was named treasurer, and William took the title of vice-president.

One of William Mellon's first tasks was to get Gulf out of a terrible contract that Guffy had negotiated. It would have required Gulf to sell oil to Shell at prices below production costs.

Shell

Marcus Samuel got his first business experience working in his father's trinket business in London. In addition to trinkets, the Shell Shop sold exotic sea shells imported from the orient. In 1890, during a trip to Constantinople (now Istanbul), Marcus realized there was more money to be made in oil than in sea shells. Two years later, he had consigned his first oil tanker, the *Murex*, and was shipping oil from the Black Sea through the Suez Canal. In 1897, his oil business grew so large that he formed a separate company called Shell Transport and Trading Limited. When he heard about the oil strike in Spindletop, he traveled to Texas and started making deals, including the aforementioned deal with Guffy.

When Samuel showed up at Guffy's doorstep, he already had an established international oil company, which gave Guffy a way to quickly sell his oil on the international market. Guffy foolishly signed a 20-year contract with Samuel to sell half of Guffy Petroleum's production to Shell at a set price of 25¢ per barrel. At the time, it seemed like a great deal. Oil was selling for only 10¢ or less per barrel. The contract didn't turn out to be such a great deal when production slowed at Spindletop. In 1903, the cost of producing a barrel rose to 35¢ per barrel.

When Mellon got directly involved in Guffy's company, he realized that the contract would require them to sell Shell oil for less than it cost them to produce! Luckily for the Mellons, the contract was poorly written and they were able to get out of it. Andrew Mellon traveled to London to renegotiate the contract, which ultimately ended Shell's involvement in Spindletop oil.

Petro-Facts

The Shell-Guffy deal made Shell Transport the first oil company with worldwide sources of production and supplies for gasoline, kerosene, and fuel oil. Not even Standard Oil could make that claim.

At the time, Samuel was busy protecting his company from another major competitor, Royal Dutch, as well as protecting himself from John D. Rockefeller's moves into the European and far-eastern markets—Standard Oil had tried to buy Shell a few times. Both Royal Dutch and Shell wanted to fend off Rockefeller, so they joined forces in 1903 and established a joint venture called the Asiatic Petroleum Company Limited (for more on this, see Chapter 10). The venture worked out well, and they realized the two companies would be stronger if they merged as one. The Royal Dutch/Shell Company was formed in 1907 with Royal Dutch holding 60 percent ownership and Shell 40 percent.

With their combined forces, Royal Dutch/Shell decided to take on Rockefeller near his own turf and in 1908 began a geological survey in Oklahoma. It opened its first refinery in the United States in California. So while Samuels never really made any money at Spindletop, he certainly got a taste for the U.S. oil market and decided that he wanted to play.

Exxon/Mobil

The connection to Spindletop for Exxon/Mobil isn't as strong as for the other major oil companies. Spindletop served as a catalyst for William Farish, who got oil in his blood when he traveled to Spindletop after the 1901 discovery, to monitor his uncle's oil investments.

Farish ran his uncle's investments at Spindletop for about four years. While living in Beaumont he met his future partner, Robert L. Blaffer. Both men moved back to Houston in 1905 and focused on the Humble oil field and other ventures north of the city. In 1917, Farish realized that if the independent oilmen were to compete with the corporate oil companies, they needed to organize. He formed the Gulf Coast Producers Association in 1916. When this failed to organize the independents, he worked with several independent oilmen, including Blaffer, to pool their assets, including wells, leases, equipment, and production, into Humble Oil in 1917. When they ran short on cash in 1919, Farish sold 50 percent of Humble to Standard Oil of New Jersey for $17 million, which later became Exxon/Mobil.

In addition to the key players who got their start at Spindletop, thousands of laborers got their training on Texas's first major oil field. These speculators and workers moved on to build today's oil industry in Texas and other parts of the United States.

They Owe It All to the Automobile

Texas oil wasn't pure enough for kerosene, but it was just right for various kinds of fuel oils needed for the budding transportation industry. Texas oils were also eventually refined for fuels to be used by airplanes, ships, and trains. Just like Rockefeller, Spindletop speculators and the entire Texas oil industry owe their success to the invention of the car, which helped to catapult the industry into the mammoth business success it is today.

Another major event would give the Texas oil industry a big boost—the breakup of Standard Oil.

The Least You Need to Know

◆ The first major Texas Oil field was at Spindletop in Beaumont, Texas. At its peak, it produced 21 million barrels a year.

◆ Texas drillers discovered that they could use mud to prevent cave-ins during drilling.

◆ More than 100 oil companies were formed to exploit Spindletop's oil. Two of these companies became major international players in the industry: Gulf and Texaco. Shell got its first foothold in the United States at Spindletop.

Chapter 9

Breaking Up Was Hard to Do

In This Chapter

♦ Exposing Standard's monopoly

♦ *The U.S. Government v. Standard Oil*

♦ Setting new standards in anti-trust

♦ Breaking up Standard Oil

Today when we think of oil wars, we think of battles for oil fought by armies, but in the late 1800s and early 1900s, the wars were waged between corporations or trusts and were fought—often secretly—by businessmen. The general of these corporate wars in the United States was John D. Rockefeller, head of the behemoth Standard Oil. Numerous weak attempts were made to expose John D. Rockefeller's business tactics, but it wasn't until a muckraking journalist uncovered the depth of his monopolist strategies that there was enough public outrage to take legal action against him. In this chapter, we'll take a look at the long struggle to break up the Standard Oil monopoly and what happened to the companies after the breakup.

Taking On Rockefeller

Commissions, unions, and politicians all attempted to reign in John D. Rockefeller's monopoly building tactics over the years, but the giant wouldn't fall. U.S. Congressional Committees attempted two investigations of Standard Oil's business practices, one in 1872 and one in 1876. Pennsylvania, New York, and Ohio legislatures investigated reports of illegal rebates from railroads and practices that restrained free trade. In all cases, political agreements or private, behind-the-scenes settlements ended the investigations.

It took muckraking journalist Ida Tarbell's 19-part series about Standard Oil, published in *McClure's Magazine* between November 1902 and October 1904, to generate enough public outrage to successfully take Rockefeller and Standard Oil to court.

Why Americans Didn't Trust Rockefeller's Trust

Before reviewing Tarbell's work more closely, you need to understand the concept of trusts as they operated in the late 1800s and early 1900s. Today, talk of trusts primarily refers to various tools used as part of estate planning, but trusts were very different entities during the time of the Standard Oil Trust.

The way the trust concept worked then was that shareholders transferred their shares to a single trustee or board of trustees, who then exercised complete control over the management of the combined shares, or trust. In building his trust, Rockefeller eventually got the owners of more than 90 percent of oil assets in this country to transfer their shares under the umbrella of the Standard Oil Trust. While there were Standard Oil companies in many states, such as Standard Oil of New Jersey and Standard Oil of Ohio, in reality all were controlled by Rockefeller and his trust.

In exchange for turning over shares to the trust, the shareholders would be entitled to a share of the profits of the trust. Rockefeller and other trust builders at the time liked trusts better than corporations because, unlike corporations, trusts didn't require state sanctions. Trusts had a lot more freedom to do what they wanted with a lot less government involvement.

Trusts were able to integrate and control many facets of an industry so they could mandate supply levels and dictate prices. For example, using the trust concept, Rockefeller controlled oil from the time it was taken out of the ground until the time it was sold to consumers by buying up refineries, oil operations, and consumer outlets. Instead of owning the means of transporting oil by buying up the railroads, Rockefeller used his power to get illegal rebates from the railroads, which they had to pay in order to get Rockefeller's business.

There was enough public animosity toward trusts, especially Standard Oil's version, that the Ohio Supreme court dissolved the trust in 1892 and ordered the companies to begin operating separately. Rockefeller got around this ruling by reorganizing as a holding company in New Jersey in 1899, under the umbrella of Standard Oil of New

Jersey. New Jersey's corporate laws allowed a company to own stock in other companies, so he could essentially rebuild the Trust using the holding company structure.

Tarbell Takes on the Trust

Let's look at how all this worked and how it was finally exposed by Tarbell. Her work was published in a treatise considered by many to be one of the best investigative journalist works ever written about a U.S. business. Her original stories appeared as a series in *McClure's*.

> ### Slick Sayings
>
> Her tenacious research, her meticulous attention to detail, and her scrupulous devotion to the truth exposed the illegal activities of Rockefeller's trust for all the world to see. It quickly became a hallmark of a new breed of investigative journalism. An angry, irritated President Theodore Roosevelt labeled this new generation of journalists, epitomized by Ida Tarbell and her History of Standard Oil, "muckrakers." And Ida Tarbell was known as the foremost "Lady Muckraker" of her time. As a consequence of her work, the U.S. Government brought suit against Standard Oil for violation of the nation's anti-trust laws, and in 1911 the nation's most powerful monopoly was broken.
> —Paula Treckel on October 7, 2000, inducting Ida Tarbell into the National Women's Hall of Fame

Tarbell's passion for writing about Rockefeller and Standard Oil stemmed from her upbringing. She was born in the late 1800s in a log home in northwestern Pennsylvania—the heart of Pennsylvania's oil region. Her father built wooden oil storage tanks and later became an oil producer and refiner. The family was well off financially until a secret agreement between the railroad and refiners designed by Rockefeller disrupted their lives. The personal affront drove Tarbell to undertake her major investigation nearly 20 years later, as the following quotation indicates: "Out of the alarm and bitterness and confusion, I gathered from my father's talk a conviction to which I still hold—that what had been undertaken was wrong."

Tarbell wove together an incredible story of the secret dealings and threats used by Rockefeller and his partners to eventually control 90 percent of the U.S. oil industry, starting with his days at Standard Oil of Ohio, his use of the Southern Improvement Company to control refineries and railroads, his building of the Standard Oil Trust, and his reshaping of the company as a holding company, the Standard Oil Company of New Jersey, when the trust was disbanded. She scoured congressional hearings, court files, probate papers, and land deeds. She even befriended a key executive at Standard Oil, H.H. Rogers, who ran the pipeline and natural gas parts of the business. He allowed her to do her research in Standard Oil's offices until he realized the impact that her journalism was having, after which he broke off contact with her.

Petroleum People

Henry Huddleston (H.H.) Rogers was known as the "Hellhound of Wall Street," in the 1880s. He was considered the mastermind behind U.S. Steel and Anaconda Copper, as well as one of the most powerful financiers of his time. He also partnered with John D. Rockefeller and helped to build Standard Oil. Rogers enjoyed helping others. One of his key benefactors (and poker and drinking buddies) was Sam Clemens (a.k.a. Mark Twain), whose books he admired and whom he once rescued from bankruptcy. Rogers's philanthropy didn't stop with Twain. He endowed his hometown of Fairhaven, Massa-chusetts, with a school, town hall, library, roads, and a Unitarian church. He provided financial backing for Booker T. Washington's Tuskegee Institute, and paid for Helen Keller's college education at Radcliff.

Tarbell didn't paint an entirely negative portrait of Rockefeller. She obviously admired his business acumen, as the following passage from her series indicates:

> And here is how he learned the value of investing money: "Among the early experiences that were helpful to me that I recollect with pleasure was one in working a few days for a neighbour in digging potatoes—a very enterprising, thrifty farmer, who could dig a great many potatoes. I was a boy of perhaps 13 or 14 years of age, and it kept me very busy from morning until night. It was a 10-hour day. And as I was saving these little sums I soon learned that I could get as much interest for 50 dollars loaned at 7 per cent—the legal rate in the state of New York at that time for a year—as I could earn by digging potatoes for 100 days. The impression was gaining ground with me that it was a good thing to let the money be my slave and not make myself a slave to money." Here we have the foundation principles of a great financial career.

Tarbell concluded her series with a two-part character study of Rockefeller, writing that "Our national life is on every side distinctly poorer, uglier, meaner, for the kind of influence he exercises."

Tarbell detailed the scheme that later proved to be the foundation of the Standard Oil monopoly—the South Improvement Company. She found details about this scheme by reading the congressional testimony of Henry M. Flagler, Rockefeller's primary partner.

Tarbell summarized his testimony about the formulation of the scheme:

> … certain Pennsylvania refiners, it is not too certain who, brought to them a remarkable scheme, the gist of which was to bring together secretly a large enough body of refiners and shippers to persuade all the railroads handling oil to give to the company formed special rebates on its oil, and drawbacks on that of other people. If they could get such rates, it was evident that those outside of their combination could not compete with them long and that they would become eventually the only refiners. They could then limit their output to actual demand, and so keep up prices. This done, they could easily persuade the railroads to transport no crude for exportation, so that the foreigners would be forced to buy American refined. They believed that the price of oil thus exported could easily be advanced fifty per cent. The control of the refining interests would also enable them to fix their own price on crude. As they would be the only buyers and sellers, the speculative character of the business would be done away with. In short, the scheme they worked out put the entire oil business in their hands. It looked as simple to put into operation as it was dazzling in its results. Mr. Flagler has sworn that neither he nor Mr. Rockefeller believed in this scheme. But when they found that their friend Peter H. Watson, and various Philadelphia and Pittsburg parties who felt as they did about the oil business, believed in it, they went in and began at once to work up a company secretly.

> **Petroleum People**
>
> Henry M. Flagler was a co-founder of the Standard Oil. He used his fortune to finance his dream—the Florida East Coast Railroad extension. This railroad took people through the Florida Keys to Key West and opened the Florida Keys to the world. It ran from 1912 until a hurricane destroyed it in 1935.

Tarbell described how they bought a charter from a liquidated estate for a company called the Southern Improvement Company, which was started by the railroads to control coal transport, as discussed in Chapter 7. In those days, a charter gave its owners the right to engage in business in any country and in any way. Once they bought that charter they sought out other partners, all of whom pledged secrecy.

In addition to controlling the refineries, Rockefeller also sought to control the means of transporting the oil—the railroads. Southern Improvement Company was eventually able to force special deals with the railroads. Tarbell cites an example in which the "open rate" for shipping crude to New York was $2.56 per barrel, but the Southern Improvement Company received a $1.06-per-barrel rebate on this price. In addition, the railroads kicked back another $1.06 for each barrel of crude parties outside the secret pact shipped.

Tarbell showed how this agreement with the railroads helped Rockefeller and his partners get control of the refineries. Citing 1877 congressional testimony by Rockefeller's brother, Frank, when he appeared before a committee considering a new bill to regulate interstate commerce, she wrote:

> We had in Cleveland at one time about 30 establishments [refineries], but the Southern Improvement Company was formed, and the Cleveland companies were told that if they didn't sell their property to them it would be valueless, that there was a combination of railroad and oil men, that they would buy all they could, and that all they didn't buy would be totally valueless, because they would be unable to compete with the Southern Improvement Company, and the result was that out of thirty there were only four or five that didn't sell.

Numerous court cases were brought against Standard Oil company over the years in individual states, but Rockefeller and his partners were able to quietly settle any problems until Tarbell aroused the public's anger. President Theodore Roosevelt took advantage of that outrage by ordering the Justice Department to file suit.

Standard Oil would face its first loss as a plaintiff in the courts before the Honorable Kennesaw Mountain Landis, who later in life became the first commissioner of baseball. (Landis's father chose that name for him because his father lost his leg on Kennesaw Mountain, Georgia, during the Civil War. Landis was born shortly after that in 1866.)

Landis was appointed to the federal courts by President Theodore Roosevelt in 1905. Just two years later, in 1907, he fined Standard Oil $29,240,000 for accepting illegal rebates on oil shipments on the Chicago and Alton Railroad. The decision didn't hold up on appeal, however, and its only claim to fame was that it was the first time Standard Oil lost in court and was ordered to pay a fine.

Taking It to the Supreme Court

A much more serious and extensive case that actually made it to the Supreme Court was driven by the Justice Department at Roosevelt's request in 1906. The case was brought against the Standard Oil Company of New Jersey and 33 other corporations, John D. Rockefeller, William Rockefeller, Henry Flagler, and four other defendants. The record included 12,000 pages of testimony about various business transactions over a 40-year period. It wasn't until 1909 that a Missouri court ruled on *U.S.* v. *Standard Oil* and ordered the breakup of the Standard Oil Trust. The decision was appealed to the Supreme Court, and Chief Justice White delivered the opinion of the high court on May 15, 1911. The court broke up the record into three periods—1870 to 1882, 1882 to 1899, and 1899 to the time of filing of the case. Here are the Supreme Court's findings:

◆ Charges stemming from 1870 to 1882 centered around the 1870 formation of the Standard Oil Company of Ohio. In 1872, the corporation had acquired substantially all but three or four of the 35 to 40 oil refineries located in Cleveland, Ohio. It alleged that by controlling these refineries, Standard Oil Trust members "obtained large preferential rates and rebates in many and devious ways over their competitors from various railroad companies." Refineries either had to sell out to Rockefeller's company or be driven out of business. Rockefeller and his partners acquired a large number of refineries of crude petroleum, situated in New York, Pennsylvania, Ohio, and elsewhere. Rockefeller also obtained control of the pipe lines available for transporting oil from the oil fields to the refineries in Cleveland, Pittsburgh, Titusville, Philadelphia, New York, and New Jersey. During this period Standard Oil Trust had "obtained a complete mastery over the oil industry, controlling 90 percent of the business of producing, shipping, refining, and selling petroleum and its products, and thus was able to fix the price of crude and refined petroleum, and to restrain and monopolize all interstate commerce in those products."

◆ For the second period (1882 to 1889), the Justice Department alleged that the "defendants entered into a contract and trust agreement, by which various independent firms engaged in purchasing, transporting, refining, shipping, and selling oil and the products thereof turned over the management of their business to nine trustees, composed chiefly of [John D. Rockefeller, William Rockefeller, and Henry M. Flagler], which said trust agreement was in restraint of trade and commerce, and in violation of law."

◆ Charges during the third period starting in 1889 were "that the said individual defendants operated through the Standard Oil Company of New Jersey as a holding corporation, which corporation obtained and acquired the majority of the stocks of the various corporations engaged in purchasing, transporting, refining, shipping, and selling oil into and among the various states and territories of the United States and thereby managed and controlled the same, in violation of the laws of the United States."

The final decree ordered the breakup of the Standard Oil Company of New Jersey and its related 36 domestic companies and one foreign company within six months. The court found that Standard's misdeeds included the following:

> Rebates, preferences, and other discriminatory practices in favor of the combination by railroad companies; restraint and monopolization by control of pipe lines, and unfair practices against competing pipe lines; contracts with competitors in restraint of trade; unfair methods of competition, such as local price cutting at

the points where necessary to suppress competition; espionage of the business of competitors, the operation of bogus independent companies, and payment of rebates on oil, with the like intent; the division of the United States into districts, and the limiting the operations of the various subsidiary corporations as to such districts so that competition in the sale of petroleum products between such corporations had been entirely eliminated and destroyed; and finally reference was made to what was alleged to be the enormous and unreasonable profits earned by the Standard Oil Trust and the Standard Oil Company as a result of the alleged monopoly.

Changing Antitrust Law

The case against Standard Oil was brought on the basis of the Sherman Anti-Trust Act. The act was passed in 1890 to "prohibit every contract, combination, or conspiracy in restrain of trade," and it provided for imposition of substantial penalties for violations. The act was named after Senator John Sherman, who proposed the legislation to address increasing concerns about the rapid dominance of large corporations, corporate trusts, and other business combinations.

The Sherman Anti-Trust Act was not successfully used in court for several years because certain Supreme Court decisions made it clear that Congress needed to pass supporting legislation and establish agencies that would enable the government to successfully challenge anticompetitive activities. President Roosevelt's "trust busting" campaigns helped to turn the tide of public opinion and ultimately the position of the Supreme Court.

After the success of the case against Standard Oil, Congress started working on improvements to the law. In 1914, Congress amended the Sherman Anti-Trust Act to clarify provisions. This effort was led by Henry DeLamar Clayton, and the new act was called the Clayton Anti-Trust Act. This legislation created the Federal Trade Commission in 1914. It also prohibited local price cutting to freeze out competitors, rebates, exclusive commercial relationships, buying out competitors, and incestuous boards. Labor unions and agricultural cooperatives were excluded from these forbidden combinations. Most of these changes related directly to the types of activities that were exposed during the Standard Oil trial.

Rockefeller's Company Rocks On

The breakup of Standard Oil into a number of so-called regional "Baby Standards" certainly didn't hurt any of the major stockholders. In fact, the value of most of the individual companies doubled in about a year. Rockefeller maintained a 25 percent ownership in the more than 30 new companies formed after the breakup. He had unofficially retired from the day-to-day administration of the company in the mid-1890s, but he kept the title of President until 1910. He spent 20 years in retirement on philanthropic activities including the formation of The Rockefeller Foundation, to which he gave an initial endowment of $3 billion dollars plus $100 million annually until his death in 1937 at the age of 97.

Slick Sayings

The breakup did have the enduring effect of strengthening the government's hand, providing a necessary balance in dealing with the massive U.S. industrial and capitalist machine that has lasted until today.

The breakup also had the unintended effect of ensuring Rockefeller's legacy. At the time of his antitrust defeat, Rockefeller was on par with Andrew Carnegie as the richest American and the richest man in the world.

In the decade following the breakup, Rockefeller's holdings increased in value by a factor of five, and his wealth surpassed that of Carnegie by a factor of two.

—From *The Color of Money*, by Michael Economides and Ronald Oligney

Rockefeller's Baby Standards initially maintained the specific regions they were assigned—not much different than what we saw after the breakup of AT&T in 1981 and the Baby Bells during the early years.

Standard Oil Companies Today

Many of the oil companies that lead the industry today were part of that Supreme Court mandated breakup. Initially the Baby Standards continued to use the Standard identity, but today none of the original Standards use that name. Let's take a look at where these Babies are today:

◆ **Standard Oil of New Jersey** changed its name to Exxon in 1972 and then merged with Mobil in 1999.

◆ **Standard Oil Company of New York** (Socony) changed its name to Mobil in 1920 and is now back with one of its former friends, Exxon (formerly Standard Oil of New Jersey).

◆ **Standard Oil of Ohio** changed its name to Sohio. British Petroleum (BP) began investing heavily in Sohio in the 1980s. By 1991, the Standard Oil name had completely disappeared in Ohio and all stations went under the name BP.

- **Standard Oil of Indiana** changed its corporate identity to Amoco in 1973. It merged with BP in 1998.

- **Standard Oil of California** (Socal) began marketing under the name of Chevron. In 1984, Chevron became its official identity. Chevron merged with Texaco in 2001.

- **Standard Oil of Kentucky** was bought out by Standard Oil of California in 1960. Its remnants are now part of Chevron/Texaco.

- **Standard Oil of Kansas** was bought by Standard Oil of Indiana in 1948 and its remnants are now part of BP.

- **Standard Oil of Brazil** today operates under the name of Esso.

Some of the Standards never really made it as companies. These included Standard Oil of Nebraska, Standard Oil of Louisiana, Standard Oil of Colorado, and Standard Oil of Missouri.

Petro-Facts

The only company operating under the Standard Oil name is **Standard Oil of Connecticut**, which was originally chartered as Standard Coal and Charcoal Company in 1915 and changed to Standard Fuel after World War II. This company was never part of Rockefeller's monopoly. When Esso was rebranded as Exxon, the local namebrand for Standard Oil became available and Standard Fuel took the opportunity to become Standard Oil. Today it is a family-owned heating oil company.

Not all the companies involved with Standard Oil operated under the name Standard. Here is what happened to some of the others:

- **Atlantic Refining** merged with Richfield Oil of California in 1966 and took the name Atlantic Richfield Company or Arco. Arco discovered oil on Alaska's north slope in 1968. Pieces of Arco went two different companies—part went to BP and part to Sunoco.

- **Ashland Oil** bought out three other Standard companies—**Cumberland PipeLine Company** (1931), **Southern Pipeline Company** (1949), and **Galena-Signal Oil** (1950s). Today it focuses on petrochemicals.

- **Sinclair Oil** bought out Prairie Oil and Gas, which purchased Long Oil Company in 1931. Sinclair was bought by Arco in 1969.

- **Continental Oil Company** (Conoco) merged with Phillips Petroleum in 2001.

- ◆ **The Ohio Oil Company** took on the name Marathon Oil in 1934.

- ◆ **Buckeye Pipe Line Company** purchased Indiana Pipe Line in 1942 and changed its name to Buckeye Partners in 1986. The company was bought out by its employees in 1996.

- ◆ **South Penn Oil Company** changed its name to Pennzoil in 1936 for its markets in Pennsylvania, Ohio, and West Virginia and to Pennzip in New York. It bought out Eureka Pipe Line Company in 1947.

- ◆ **Vacuum Oil** merged with Socony in 1931 and its remnants are now part of Exxon/Mobil.

Many of today's major oil companies have historical ties to Standard Oil, including Exxon/Mobil, BP, Chevron/Texaco, ConocoPhillips, Marathon, Ashland Oil, and Pennzoil.

While the oil industry was being shaken up in the United States, there were similar corporate wars going on in other parts of the world. We'll take a look at those next.

The Least You Need to Know

- ◆ Standard Oil's business practices were exposed to the public by Ida Tarbell in one of the first major pieces of investigative journalism.

- ◆ Numerous unsuccessful attempts were made to try to control the monopolistic tendencies of Rockefeller and his Standard Oil policies; the government was finally successful in 1911 when the Supreme Court ordered the breakup of Standard Oil into smaller regional companies.

- ◆ The so-called "Baby Standards" grew into many of today's major oil companies.

International Players in Oil Politics

In This Chapter

- ◆ Russian losses
- ◆ Persian gains
- ◆ Mexico's rise and fall
- ◆ Venezuelan beginnings

In the late 1800s and early 1900s, the race to find oil spanned the globe, with many of the same faces turning up in the same places. And although Standard Oil (which at the time hadn't yet been broken up) had a strong foothold in international markets, the battle to control oil outside the United States was much more difficult and involved much stiffer competition. For Rockefeller, that simply meant that he had to try harder and play dirtier.

Losing the Lead in Russia

As noted previously, the first modern oil wells were sunk in the Baku peninsula of Russia. The development of the Russian oil industry was led by the Nobel family, who would one day claim Alfred Nobel as its most famous member. A large portion of the funds Alfred Nobel contributed for the Nobel Prizes came from shares in the Nobel Brothers' Oil Producing Company, which was run by Alfred's brothers Ludwig and Robert.

Petroleum People

The Nobel brothers, Ludwig, Robert, and Alfred, formed the Nobel Brothers' Oil Producing Company in 1879 and became major players in the development of the Russian oil industry. Alfred Nobel is better known as the inventor of dynamite, but a majority of his fortune came from the oil industry. He held more than 350 patents for his inventions and had laboratories in more than 20 countries. His efforts to promote peace were well known, and in 1985, when he drew up his final will and testament, he set aside a majority of his estate for the formation and funding of the Nobel Foundation, which today awards the Nobel prizes. Alfred Nobel died in December 1896. The Nobel Foundation was established on June 29, 1900.

Over a 10-year period between 1874 and 1884, the Nobels were the main drivers in developing Russia's oil industry and were a critical force in increasing Russian annual oil output from 600,000 barrels to 10.8 million barrels. Russia didn't need that much oil, so the Nobels started looking for markets outside Russia and the means to transport it to them. They started to build a railway between Baku (now in the break-away nation of Azerbaijan) and the Black Sea port of Batum (which is in the Republic of Georgia) in the early 1880s, but ran short of cash. To finish the project, the Nobel's turned to another major financial family, the Rothschilds, for help financing the railway project.

The Rothschilds Step In

The Rothschilds needed oil for their refinery at Fiume on the East Coast of the Adriatic, so they decided to bankroll the railway in order to have a secure oil supply. Ultimately, they started their own oil company, the Caspian & Black Sea Petroleum Company. These moves brought Russian oil to the European market, thereby putting it in direct competition with Standard Oil, which until that point had nearly 100 percent of the global market.

The infusion of cash from the Rothschild family helped to increase Russian output to 25 million barrels per year by the end of the 1880s. By 1891, Russian exports had captured about 30 percent of the global oil and kerosene market. That much oil fueled Rockefeller's competitive drive, and he started putting pressure on the Rothschilds and Nobels by lowering his international oil prices.

Petroleum People

The Rothschild banking business was started by five sons of a coin and bill dealer in Frankfurt named Mayer Amschel. The sons fanned out across Europe to set up their banking business. Nathan established his in London. James started his banking house in Paris. Salomon decided on Vienna for his bank. Carl set up in Naples. Amschel, the eldest, ran the Frankfurt bank established by his father. They funded many ventures including searches for gold, as well as building the Suez Canal, railways, and oil. The Rothschilds have been leading financiers for more than 200 years, and while their total accumulated wealth is a mystery, it has been estimated to be in the trillions of dollars.

Samuels to the Rescue

The Rothschild family realized they needed to open new markets and decided to turn to the Far East, where there was a growing demand for kerosene, but first they needed to solve two major problems: how to transport the kerosene and how to distribute it once it reached its destination. Marcus Samuels and his Shell Transport and Trading Company came to the rescue—Samuels developed a fleet of tankers and, using his established contacts in Asia, created a network of storage tanks in key Asian port cities such as Hong Kong, Bangkok, and Shanghai.

In addition, with help from the Rothschilds, he obtained permission to move oil through the Suez Canal, drastically cutting the time it took to ship oil to the East. Finally, he signed a nine-year exclusive license with the Rothschilds to market Russian kerosene in the Far East. In the late 1890s, Samuels's Shell Transport and Trading Company had 10 bulk tankers moving kerosene from Baku to the Far East.

Samuels wasn't alone in peddling petroleum products to the Far East. The Royal Dutch Company delivered its first cases of kerosene to Eastern ports in 1892 from its oil wells on the Indonesian island of Sumatra. By the end of the 1890s, Shell and Royal Dutch had over half of all oil sales in the Far East. Mr. Rockefeller was losing ground.

Strength in Numbers

While still trying to take back significant market share with price cuts and threats, Rockefeller began separate negotiations with Shell and Royal Dutch to buy them out.

As noted in Chapter 8, Shell and Royal Dutch realized that if they continued to battle each other they could ultimately lose the war to Rockefeller. In December 1901, Samuels signed an agreement with Royal Dutch. Then in June 1903, the Rothschilds joined Royal Dutch/Shell in a joint venture, the Asiatic Petroleum Company, whose day-to-day management would be run by Henri Deterding of Royal Dutch. The joint venture strengthened their hand against Rockefeller.

Both Shell and Royal Dutch were suffering financially. Samuels lost an anticipated long-term oil source at Spindletop (see Chapter 8). Royal Dutch lost its largest oil supply as strikes, the Russo-Japanese war, and the Russian revolution cut off access to Russian oil. These Russian events combined destroyed two thirds of Russia's oil wells by 1905.

Petroleum People

Henri Deterding was the founder of Royal Dutch. He started as a banker in the Dutch East Indies and was appointed the chief executive of the Royal Dutch Petroleum Company in 1900. Deterding was a tough businessman and pushed Samuels to agree to a 60/40 split in the 1907 merger of Royal Dutch/Shell.

Petro-Facts

In 2002, Royal Dutch/Shell ranked 8 on the *Fortune* Global 500, and Exxon/Mobil, Standard Oil's most successful baby, ranked 2 on the list. British Petroleum (BP), who ranked 4, didn't yet exist in 1906, but its predecessor would soon take form in Persia.

At first Samuels thought about combining forces with Rockefeller after losing the Spindletop contract, but the two parties couldn't work out a deal. Deterding pushed Samuels to agree to an alliance with Royal Dutch in 1906. Sixty percent of the new company would be owned by Royal Dutch and 40 percent by Shell. That 60/40 distribution still stands to this day for what has become the number eight company on *Fortune Magazine*'s Global 500 company list.

Rockefeller now had much stronger adversary. In 1906, Royal Dutch/Shell had a production base in Asia, a long-term-supply contract for Russian crude (through the Rothschilds), and production capability of 151 million barrels of oil per year, which represented about 26 percent of the global oil output.

Royal Dutch/Shell decided it was time to wage battle with Rockefeller on his own turf—the United States. Between 1910 and 1914, at the same time Standard Oil was battling its court cases that ultimately resulted in the breakup of the monopoly, Royal Dutch/Shell looked to open a front in the United States market for the corporate oil wars. Deterding started on two fronts—California and Oklahoma.

Meanwhile, the Russian oil fields were in shambles and the Rothschilds decided it was time to get out. In 1911, they sold their oil interest in Russia to Royal Dutch/Shell. The deal was struck in 1912, and the Rothschild assets were traded for stock in Royal/Dutch Shell. Deterding became a major player in rebuilding the devastated Russian oil industry. (These maneuverings and their impact on future political decisions were not visible until the World Wars. We'll talk more about this in Chapter 13.)

Fighting Over Persia

With all this talk of oil in Russia, the United States, and the East Indies, you may be wondering, "What about today's major player, the Middle East?"

The story of Middle East oil begins in Persia, whose civilization dates back to about 3500 B.C.E., when the area was inhabited by Sumerians. From 247 B.C.E. to 228 C.E., Persia was the center of the Parthian Empire, which included areas now in Iran, Turkey, Armenia, Georgia, Azerbaijan, Turkmenistan, Afghanistan, Tajikistan, Pakistan, Syria, Lebanon, Jordan, Palestine, and Israel. Invasions by Greeks, Arabs, Mongols, and Turks brought down this empire and Persia ended up under Arab rule.

Persia didn't again gain independence until 1499. Its next major battle was with the Afghans, who seized the country in 1722 and weren't ousted until 1794 when Aga-Mohammed became Shah, which is generally regarded as the start of present day Iran or Persia. The Shah did battle with Russia to reclaim territory in what is today the Republic of Georgia, but was unsuccessful and ended up losing even more northern territory to Russia. The final battle in 1827 set the northern boundary of Iran that is still pretty much in existence today.

The Persians first came in contact with England in 1821, when they tried to regain territory in Afghanistan, which at that time was under an English protectorate. In 1837, when diplomacy failed, the Shah seized Herat in Afghanistan for 10 months. England defended Afghanistan, while Russia cheered on the Shah. England prevailed and Persia tried again in 1856, which resulted in England actually declaring war against Persia. A peace agreement was worked out before any serious fighting took place.

Persia then became a pawn in the diplomatic battles between England and Russia, each trying to secure their spheres of influence. Persia essentially was stuck in the role of buffer state between the two powers. Russia ended up controlling the northern portion of Persia near its Asiatic borders while England took on the role of advising most of what was left of Persia, with Britain's primary goal being to protect its Indian Empire.

These diplomatic battles became more serious as Persia's oil potential was revealed. The first person to write about Persian oil potential was a French geologist named de Morgan in the 1890s. According to a history written by British Petroleum, de Morgan was consulted by a British Ambassador, a Persian General, and the director of Persian Customs to discuss this oil potential. They wanted to pursue its development, but had a major problem—no money. But one of the men thought he knew just the person who could bankroll it—William Knox D'Arcy.

Petroleum People

Willam Knox D'Arcy was born in England in 1849, but moved to Queensland, Australia, with his family in 1866, where he studied law. He bought an interest in a gold mine from which he made millions. In 1900, he was asked to finance an exploration for oil in Persia and he decided to take on the challenge. By 1901, he negotiated a concession to explore for oil. His engineers struck oil in 1908, and he formed the Anglo-Persian Oil Company in 1909, which was renamed British Petroleum in 1954. D'Arcy made his second fortune in oil. He held a seat on the Anglo-Persian board until he died in 1917.

Working with Persian connections, D'Arcy was able to successfully negotiate a 60-year *concession* to explore for oil in the Persian empire. The Russians protested the agreement because they wanted the oil concession, but D'Arcy came up with money to tilt the deal in his favor.

Drill Bits

An **oil concession** is a contract between the country that owns the land and a company that wants to explore the lands for oil or other mineral potential. The agreement usually includes payments to the country for the right to explore as well as some percentage of any profits.

D'Arcy hired an engineer, G. B. Reynolds, who had worked in India and had experience drilling in Sumatra, to head the drilling operations in Persia. They had decided on two possible locations to start drilling. One was at Chiah Surkh, which was near the frontier of Iraq (then part of the Turkish Empire) and the other was a southern site near Ahwaz. They chose Chiah Surkh but found development very difficult. They struck oil in 1904, but the flow quickly declined. By this time, D'Arcy needed more cash and convinced another British Company, the Burmah Oil Company, to get involved.

Finally they hit pay dirt. They moved to Masjid-I-Suleiman, and stuck oil at the depth of 360 meters on May 26, 1908. This was the first oil operation in the Middle East region. A pipeline was constructed to take the oil from Masjid-I-Suleiman to a refinery at Abaden in 1912, which is an island off Iran on the Persian Gulf. The refinery had a daily capacity of 2,400 barrels and was the first oil refinery in the Middle East.

By the time the Anglo-Persian Company was formed in 1909 to develop the new oil field, 97 percent of the common shares were owned by the Burmah Oil Company and the rest were owned by Lord Strathcona, the first chairman of the new company. D'Arcy served as a director for the new company and served on the board, but he never played a major role in the company's day-to-day affairs. His role for Anglo-Persian was one of risk-taking investor.

Petro-Facts _____

Over the years, more than 375 wells have been drilled on the Masjid-I-Suleiman field and 14 are currently producing oil. In 2003, Iran had plans to further develop the field. Canadian independent oil company Sheer Energy, in a joint venture with Iran's Naftgaran Engineering Services, which is a branch of the Oil Industry Investment Company of Iran, are leading up the development. Sheer estimates there are more than 6 billion barrels of oil at an average depth of 200 to 300 feet. They estimate an overage output of 20,000 barrels per day after redevelopment.

In 1910, Charles Greenway, one of the founding directors of Anglo-Persian, took over as managing director and then became chairman in 1914. He was very concerned about the growing domination of Royal Dutch/Shell and turned to the British government for help. He needed new capital to develop Persian oil.

In 1914, just before the outbreak of World War I, Greenway contracted with the British government to supply oil for the Royal Navy. Royal Dutch/Shell was battling for the same deal and lost it when Winston Churchill decided he wasn't impressed with Marcus Samuels. Some said he didn't want to work with a Jew, while others thought that the Dutch influence was a problem. Whatever the reason, this new partnership with the British government catapulted the Anglo-Persian Company from a bit part to a major role in the oil industry.

The deal didn't come cheaply for Anglo-Persian, however. The money from the British government came with strings. The government became a majority shareholder in the company and had the right to appoint two directors to the board. It wasn't until 1987 that the British government was completely out of the oil business.

Developing Mexico

Back in the Americas, the excitement of finding oil at Spindletop crept over the border to Mexico, and locals there decided that they, too, could find oil. In 1901, British civil engineer Weetman Pearson was doing work for the Mexican government when he heard about the oil mania in the Mexico border town of Laredo. He quickly reviewed all the information he could find about oil potential in Mexico and bought land in Laredo that looked good for the development of prospective oil fields.

In 1908, Pearson established the Mexico Eagle Oil Company and hired Captain Anthony Lucas, who had struck black gold at Spindletop, to engineer and begin drilling explorations, to no avail. In 1909, Pearson hired new geologists who had worked for the U.S. Geological Service. With their help, he finally struck oil in Tampico, on the Gulf Coast, in 1910. The successful well produced 110,000 barrels per day.

Petroleum People

Weetman Pearson was a British civil engineer and entrepreneur who became famous for the construction projects he managed for his father's company, S. Pearson and Sons. His projects included the Hudson Tunnel in New York, railways in Spain, Mexico, Colombia, and China, dams and canals in Mexico, and docks in Egypt and Canada. He took on a title in 1910 and became Lord Cowdray. In 1919, S. Pearson & Sons became a holding company that included civil engineering operations, oil extraction and refining, real estate, and the Whitehall Trust, which was a finance and investment house. They dropped the contracting arm of the business in the late 1920s and early 1930s.

The Mexican oil boom was on! Other wells were drilled that also produced at the rate of about 100,000 barrels per day. Standard Oil became a major player in developing Mexican oil once it was discovered. Another speculator involved in the early days in Mexico was Edward L. Doheny, who established the Mexican Petroleum Company of California.

Petroleum People

Edward L. Doheny created California's first oil boom in 1892, when he realized the La Brea tar pits in Los Angeles were fed by an oil source. He dug the first well in Los Angles and struck oil in 1893 at a depth of 200 feet. After Los Angeles, he set his sights on Mexico and got involved in the Tampico area. He also sought oil sources in South American and the British Isles. In 1924, he was indicted on conspiracy and bribery charges related to his development of the Elk Hills Naval Petroleum Reserve in Kern County, California. Even though he was acquitted of the charges, he lost his oil leases at Elk Hills and his reputation was permanently stained. His name also became linked to the Teapot Dome scandal, which we will discuss in Chapter 12.

By 1920, Mexico became a critical source of oil for U.S. markets, supplying 20 percent of its domestic oil needs. Mexico's oil output by 1921 was about 193 million barrels annually, and it ranked as the second-largest oil producer in the world.

All this happened even though there was major political upheaval in the Mexico—in 1911, the Mexican president was overthrown and the Mexican revolution began. Due to the political uncertainty in that country, developing the oil industry was not only an expensive proposition for the oil companies, it also became dangerous, as oil camps were overrun or oil workers were attacked.

Doheny tried to salvage his investment in the Mexican Petroleum Company of California and even financed a private army to help protect his oil interests. He also lobbied for U.S. intervention, including an invasion of Mexico, but failed in getting any U.S. support.

Instead of trying to protect his interest in the Mexican Eagle Oil Company, Pearson opted to get out of the Mexican market. In 1918, Royal Dutch/Shell wanted to enter into the Mexican market. Deterding sent a representative to offer to purchase a major portion of Pearson's Mexican Eagle Oil Company. Pearson jumped at the chance to get out of Mexican and took Deterding up on his offer. That ended up being a very lucky move for Pearson.

Soon after Royal Dutch/Shell arrived, salt water started to encroach on major Mexican oil wells, greatly reducing their production. The problem could have been fixed with new investment, but none of the oil companies wanted to make the financial commitment given the political upheaval.

Oil production dropped dramatically, and Mexico ceased to be a major world oil exporter. Companies didn't abandon Mexico, but they stopped investing in future growth. Production dropped to only about 33 million barrels by 1931.

Mexico's political situation changed when the Partido Revolucionario Institucional (PRI), founded by Lazaro Cardenas, took power in 1929. When it was obvious that the foreign oil companies involved in Mexico were not going to invest in the growth of Mexico's oil industry, Cardenas nationalized the industry in 1938 and put it under the management of Pemex. Daniel Yergin in *The Prize* calls this act "a great symbolic and passionate act of resistance to foreign control, which would become central to the spirit of nationalism that tied the country together." To this day, Pemex is still a symbol of Mexican independence.

Petro-Facts

Throughout the twentieth century, many countries decided to take control of their oil riches after foreign companies had developed them. Sometimes they bought out the concessions (Saudi Arabia is one country that did this), and at other times, they simply reneged on their oil concessions, took control of the wells, and ousted the foreign companies. Russia started the trend of canceling oil concessions after the Russian Revolution.

Oil companies tried to recoup their losses, and the United States even filed suit, but Mexico never paid the oil companies what they said they were due. Mexico's oil industry suffered the consequences of this decision—they no longer had an export market for their product because they had angered all the countries whose companies lost in the nationalization process, including the United States and Britain. It wasn't until the 1970s, when the United States searched for new oil sources, that it turned once again to its southern neighbor.

Getting Started in Venezuela

As Mexico became an unstable source of crude oil, oil companies looked to Venezuela as a possible petroleum source. Locals had drilled the first well in the country at Lake Maracaibo in 1878, but it wasn't until 1907 that foreign oil companies started securing concessions there. Shell was the first to begin major exploration after World War I and was rewarded with its first major strike at Lake Maracaibo with a well that produced 100,000 barrels per day.

Standard Oil of Indiana also had early rights to Venezuela oil, but the company didn't pursue those rights after Mexico nationalized oil. It didn't want to risk Venezuela possibly following Mexico's lead and sold its Venezuelan interests to Exxon in the 1930s. Gulf also was a principal operator in the development of Venezuela oil in the 1930s. At that time, Venezuela was producing about 300,000 barrels of oil per day, which is tiny compared to 2 million bpd by the 1970s. Venezuela's oil industry really didn't get off the ground until after World War II. We'll revisit Venezuela later when we talk about today's major oil players.

These early days of oil primarily consisted of corporate wars, but after World War I, the battle for oil became much bloodier. But before we discuss the bloody battles, let's first look at why we are so dependent on oil and the forces behind oil politics.

The Least You Need to Know

◆ Russia's oil industry was destroyed during the first revolution. Royal Dutch and Shell were major players in rebuilding it.

◆ British Petroleum, then operating under the name of the Anglo-Persian Company, won rights to develop Persian oil.

◆ Mexico was a major oil producer in the 1920s, but lost its place after a revolution destabilized the country and oil wells encountered technical difficulties. Mexico nationalized its oil industry in 1938.

◆ The Venezuelan oil industry was a minor player before World War II.

11

Getting Our Petroleum Fix

In This Chapter

- ◆ Who consumes the world's oil
- ◆ How a barrel of oil is used
- ◆ Oil and the petrochemical industry
- ◆ Products made from oil in our daily lives

Oil fuels our cars, trucks, and planes. But only about 50 percent of what's distilled from a barrel of crude oil is pumped into our vehicles' gas tanks. What about the other half of the barrel—what happens to it?

Unlike in the past, when refiners would dump what they couldn't use into our waterways or fields, today refiners put almost every last drop of a barrel of oil to use. In this chapter, we're going to take a look at how much oil is consumed in a day, and how it's used.

Consuming the Brew

The United States is the world's undisputed oil hog, using almost 20 million barrels of oil per day. The next closest consuming country is Japan, which uses 5.4 million barrels per day. The following table, which lists the top 20 oil users in the world, shows that the United States consumes more oil than all the countries *not* on this chart combined.

Oil Consumption in 2001

Country	Barrels Per Day
United States*	19,993,000
Japan	5,423,000
China	4,854,000
Germany	2,814,000
Russia	2,531,000
South Korea	2,126,000
Brazil	2,123,000
Canada	2,048,000
France	2,040,000
India	2,011,000
Mexico	1,932,000
Italy	1,881,000
United Kingdom	1,699,000
Spain	1,465,000
Saudi Arabia	1,415,000
Iran	1,109,000
Indonesia	1,063,000
Netherlands	881,000
Australia	879,000
Taiwan	846,000
First 20 Countries	**59,134,000**
Rest of the World	**16,854,000**
World	**75,988,000**

The numbers in this chart are slightly different than those released by the U.S. Department of Energy for 2001, which puts U.S. consumption at 19,649,000 per day.

(Source: ENI, an Italian energy company)

More than half of the oil consumed by the United States comes from imports, which total 10.9 million barrels per day. People often assume that the majority of our oil comes from the Middle East; however, only 2.757 million barrels come from the Persian Gulf region. Our largest single course of oil is Canada, and the majority of our oil comes from North and South America.

In 2002, the United States imported oil from more than 50 countries. The top seven countries that dominated U.S. oil imports are listed in the following table.

Where Our Oil Comes From

Country	Barrels Per Day
Canada	2,082,000
Saudi Arabia	1,851,000
Mexico	1,772,000
Venezuela	778,000
Nigeria	650,000
United Kingdom	415,000
Iraq	366,000

(Source: The American Petroleum Institute)

So what do Americans do with their nearly 20 millions barrels of oil per day? Let's take a look.

What Does a Barrel of Crude Oil Make?

According to the American Petroleum Institute, a barrel of crude oil provides Americans with the following products, in these quantities:

Product	Gallons per Barrel
Gasoline	19.4
Distillate Fuel Oil	9.7
Kerosene-Type Jet Fuel	4.3
Petroleum Coke	2.0
Residual Fuel Oil	1.9
Liquefied Refinery Gases	1.9
Still Gas	1.8
Asphalt and Road Oil	1.4
Petrochemical Feedstocks	1.1
Lubricants	0.5
Kerosene	0.2
Other	0.4

This totals 44.6 gallons, but there are only 42 gallons in a barrel of crude oil. The processing of crude oil actually results in a slightly higher volume of products. You probably recognize many of these products, but let's break them down into everyday uses.

- **Gasoline** can be produced for use in cars or airplanes with piston engines, depending on the distillation process.

- **Distillate Fuel Oil** is a light fuel oil used primarily for space heating, diesel engine fuel, railroad engine fuel, agricultural machinery, and electric power generation.

- **Kerosene-Type Jet Fuel** is used for airplanes with turbine power units. This is different than the gasoline produced for aviation piston engines.

- **Petroleum Coke** isn't a soft drink. It's a black solid residue of the distillation process, and it is used to heat steel-industry ovens, in electrode manufacturing, and for the productions of chemicals.

- **Residual Fuel Oils** are heavy oils used as fuels in industry, for marine transportation, and for electric power generation.

- **Liquefied Refinery Gases** consist mainly of hydrogen, methane, ethane, and olefins, which are used by the petrochemical industry. We'll talk more about petrochemicals later in this chapter.

- **Still Gas** is used as a refinery fuel and a petrochemical feedstock. Its principal constituents are methane, ethane, ethylene, normal butane, butylene, propane, and propylene, which are all important in the petrochemical industry.

- **Asphalt and Road Oil** is used to build our streets and highways.

- **Petrochemical Feedstocks** are used by the petrochemical industry to produce synthetic materials for use by consumers, agriculture, and industry.

- **Lubricants** are used in engines and other machinery to reduce friction between bearing surfaces.

- **Kerosene** is now a very minor product produced from oil, but is still used for lighting and heating.

Let's look at how the petrochemical industry uses these byproducts of oil.

Petrochemicals: The Other Oil Industry

In addition to the transportation fuel industry, another industry is built almost entirely around products from crude oil, and it's called the petrochemical industry. This industry uses products derived from oil and natural gas to make things like synthetic rubber, synthetic chemicals, plastic, and synthetic fibers.

Petroleum People
Vladimir Haensel was one of the leading pioneers in the petrochemical industry. He immigrated to the United States from Germany at the age of 16. He landed his first corporate job for Universal Oil Products as a lab assistant in 1937 and was a vice-president of the firm by 1951. During his 60-year career he was awarded more than 145 U.S. patents and 400 foreign patents and published more than 120 scientific and technical papers. He will probably be most remembered for his articles, "Lucky Alva" and "Lucky Proteus, of How Not to Hire a Genius." In these tongue-in-check fables he warns of the danger to science and innovation if contributions to the "bottom-line" rule how scientific research is measured.

Many of the major oil companies have petrochemical divisions, but other major corporations also play a role in this field including DuPont Worldwide, Monsanto Company, Dow Chemical Company, and these corporate behemoths' subsidiaries. In addition, hundreds of smaller companies are involved in petrochemical processing.

Most of the petrochemicals are used to make end products, so unless you work in the petrochemical industry, you wouldn't encounter them in their raw form. However, you encounter them in their finished form everyday, throughout the day.

Ethylene is the most common byproduct from crude oil that is used in the petrochemical industry. It is used in antifreeze, synthetic rubber, plastic, fabric finishes, and latex paints. The acetylene family of chemicals, also byproducts of crude, are used to make vinyls, adhesives, plastics, and coatings.

Everyday Uses

Let's look at products that you use in your everyday life and how petrochemicals fit in:

◆ **Agriculture and food**   Ammonia is the most important petrochemical product in this arena. It's used for nitrogen fertilizers, crop-protection chemicals, animal feed, and food additives.

◆ **Clothing**   Only 3 of the 20 synthetic fibers used to make clothes today are *not* made from petrochemicals. We'll just name the three that aren't: acetate, rayon, and acetic anhydride.

◆ **Housing**   You'll find petrochemicals throughout your house. They are used in vinyl siding, insulation, seal and caulking materials, adhesives, furniture fabrics, carpeting, paints, roofing, and wallpaper. If it weren't for petrochemicals, many of the objects in your home wouldn't exist—at least in their current form.

Petro-Facts

Hundreds of products in homes are made using petrochemical industry. These include balloons, blenders, cameras, candles, compact discs, computers, crayons, credit cards, dentures, deodorants, diapers, digital clocks, dinnerware, dyes, eyeglass frames, garbage bags, glue, golf balls, hair dryers, infant seats, ink, lipstick, luggage, patio screens, photographic film, shampoo, shaving cream, slippers, soft contact lenses, sunglasses, telephones, toothpaste, toys, and umbrellas.

♦ **Medicine**   We talked earlier about oil being used as a cure for many things in the early days of humans. It still plays a major role in today's medicine. Petrochemicals are used in making antihistamines, antiseptics, artificial hearts, bandages, decongestants, antihypertensives, aspirin, acetaminophen, vitamin capsules, heart replacement valves, pacemakers, surgical equipment, syringes, and medical equipment.

♦ **Transportation**   Gasoline isn't the only thing crude oil is used for in transportation. Petrochemicals are used to create polyester for car and truck bodies, acrylic automobile finish coats, car bumpers, tire treads and hoses, vinyl seat covers, traffic lights, road signs, and vinyl road paints.

This only scratches the surface of the types of products made using petrochemicals. People use thousands of them everyday. Knowing all this, can you imagine a world without oil?

A reduction in oil supplies would have a major impact on your life. In the next chapter, we'll look at some of the measures that the U.S. government takes to ensure a constant oil supply.

The Least You Need to Know

♦ The United States is by far the largest consumer of oil, and more than 50 percent of that oil is imported.

♦ Oil provides more than just fuel for our transportation. Thousands of everyday products are made using petroleum products.

♦ Petrochemicals are used in the production of synthetic rubber, synthetic fibers, and plastics, as well as medicine and medical equipment.

Part 3

Bloody Wars: Fighting for Fuel

By the early to mid-nineteenth century, oil had become such a necessity that countries werc willing to go to war to keep it flowing freely. In the following chapters, we recount how oil has been booty in some of history's most important wars, and we consider arguments that the wars fought as part of the War on Terror may be as much about oil as they are about terrorism, especially in Iraq.

Chapter 12

Making Oil a National Priority

In This Chapter

- ◆ Setting aside oil lands
- ◆ Uncovering the Teapot Dome scandal
- ◆ Turning oil reserves over to industry
- ◆ Establishing the Strategic Petroleum Reserve

Oil's importance for strategic purposes was quickly recognized as the United States converted its coal-powered naval ships to oil-burning vessels in the early 1900s. The Navy needed to be certain it would have a dependable supply of oil to power its ships, and policy makers wanted to guarantee that supply in case of a national emergency.

In 1910, Congress passed legislation authorizing the president to set aside land in California and Wyoming believed to have underground oil reserves as a Naval Petroleum Reserve. Control of these critical lands changed hands within the government numerous times over the years until most of it was finally sold or leased to private oil companies.

These lands were political hot potatoes even before they were officially established. In addition, they were the subject of a well-known political scandal in U.S. history— the Teapot Dome Scandal. In this chapter, we'll take a look at what happened to the Naval Petroleum Reserves and how the United States converted to a system today called the Strategic Petroleum Reserve.

Setting Aside the Oil-Rich Lands

The early quest for oil in many ways mirrored the early gold-rush days in California. Prospectors who flooded areas believed to be rich in black gold in the 1870s even fell under the same rules as other mining operations. Those rules stipulated that prospectors couldn't make a claim on the mineral rights to an area until they actually found the mineral that they sought. Unlike gold, however, petroleum was rarely found on or near the surface. Oil prospectors had to drill to hit pay dirt, which often cost a lot of money and time. The problem was that as soon as a prospector set up an oil rig, others would see what he was doing and set another one up nearby. If one of them struck oil, chances were good that all of them would strike oil, and they would all compete for the same mineral rights.

Petro-Facts

When the U.S. Navy started converting ships from coal to oil, oil-rich lands suddenly became very valuable. At about this time, the movement to conserve federal lands for public use was getting underway. These political issues were at loggerheads. Battles to set up the National Petroleum Reserve took about 10 years to sort out between Congress, the courts, and the executive branch.

The existing law—the Mining Law of 1872—didn't require that prospectors pay the federal government royalties on oil extracted from federal land. Remember that in 1872, oil was still considered black crud by many, and its true value was just being recognized. Federal law had not yet caught up with the new realities of this black gold. In 1896, still not yet aware of oil's potential, the Secretary of the Interior determined that petroleum was classified by scientists as a mineral only "as a sort of distinction from a vegetable product" and exempted oil from the Mining Law altogether.

Setting the Precedent for Reserving Natural Resources

Today we take for granted that the United States should control certain natural resources. Various government agencies control national forests, national parks, as well as lands rich with oil. That wasn't the case in the late 1800s and early 1900s. The battle for the establishment of national forests was fought and won by President Theodore Roosevelt and the first Forest Service Chief Gifford Pinchot. This battle paved the way for the later fight to preserve lands thought to contain significant petroleum potential.

In the early 1900s, the United States was trying to encourage people to populate areas—mainly out west—that it considered to be unpopulated. People could purchase a homestead in California or Wyoming, for instance, fairly cheaply. Since there were no laws recognizing the potential of oil and the value of the lands on which it sat, people were able to buy oil-rich lands with no regard for their resource potential. Mining speculators who recognized the value of oil were gobbling up the petroleum-rich property relatively cheaply.

The battle lines for oil were drawn on September 17, 1909, when the director of the Geological Survey sent a report to the Secretary of the Interior concluding that oil lands were passing into private control so rapidly that it would "be impossible for the people of the United States to continue ownership of oil lands for more than a few months. After that, the Government will be obliged to repurchase the very oil that it has practically given away."

President William Howard Taft acted quickly on this report by issuing an executive order on September 27, 1909. The order was called the Temporary Petroleum Withdrawal No. 5 and it withdrew more than 3 million acres of land in California and Wyoming that had been available to the public for development. At the same time, it proposed legislation that would control the use and sale of the petroleum deposits on these lands currently in the public domain.

Many questioned whether President Taft had the authority to withdraw these lands. Congress indirectly supported his decision with the Pickett Act, passed on June 25, 1910, which gave the President the authority to withdraw public lands for water-power sites, irrigation, or other public purposes. The Act did not, however, make the law retroactive to the date that Taft issued his executive order or specifically support his temporary order.

The First Naval Petroleum Reserves

Using this newly granted authority, President Taft started to set aside lands to conserve oil for naval purposes. In 1912, Taft set aside Elk Hills, California, as Naval Petroleum Reserve No. 1 and Buena Vista Hills, California, as Naval Petroleum Reserve No. 2. Teapot Dome, Wyoming was established as Naval Petroleum Reserve No. 3 in 1915. The most controversial site today, Naval Petroleum Reserve No. 4, in Alaska, was set aside in 1923. In addition, President Taft set aside Naval Oil Shale Reserves in Colorado and Utah in 1916.

Legislation to set up the laws governing leasing federal land for mining gold, oil, and other valuable minerals was not passed until 1920, and lands set aside for military or naval uses were excluded from the legislation. This 10-year struggle between the passing of the Pickett Act and the Mineral Leasing Act was fraught with political battles between the conservationists and the pro-development forces.

Slick Sayings

I do not know, Mr. President, whether you have ever been in the section of California where oil in quantity was first discovered, but a coyote has to carry his rations with him if he expects to stay overnight anywhere upon the Mohave Desert and that section of California lying immediately to the east of it. These men, however, went there … and built roads, laid waterpipes, then sunk their shafts and discovered oil. What geologic bureau, what paid Government prospector—if such a thing can be imagined—what impulse or influence except the impulse or influence of gain … would ever have driven men into such inhospitable regions, impelled them to expend their money and their time, and incur all of the dangers which inhere in such climatic conditions, except that they knew and were told by the Government that their successful exploitation would be followed by a recognition of their locations?

—Statement of Senator Charles Thomas (D-Colorado) on the floor of the Senate on August 23, 1919, during debate on the Mineral Leasing Act.

Lawyers representing the oil companies that were fighting to maintain their mineral rights told their clients that President Taft's executive order to withdraw the lands in 1909 wasn't valid because he didn't have the authority. On that advice, oil companies worked rapidly to develop their rights in the nine-month period between the temporary executive order of 1909 and the permanent law of 1910. The oil companies hoped that if they bought the land before the law took effect, they would have permanent claim on it.

Congress complicated the situation by not specifically mentioning the temporary set aside in the 1910 legislation. Rather than telling companies that they lost their land, Congress left that tough job to the courts. Midwest Oil challenged the President's authority, and the Supreme Court ruled in favor of Taft in 1915 in a precedent-setting case for land-use rights entitled *United States* v. *Midwest Oil*.

Once the Mineral Leasing Act of 1920 passed, any land deemed to have mineral potential was retained by the United States. The government then sold leases for the mineral rights to companies that wanted to risk developing them. If oil, gold, or other value minerals were found, the companies were obliged to pay royalties to the government on any profits they made. (We'll talk more about the leasing process later in this chapter.)

Once the leasing system was established, the Naval Petroleum Reserves became a political football passing between the Navy and the Department of Interior (DOI). The DOI had control until 1920 the when the U.S. Navy's Fuel Oil Office took over. Then, in 1922, a soon-to-be-infamous and powerful Secretary of the Interior, Albert Fall, convinced the Secretary of the Navy, Edwin Denby, to allow him to take over control of the Reserves.

> **Petroleum People**
>
> Albert Fall was born in Kentucky and worked as a lawyer in New Mexico until he was appointed to a judgeship. He became active in the Republican Party and was elected to the Senate in 1912. In 1921, President Warren Harding appointed him Secretary of the Interior.

Scandalizing a Teapot—Dome, That Is

Once the reserves fell under his control, Fall made a secret deal to turn over leasing rights at the Elk Hills and Teapot Dome Reserve sites to two of his closest friends. At the time there was no official process for leasing the lands. Harry Sinclair of Mammoth Oil got leases to develop naval reserve lands at Teapot Dome, and Edward Doheny of Pan American Petroleum and Transport Company "won" the right to develop Elk Hills.

Soon after the deal, word spread around Washington that Fall was suddenly spending a lot more money than he used to. People started getting suspicious. The *Wall Street Journal* exposed Sinclair's lease at the Teapot Dome Reserve on April 14, 1922. President Harding defended Fall and Denby, but two senators, Robert La Follette (R-Wisconsin) and John B. Kendrick (D-Wyoming), called for an investigation. Senator Thomas Walsh, a Democrat from Montana, led the investigation that included dozens of witnesses. Finally, on January 24, 1924, Edward Doheny testified that he had "lent" Fall $100,000, which many believe was a payoff to get the lease.

Within seven days of Doheny's testimony, the Senate resolved that the leases were "executed under circumstances indicating fraud and corruption." The oil companies lost their leases, and Fall and Denby were forced to resign.

The U.S. Justice Department filed criminal suit, and Sinclair was the first to be brought to trial on conspiracy charges to defraud the United States. However, the trial came to an abrupt end after only two weeks, when it was exposed that Sinclair had hired a detective agency to follow the jury. A mistrial was declared, and Sinclair was tried and convicted for criminal contempt of court. He was sentenced to six months in prison.

Albert Fall faced trial on October 7, 1918, for accepting a bribe from Doheny. Fall was found guilty, sentenced to one year in jail, and fined $100,000. Ultimately it was proven that Fall had received a total of $400,000 in gifts and loans.

The Teapot Dome Scandal forced control of the Reserves back to the Navy, and in 1927, the Navy created the first Office of the Naval Petroleum and Oil Shale Reserves. Under the Navy, the Reserves sat idle for many years.

The Changing Role of the Reserves

Another World War once again changed the future of the Reserves, as the United States needed to feed the thirsty machines of World War II. President Franklin Roosevelt signed an executive order on October 15, 1942, which essentially gave Standard Oil of California the rights to develop Elk Hills (NPR-1). Standard shared the profits and costs of developing the field with the U.S government. The wells were shut down at the end of World War II.

There was again some production from the fields in the 1950s, but it wasn't until the Arab oil embargo of 1973 that the fate of the Naval Petroleum Reserves again became a major political issue. At that time, OPEC drastically cut oil production and created a worldwide oil shortage.

The priority for the reserves prior to 1973 was to conserve the oil for future needs, so current production was limited. Then, on April 5, 1976, President Gerald Ford signed the Naval Petroleum Reserves Production Act into law. This law allowed production, rather than conservation, to be the priority for the Reserves. About a year later, President Jimmy Carter transferred the reserves to the Department of Energy. A Navy captain directed the Energy Department program for about 20 years, and Navy Lieutenants served as engineering staffs for the California and Wyoming sites.

Petro-Facts

Elk Hills became a model for environmental protection. Its field operators developed technology that reduced nitrogen-oxide emissions, which are released in the production or use of oil, by 70 percent. Asthma and heart attacks are two of the many health hazards related to nitrogen-oxide. In 1993, the local American Lung Association awarded Elk Hills with a Clean Air Award for its success in reducing vehicle emissions by converting truck and vanpools to natural gas. Elk Hills also won awards for energy efficiency for its fleet conversion program.

Elk Hills opened for commercial production in 1976, and by July 1981, was producing 181,000 barrels of oil per day. It became the United States' eleventh top-producing field, generating about $13 billion in profits for the U.S. Treasury.

Production continued at the fields for about 20 years, with Elk Hills being the largest producer by far among the Reserve sites. In 1994, Elks Hills produced 68,000 barrels per day (BPD), Buena Vista Hills produced fewer than 4,000 BPD, and Teapot Dome produced under 2,000 BPD. In that period, the Reserves produced more than 1 billion barrels of oil, 2 trillion cubic feet of natural gas, and 3.2 billion gallons of natural gas liquids. These translated to over $16 billion for the U.S. Treasury on a $3 billion dollar investment.

Privatizing Oil Properties

As financially successful as the Reserves were, the Energy Department and some members of Congress began questioning whether the United States should be in the oil business at all. Patricia Fry Godly, Assistant Secretary for Fossil Energy, testifying before Congress on September 8, 1995, had the following to say about the government's role in the oil business:

> … the Department of Energy, as a Government agency, does not—and cannot— operate the fields to achieve their maximum value. The Federal Government, by design, is not in the business of making money. Government programs are driven by the public interest—not by profit motive. Today the public interest dictates that the Government restrict its expenditures to the highest priority of programs that are responsive to the broadest public interest. This has limited the Department of Energy's ability to make capital investments in the Naval Petroleum Reserves that would have been routine for the private sector.

The Department of Defense (DOD) also sent a letter to congress earlier in the year, stating that the DOD's "interest in the Naval Petroleum Reserves has diminished over the years as the Reserves have become depleted and otherwise less relevant as a Defense asset." The military went on to state that for readiness purposes it needed refined product, not crude oil.

The United States Congress authorized the U.S. Department of Energy to sell the assets of NPR-1 (Elk Hills, California) in the Defense Authorization Act of 1996. On Feb-ruary 5, 1998, Occidental Petroleum purchased Elk Hills from the government with a winning bid of $3.65 billion.

Sale of these government lands have generated a significant amount of cash for the U.S. Treasury. The big controversy is whether the United States is receiving adequate compensation for the lands. Some people believe that the government is in essence giving the land to the oil companies because of how much money those companies will eventually make on the oil extracted from those areas.

The sale of important oil leases isn't the only recent action that has been subject to controversy. The amount companies pay in royalties and how the royalties are calculated also raise eyebrows as well as questions—we'll talk more about that in Chapter 19.

Today's Naval Reserve Activities

The Energy Department continues to operate NPR-2 (Buena Vista Hills, California) and NPR-3 (Teapot Dome) but leases most of the lands to private companies. For instance, 90 percent of the tracts of NPR-2 that the federal government owns are leased to private oil companies. The Rocky Mountain Oilfield Testing Center at Teapot Dome is used as a state-of-the-art test center for the oil and gas industry to try out new petroleum production technology.

Petro-Facts

In April 1987, the Department of Energy transferred the Naval Oil Shale Reserves to the Northern Ute Indian Tribe. These reserves were set aside in the early 1900s because the government believed the geology had potential oil production. No one has ever found an economical way to develop oil shale.

The development of NPR-4, which today is known as National Petroleum Reserve-Alaska, still faces major political battles regarding its development of some sensitive environmental areas of Alaska. This is separate from the Alaskan National Wildlife Refuge. We'll take a closer look at those battles in Chapter 23.

The Naval Oil Shale Reserves in Colorado were transferred to the Department of Interior's Bureau of Land Management, which offers commercial mineral leasing of these properties primarily for natural gas production and future oil exploration. In 2000 and 2001, the Naval Oil Shale Reserve in Utah was transferred to the Northern Ute Indian Tribe.

Managing the Strategic Reserves

Even though the government has pretty much gotten out of the oil production business, it still sees oil as critical for national security. After all, our dependency on oil has only increased since the program was implemented in the early part of the twentieth century. The U.S. government has shifted emphasis from owning oil-rich land and leasing the mineral rights to that land to actually stockpiling crude oil that has already been extracted from the ground.

Secretary of the Interior Harold Ickes first advocated the stockpiling of emergency crude oil in 1944. President Truman appointed a Minerals Policy Commission to study the issue. It proposed the establishment of a strategic oil supply in 1952. President Eisenhower suggested an oil reserve in 1956, and a Cabinet Task Force on Oil Import Control during the Nixon Administration echoed the called for a reserve in 1970.

Even with all these calls for establishing a reserve, it took a major crisis to get Congress to act. When the Arab countries cut off oil flow to the United States in 1973 and 1974 (more on that in Chapter 14), the need for a strategic oil reserve became critical. The Strategic Petroleum Reserve (SPR), where oil is stored for emergency situations, was established with the passage of the Energy Policy and Conservation Act, which was signed into law on December 22, 1975, by President Gerald Ford. The legislation mandated the establishment of an SPR of up to one billion barrels of petroleum.

The Gulf of Mexico and its salt domes along the U.S. coast were chosen as the logical place for the SPR because many U.S. refineries and distribution points were already located there. Construction of the first site began in 1977. On July 21, 1977, the first oil—approximately 412,000 barrels of Saudi Arabian crude—was delivered as the first deposit to the SPR. Today the SPR has 700 million barrels of oil, which translates to about 53 days of supply according to the Department of Energy calculations.

The Reserves are used sparingly. During the first Gulf War in 1990 and 1991, the Department of Energy implemented a plan to draw up to 33.75 million barrels of crude oil from the SPR. Since world oil supplies and prices stabilized quickly, the United States sold only about 17.3 million barrels of the oil to 13 companies. Just the announcement by the United States that it intended to use the SPR helped to stabilize oil supply and prices.

> **Petro-Facts**
>
> The U.S. government has spent more than $20 billion to establish the Strategic Petroleum Reserves. Four billion dollars were spent on building the facilities, and $16 billion were used to buy the oil.

Periodically, the government uses the Reserves to assist U.S. oil companies facing temporary shortages. For example, when ARCO had a pipe-line blockage problem in 1996, the SPR supplied the company with 900,000 barrels of crude oil. ARCO replaced the oil as soon as the blockage was cleared.

According to language in the Energy Policy and Conservation Act, the president can draw down from the reserves if he or she decides that …

1. An emergency situation exists and that there is a significant reduction in supply which is of significant duration and scope;

2. A severe increase in the price of petroleum products has resulted from such emergency situation; and

3. Such a price increase is likely to cause a major adverse impact on the national economy.

Some policymakers wanted President George W. Bush to release oil from the SPR just before the war with Iraq in March 2003, especially since oil from Venezuela was blocked by strikes in that country. Bush decided against releasing oil from the SPR even though prices jumped at the fuel pump significantly.

Why did Bush decide not to release oil from the reserves? Political infighting plays a major role in oil-related decision-making, and many of the decisions are driven by the lobbying efforts of oil companies. In Chapter 17, we'll look at who makes up the oil lobby and the critical issues endorsed by the lobby, as well as how the lobby's influence impacts governmental decisions.

The Least You Need to Know

◆ Lands were set aside for a Naval Petroleum Reserve in 1910 just before World War I.

◆ Control of NPR lands bounced among the Department of the Navy, Department of the Interior, and the Department of Energy throughout their history. Today private companies extract most of the oil from these lands.

◆ The United States' emergency oil supply is held in salt domes near the Gulf of Mexico as part of a Strategic Petroleum Reserve.

Chapter 13

Oil as a Spoil of War

In This Chapter

- ◆ Oil and the internal combustion engine change the face of war
- ◆ The French develop a new military use for petroleum
- ◆ Hitler's unsuccessful quest for control of Russian oil
- ◆ Japan's desire for control of Far-East oil brings the United States into World War II

Prior to World War I, the battle for oil took place between corporations. Although things got nasty and there were certainly winners and losers, no human blood was shed—at least not much. Everything changed with the development of the combustion engine.

Armies became more mobile, but they needed that black blood—oil—to move. As nations realized the strategic value of oil, corporate battles turned to world wars that led to incredible death and destruction. World Wars I and II proved the strategic value of oil and set the world on a course driven by the race to control oil at any cost.

We'll take a look at the how the adoption of the combustion engine for military purposes raised the stakes and started the bloody politics that still drive the need to control oil today.

Learning the Power of Machines

Before the combustion engine, armies were transported by train or on horseback. This limited where wars could be fought and how quickly troops could get to the front. And if an opposing force disrupted the rail lines, it could severely hamper any efforts to defend a country. At the start of World War I in August 1914, troops still advanced on horseback or by train. Mechanized vehicles were not yet part of military planning.

As Germany breathed down the neck of the French and was close to taking Paris only one month after World War I began, the commander in chief of the French Army considered pulling back and leaving Paris undefended. The rail system was in shambles and there was no way to move the troops to the front line to fend off the Germans. Or at least that's what he thought.

Driver, Take Me to the Front Line

The French Commander enlisted the help of a retired French General, Joseph Gallieni. Gallieni had initially planned to use taxi cabs to evacuate Paris, but then had an epiphany. Why not instead use the taxicabs to get the troops to the front? The taxis would be an excellent and quick way to transport troops to the front to reinforce the French position and stop the German advance.

Gallieni's unorthodox methods showed the value of the newly developed combustion engine for military purposes. Once the French stopped the German advance, the opposing armies began the long war of attrition. The front lines didn't move more than 10 miles in either direction during the first two years of WWI. Both sides had reached a stalemate, and they needed something dramatic to break it. That "something dramatic" would be Little Willie.

Petroleum People

General Joseph Gallieni was retired at the start of WWI, but had a long military career that included service during the Franco-Prussian War of 1870 and 1871 and a stint as governor of French Sudan where he successfully stopped a rebellion. He was widely supported to be supreme commander of the French Army in 1911, but declined because of age and ill health. Gallieni was recalled in August to help defend Paris. He helped saved Paris by moving troops in Parisian taxicabs to reinforce the front.

Little Willie to the Rescue

"Little Willie" was the nickname for the first tank fueled by gasoline. In reality, Little Willie wasn't so little: It weighed 14 tons and could carry three people. Key people in the British military—including Winston Churchill, who was then First Lord of the Admiralty at the time—had been pushing for its development for military use. Finally, in January 1916, they got their wishes. The first British combat tank was ready January 1916. The fastest it could travel was 3 miles per hour on level ground and 2 miles per hour across rough terrain.

Petro-Facts

Tanks, which are a major part of any ground force today, were first developed by the British in 1916. The British had 150 tanks by the end of 1916. By the end of World War I (1918), all the major forces involved had their own tanks. The British fleet had 1,391 tanks, France had 4,000, Germany had 20, Italy had 6, and the United States had 84.

Other forms of mechanized vehicles also played a major role in World War I. By the end of the war, Britain was using 56,000 trucks, 23,000 cars, and 34,000 motorcycles in its war effort. The United States added 50,000 vehicles when it entered the war. Germany continued to depend primarily on the railways to move troops, which ultimately proved to be a key factor in its defeat.

The first successful demonstration of tanks on the battlefield was on November 20, 1917, when the British Tank Corps, with its 474 tanks, breached 12 miles of the German front and captured 10,000 German prisoners. Unfortunately, the British didn't have enough infantry in the area to exploit the breach, but it still showed the power of this new weapon. The U.S. Army was impressed enough to start developing its own tank (the French had already developed their version of the tank and had 400 ready by 1917).

Tanks weren't the only weapons of war that depended on oil and the combustion engine. The British and U.S. navies were also using oil to fuel their ships.

Planes for Bombing and Spying

Another major invention that relied on petroleum and that proved its worth during World War I was the airplane. The Italians were actually the first to use the airplane in a battle situation when they fought the Turks in Tripoli in 1911, but it wasn't until 1916 that the fighter plane arrived on the scene. The idea of tactical bombing was introduced at that time as well.

The British bombed both Turkish and German troops, but it was Germans who really took the lead in launching strategic attacks against cities when it bombed England. The British didn't attack German cities until the war was almost over.

Airplanes were rapidly developed not only for bombing but also for surveillance. During the war, the British built about 55,000 planes, the Germans about 48,000, the French took the lead with about 68,000 planes, and Italy had about 20,000. The United States had the smallest fleet with 15,000 planes.

Denying Oil Access

All these taxis, tanks, ships, and planes needed fuel—a fact that quickly turned petroleum into a strategic necessity. It didn't take long for the military strategists on both sides of the war to realize that cutting off an army's access to oil could be a decisive blow to the enemy. Once they came to this conclusion, the deadly race to cut enemy oil supplies began.

The Allied forces of Britain, France, and Italy got 80 percent of their oil from the United States by tanker. Shell and Standard Oil tankers were the primary suppliers. Russia had supplied oil to the European nations, but access to that oil had been cut off by the German advance as well as the reduction in supplies because of the Russian revolution (see Chapter 10).

Germany, in an attempt to cut off the U.S. supply, started attacking tankers on the open seas in 1916 using their submarine fleet. By 1917, Germany had sunk six Standard Oil of New Jersey tankers as well as the flagship *Murex* run by Royal Dutch/Shell. Not willing to stand by and let Germany attack its vessels at will, the United States entered World War I on the side of the Allies. In addition to drawing the United States into the war, the German submarine campaign also broke down the divisions among the oil companies and the Allies and led to a system in which Standard Oil and Royal Dutch/Shell temporarily stopped competing and instead worked cooperatively to help the Allies win the war.

In retaliation for the German submarine campaign, the Allies blocked Germany's access to any oil shipments by water. That left Germany with only one alternative—Romania, which was the only oil producer in Europe. However, Romania did not voluntarily turn over its oil to the Germans. The Germans, refusing to take no for an answer, invaded Romania. The British government came to Romania's aid, but it also realized that if Romania fell, they would have to destroy the oil fields rather than let Germany have access to the oil.

The Romanian government didn't want to destroy its one source of national wealth and resisted allowing the destruction until November 17, 1916, when Germany broke through their lines. Britain had a colonel in place whose job was to destroy the oil if German crossed into Romania. He ordered that explosives be placed in the refiners and that all of the oil in storage be released to create lakes of black liquid in the refineries and around other equipment. The lakes were then set on fire. When the Germans arrived on the scene, they found that their prize had been destroyed.

The Germans weren't able to get Romanian oil production started again for five months, and even then the production was only a fraction of the 1914 levels. It took another year to get production levels back up to normal.

The Germans also set their sites on the Russian oil fields in Baku to get the oil they so desperately needed. Britain teamed with Russians, Turks, and Armenians to stop the German advance to Baku and prevent Germany's access to oil there.

By mid-1918, Germany had only enough oil to keep its air and land campaign fueled for about two more months. Denying Germany its oil was the final blow, and the armistice was signed on November 11, 1918, ending World War I.

Rebuilding Russian Oil Fields

After the war, Russia's oil concessions were in total chaos thanks to the Russian revolution and the battles fought during that revolution for ultimate control. The Nobels, deciding it was time to get out of the oil business, started negotiating with Deterding of Royal Dutch/Shell. As we discussed in Chapter 10, Deterding had already worked out a deal with the Rothschilds to take control of their oil stake in Russia.

When negotiations between Royal Dutch/Shell and the Nobels broke down, Standard Oil of New Jersey, seeing an opportunity to increase its market share, quickly stepped up to the plate. Meanwhile, the *Bolsheviks* captured the Baku oil fields and quickly nationalized them. Standard Oil, which didn't believe that the Bolsheviks would maintain control at the end of the revolution, decided to buy about half of the Nobels Russian stake anyway. This deal gave Standard Oil control of about a third of the

Drill Bits

Bolshevik means majority in Russian. The Bolshevik party was formed in 1903 with the idea to set up a Socialist state. The Bolsheviks were led by Vladimir Lenin; they believed that a revolution was the only way to improve the plight of the workers.

Petro-Facts

Today Russian oil companies are trying to stop Iraq from voiding its oil contracts. Since Russia essentially set the precedent on the matter by nationalizing its oil fields after the Russian revolution, it may have a hard time defending its claims in international courts in 2003. We'll talk more about Iraq's postwar oil industry in Chapter 15.

Russian oil output, 40 percent of the Russian refinery capacity, and about 60 percent of the internal Russian oil market.

Dealing with the Bolsheviks proved to be more difficult than Standard Oil anticipated, and the company essentially took a loss on its investment. The Russians nationalized the oil properties and never really compensated the owners. This was the first time a country nationalized its oil industry and kicked out foreign oil companies. It was a pattern that would be repeated by many countries after that.

Nazi Drive for Oil

Germany lost everything after its defeat in World War I. Prior to the war, it was the most industrialized nation in Europe. After the war, its African colonies were seized by Britain. France shared Germany's spheres of influence in the Middle East, Eastern Europe, and China with Britain. Almost all wealth left in Germany was used to pay war reparations, creating an increasingly angry German citizenry. The country, spurred on by its new fascist leader Adolf Hitler, was beginning to believe that the only way it was going to recover from the financial destruction forced on it after World War I was to again fight a war.

Adolf Hitler initially drew a lot of support from Wall Street, Washington, London, and Paris because of his anti-communist/anti-Russian stance. At the time, the fear of communism and Russia was greater than the fear of the burgeoning Nazi war drive. Most countries assumed that Hitler would take care of the so-called "Russian problem" of communism, but none expected him to first conquer the European nations. The West even supplied Hitler with the oil, rubber, and money that he needed to build his war machine.

By the time Hitler actually got around to attacking Russia, he had already occupied most of Eastern Europe (or had an alliance with the countries involved), Holland, Belgium, and Norway, and was in the middle of invading France. Making matters worse, oil-rich Romania and Mussolini's Italy joined forces with Hitler fairly early in the campaign.

Hitler's obsession with oil drove much of his battle plan. World War I had taught everyone how important control of oil was to the new mechanized fighting forces. Learning a thing or two from World War I, Hitler tried to reduce his country's dependence on foreign sources of oil by backing the development of synthetic fuels through a new process called *hydrogenation*. The process was developed by German chemist Friedrich Bergius, and the patent for the process was controlled by the German company I.G. Farben.

Hitler guaranteed prices and markets to I.G. Farben, giving the company the government support it needed to develop the synthetic fuels industry. Farben had proved to Hitler and his air force, the Luftwaffe, that it could produce a high-quality aviation gasoline for its airplanes. By the late 1930s, I.G. Farben became an industrial arm of the Nazi state.

Drill Bits

Hydrogenation is a process used to extract a liquid fuel from coal. It works by adding hydrogen to coal using high temperatures and pressure. Today, hydrogenation is a key purification process used in both the refining and petrochemical industries.

By the time Hitler invaded Poland in 1939, I.G. Farben had 14 hydrogenation plants in operation and six under construction. Most of these plants relied on concentration-camp labor. The aviation fuel output of these plants satisfied more than 90 percent of the German air force's needs.

With synthetic sources of fuel, in addition to his early success in conquering European countries and taking control of their oil reserves, Hitler was able to build up Germany's reserves. Now he had everything in place to fuel his drive to his primary prize—the Russian oil fields. Hitler invaded the Soviet Union on June 22, 1941, with more than 3 million Nazi troops. German military experts expected this to be a quick six-week campaign, but after four years, Hitler never even got close to taking control of Russian oil. By this time, Hitler was once again facing a crisis in his oil supply.

As with World War I, the battle in the seas around Europe was a battle to control access to oil shipments. During the early stages of World War II, Hitler's U-boats (submarines) were successful in cutting off U.S. oil from Britain, by sinking U.S. tankers and supply ships. Once the Allies got control of the seas, they turned the tide and started cutting off the supply lines for Hitler's troops. The German troops found themselves deep in Soviet Union territory with their supply lines cut off both on land and sea. When things started looking bleak, Hitler committed suicide, the Russians took Berlin, and Germany once against suffered a devastating defeat.

Ultimately, the amount of oil used during the four years of World War II was about 100 times the amount used during World War I. Let's look at some other ways that oil was a factor in the Second World War.

Japan, Oil, and Pearl Harbor

Germany didn't drive the United States into the war this time. Until Japan attacked Pearl Harbor, the United States was relatively content to sit back and watch the war unfold from a safe distance. The Allies were expecting Japan's first major move to be an attempt to take control of the oil sources in the Far East. Japan's market was dominated by two Western companies—Royal Dutch/Shell and Standard Oil/Vacuum (a partnership of two baby Standards—Standard of New Jersey and Vacuum, formerly Standard of New York, which was also known as Stanvac). Once Japan entered the war, it knew the American and British companies would cut off their oil supply, which primarily came from these companies' production facilities in the Far East.

Petro-Facts

When Marcus Samuels started developing oil production facilities in the Dutch East Indies, on the Islands of Sumatra, Java, and Borneo in the late 1800s, many people thought he was crazy. No one imagined these islands would become a key military target in a world war.

Japan was very nervous about depending on foreign oil, and required its suppliers to maintain at least six months of oil reserves in Japan so that it could build up its refining industry. Roosevelt considered cutting off Japan's oil supply, but delayed action because he feared that strong economic sanctions, especially the cut-off of oil, would drive Japan to attack the oil industry in the Dutch East Indies. Roosevelt considered the German threat to be more significant than anything Japan could do, and he didn't want to start a war in the East since it was likely the United States would be pulled into the war in Europe.

In 1940, the Japanese government allied its forces with Germany, and by 1941, Japan had taken over all of Indochina. As it became more and more apparent that Japan planned to attack the East Indies, the United States moved its fleet to its base at Pearl Harbor, so that it would be in the right position in case Japan moved against the Dutch East Indies.

Before attacking the East Indies, Japan knew it needed to weaken the U.S. Naval forces. Japanese Admiral Isoroku Yamamoto decided that the best way to do this would be to attack the fleet at Pearl Harbor, which it did at dawn on December 7, 1941.

Fortunately for the United States, none of its aircraft carriers were in the harbor at the time of the attack. Japan also failed to strike the extensive oil reserves held at Pearl Harbor. If Japan had destroyed the oil supplies, the Navy would have had to wait for more oil to be shipped from the mainland, which was more than 1,000 miles away. With its oil and carriers intact, the United States quickly declared war and sent its fleet to battle in the Pacific.

Japanese forces were already in place to attack the oil industry in the East Indies. However, just as with Romania during World War I, plans were in place to destroy the oil facilities on the islands before they could fall into enemy hands. Japan was prepared for this, though, and had more than 4,000 workers ready to repair the damage. The destruction of the oil fields did slow Japan down a bit in 1942. They produced just under 26 million barrels that first year, but almost doubled production the following year. This fuel kept the Japanese fleet going during the war.

The allies fought back with their submarine and carrier force and sunk more than 80 percent of Japan's ships and damaged another 10 percent. The campaign prevented Japan from shipping its oil home, and so the homeland was starved for oil. By June 1944, Japan had to cut back its military operation because of lack of fuel. Even before the United States ended the war with the dropping of the atom bombs in 1945, Japan's oil consumption in the homeland had been cut to just 4 percent of what it had been in 1940.

The world wars taught all powers how important the control of oil was to the security of their own countries. During the years between the two wars, much maneuvering was going on to control the world's largest oil resources—the Middle East—but it wasn't until after the world wars that the world would really understand the size of those resources.

The Least You Need to Know

- Oil domination proved to be the key strategic means to win a war once the combustion engine was invented.

- Adolf Hitler was obsessed with oil and planned his campaign to gain control of oil resources in Europe and Russia.

- Japan knew that it was overly dependent on foreign oil and designed its war strategy to take control of the prize in the Pacific—oil in the Dutch East Indies.

Chapter 14

Battling for Middle East Control

In This Chapter

- ◆ Middle-East oil as a spoil of war
- ◆ Western powers' use and abuse of oil concessions before, during, and after the World Wars
- ◆ Iran, Iraq, Saudi Arabia, and Kuwait regain control of their oil
- ◆ The first Gulf War

As the two World Wars were waged, the West saw the Middle East as mere pawns in a chess game being played on a global scale. Instead of recognizing the rich cultural, political, and religious history of the area, most Western leaders focused on what lay below the surface: oil. And so, although those in power frequently promised Middle-Eastern people independence in exchange for political alliances or key oil concessions, when victory was declared, the Middle East was usually viewed as a spoil of war. Many people argue that this lack of understanding for and interest in the people of the Middle East has cultivated their animosity toward Western cultures, especially the United States and Great Britain.

In this chapter, we'll look at how the two world wars as well as other Middle-East wars have impacted the development of the Middle-East oil industry. The chess game for Middle-East oil has certainly been a bloody one, and probably will continue to be so for many years to come.

Dividing the Spoils

As noted in Chapter 13, World War I proved the strategic importance of oil, and all developed nations were seeking new sources for that prize. The Middle East was the new oil frontier, and everyone wanted a piece of the action.

Britain had the earliest foothold in the Middle East. Its Anglo-Persian company had gained concessions to extract oil in Persia (Iran) in 1909 (see Chapter 10). The British had also established footholds in Iraq and, in 1912, they formed the Turkish Petroleum Company as a means of getting their hands on oil in the Ottoman territories. Britain promised to provide military protection for the Ottoman sheikdoms in exchange for oil rights.

Before World War I, the Ottoman Empire had controlled Syria, Palestine, Arabia, and Mesopotamia (Iraq). The Ottomans, disregarding their agreement with Britain, fought on Germany's side in the war, and so, after World War I, its holdings became part of the spoils to be divided. Syria fell under French control. Britain took control of Palestine, Saudi Arabia, and Iraq.

In dividing the spoils, the Allies made a fatal error—one that still haunts the world today. Since the Allies only saw the Middle East as a big desert, they drew straight lines to establish borders, but didn't factor the local cultures and tribes in the equation. In some areas, the new borders divided people of the same tribes, while in other areas, rival tribes were put into the same country.

Today we still see the tensions created in the region by these nonsensical borders. For example, the *Kurds* were divided among Iraq, Turkey, and Iran. Two Muslim sects, the *Sunnis* and the *Shiites*, vie for power in Iraq. Trading partners Basra and Kuwait were divided when Basra became part of Iraq, and Kuwait was made a separate British protectorate. Tribal territories were also ignored when establishing the border between Iraq and Saudi Arabia. Control of potential oil reserves was more important than the traditions of the local tribes.

Let's take a brief look at how the key Middle-Eastern oil countries developed after World War I.

Drill Bits _____

Kurds are a nationality of about 25 million people inhabiting parts of Iraq, Iran, and Turkey. They have been seeking autonomy since the borders were redrawn after World War I.

Shiite Muslims make up less than 5 percent of the worldwide Muslim population, but they constitute 60 percent of Iraq's population, and almost all of Iran's population is made up of Shiite Muslims. Iranian Shiites are Persians who have not been particularly friendly with the Iraqi Shiites, who identify with the Arab world. One of the big questions in present-day Iraq is whether this age-old difference can be put aside as Shiites vie for control and possibly get assistance from Iran.

Sunni Muslims are by far the vast majority of Muslims worldwide—more than 95 percent of the Muslim world. They are the Muslim minority in Iraq, though, making up only about 30 percent of the population. This minority population controlled Iraq under Hussein through the Ba'th Party (more on that later).

Iraq

The British promised the people living in the Middle-Eastern countries under its control that British rule would be temporary until independent governments could be established. However, instead of allowing for Iraqi self-rule, Britain placed foreigners from India in charge of the new government in Iraq. When that didn't work, the British then turned to Prince Faisal, who was part of a royal Hashemite family, which was respected in the area that would later become Saudi Arabia. While this family was pro-British and claimed to be descended from Mohammed, it was not Iraqi.

Britain got the oil concessions it wanted in Iraq from King Faisal, but the Iraqis never saw him as a legitimate leader. Faisal signed an agreement with the British that essentially made Iraq a puppet of Britain both politically and economically. While King Faisal reigned, Britain maintained control, but when he died, his son and heir to the throne, Ghazi ibn Faisal, was anti-British and wanted to ally with other Arab nations.

Leadership changed numerous times in Iraq. By the time World War II had begun, Iraq was led by a coalition government that included the Shiites, Sunnis, and Kurds under an Iraqi Army General named Nuri as-Said. The first truly independent elections were held in March 1940, and an Arab nationalist was elected, Rashid Ali al-Gailani, who wanted to kick the British out of Iraq once and for all. However, Britain believed that it needed its Iraqi alliance both for the oil it provided and to protect its access to India. After sending troops from Iran and India, the Iraqis quickly capitulated and Britain regained control.

Petro-Facts _____

The Turkish Petroleum Company (TPC) was formed in 1928 by an Armenian from Turkey who convinced the Dutch Shell Group, the French CFP group, and the Near East Development Corporation (American oil companies) to join him in his quest for Iraqi oil. The TPC was formed as a nonprofit British company that produced crude oil for a fee to be divided among the owners based on their shares. The company was limited to refining and marketing enough oil to satisfy Iraq's internal needs, so it did not compete with any of the parent companies outside Iraq.

Throughout this period, the oil industry was run by the Iraqi Petroleum Company (IPC) (formerly the Turkish Petroleum Company). Its shareholders included the Anglo-Persian Oil Company, the Dutch/Shell Group, the French CFP, and the Near-East Development Corporation (American oil companies). Each of the four owned 23.7 percent of the shares. Calouste Gulbenkian, an Armenian from Turkey who engineered the deal, held 5 percent.

Iraq was slated to receive 20 percent of any oil revenues from the field. However, IPC delayed development of the oil fields because some of the shareholders wanted to keep the Iraqi concession in reserve. The primary drivers behind that decision were the British Anglo-Persian Oil Company and U.S. Standard Oil of New Jersey because they had other oil sources available to serve their needs. The French wanted more oil, and Gulbenkian and the Iraqis just wanted to make money.

Iraq ended the concession with IPC in 1931 because it failed to meet performance requirements, which included construction of pipelines and shipping terminals. To regain control, IPC had to give the Iraqi government additional payments and loans and promise to complete two oil pipelines to the Mediterranean by 1935. It wasn't until 1938 that Iraq began exporting oil in significant quantities, which averaged 4 million tons per year until World War II.

After World War II, the Iraqi oil industry began to flourish, and the Iraqi government renegotiated its share from 20 percent of revenues to 50 percent of revenues in 1952. Oil revenues never made it to the people, though. Instead, they were pocketed by government officials while the populace continued to live in poverty. After a rebellion and other unrest in Iraq, the British turned over control of its oil share to the United States in 1954. The Hashemite monarchy installed by the British was finally overthrown in 1958, and the Ba'ath Socialist Party took control. That control was challenged numerous times until July 17, 1968, when the Arab Ba'ath Socialist Resurrection Party took control under the leadership of Saddam Hussein.

Kuwait

Kuwait's border was actually set by the Turks in 1913, before the First World War, and became permanent in 1922, when the Allies were dividing the spoils. At that time, no one thought Kuwait had any oil reserves. Britain's primary interest in Kuwait was its port, which could accommodate British ships because it was the only deep-water port in the northern Persian Gulf.

Britain signed an agreement with the Shaikh of Kuwait in 1899, in which it promised protection in exchange for an agreement that Kuwait would not conduct foreign policy or sell or lease land without first consulting the British government. In 1913, the granting of oil concessions was placed under the same agreement.

The Anglo-Persian Oil Company began exploring for oil in Kuwait in 1935, by which time it had a U.S. partner, Gulf. The companies made their first major oil strike in 1938. It wasn't until after World War II that the oil industry really started to bring in profits, however.

Britain withdrew from Kuwait completely by early 1960. Saudi Arabia took over the defense of Kuwait at that time, but economic ties to Britain continue today. We'll take a closer look at the border struggles between Kuwait and Iraq later in this chapter when we discuss the Gulf War.

Saudi Arabia

The Saudi regime can trace its roots back to ancestors in the mid-fifteenth century, but it was King Ibn Saud who established modern-day Saudi Arabia after the fall of the Ottoman Empire in 1915, when the British acknowledged Saudi independence. King Ibn Saud named the country the Kingdom of Saudi Arabia in 1932, which was formed as a dynastic monarchy.

Petroleum People
Ibn Saud is considered the founder of Saudi Arabia. He was raised in Kuwait, where his family was living in exile. Britain supported his rival for control of what was to become Saudi Arabia, but he consolidated his power over the Arabian Peninsula by 1932, when he named it the Kingdom of Saudi Arabia. In 1935, he granted oil concessions to U.S. oil companies, which began a Saudi friendship with the United States that continues today. During World War II, he remained neutral but favored the Allies. His eldest son Prince Saud succeeded him after he died in 1953.

Standard Oil of California (now Chevron) secured Saudi oil concessions in 1933, thanks to the help of Harry St. John Philby, who had been a British advisor to King Ibn Saud until he resigned from the British Foreign Service in 1930 and became a Muslim. Philby left the Service because he disagreed with British foreign policy in the Middle East.

The agreement Philby helped to arrange with Standard Oil of California laid the foundation for what is today the Saudi oil company Aramco. The company started as the California Arabian Standard Oil Company (Casoc). Texas Company (later Texaco) took a 50 percent share in Casoc in 1936. Saudi Arabia had its first successful oil strike in 1939.

In 1944, Casoc changed its name to Aramco (Arabian American Oil Company). The Saudi government acquired its first portion of ownership in the company—25 percent— in 1973 and purchased the rest by 1980. Rather than nationalize the industry and just kick out the foreign oil companies, Saudi Arabia made a fair offer to buy them out. The friendship between the Saudi government and the United States is still strong today and American oil companies still work closely with Saudi Arabia.

Iran

We discussed Britain's discovery of oil in Iran in Chapter 10. Russia also had a stake in Iranian oil, which they gave up after World War I. Even though U.S. companies also tried to get a foothold in Iran, Britain won out.

Iran played a vital role in World War II even though its original intention was to stay neutral. British, U.S., and Soviet forces occupied the country and used it as a strategic area over which to move 5 million tons of munitions and other war materials needed to aid the Soviet Union's defense against Germany. Iran finally signed an alliance with Britain and the Soviet Union in 1942, after the two countries promised to withdraw all troops within six months of the end of World War II.

In 1944, U.S. and Russian oil companies began negotiating for oil concessions in Iran. However, the Iranian government put off all discussions about oil concessions until after the war. After the war, the United States and Britain held up to their part of the bargain and removed their troops from Iran, but the Soviet troops didn't budge. Soviet leader Joseph Stalin dug in his heels and said that he wouldn't remove his troops until he got an oil concession from the Iranian Prime Minister. He never got his concession, and he finally withdrew his forces. The Soviet influence was completely diminished when the United States signed a military aid agreement with Iran in 1947.

Britain maintained its control over Iranian oil interests until March 20, 1951, when Iran nationalized its oil industry. Even though the United States signed a military aid agreement with Iran, it never got access to the country's oil.

Destabilizing Forces

As you can see, the seeds for unrest in the region were laid as agreements for Middle-East oil were made to satisfy the world's thirst for petroleum rather than the needs of the people of the Middle East. This string of concessions and political maneuverings has contributed to the major rift between the Muslims and Western powers. But by far the most destabilizing factor for the region was the establishment of Israel by the UN General Assembly in 1947, which the Arabs opposed unanimously. Palestine was divided into two countries, one for the Jews and one for the Arabs. The Arab portion was very similar to what today constitutes the Gaza Strip and the West Bank. At the time, the Palestinians did not consider themselves a separate nationality. Even so, over the years they recognized themselves as a nationality, and their plight was taken on by all Arabs who wanted rid the Middle East of what they considered to be the "Jewish menace."

The establishment of the State of Israel has lead to many conflicts in the region.

Battle for Suez Canal

Construction of the Suez Canal began in 1854 by a French engineering company after signing a concession with the Egyptian government, and it was finally completed in 1869. Strategically, the Canal was important because it linked two oceans and two seas—the Atlantic and the Mediterranean and the Indian Ocean and Red Sea—making it very important to commerce in the Middle East, including the transport of oil. The British and the French controlled the canal.

Egypt nationalized the Suez Canal in 1955, which didn't go over well with the Brits or the French. Making matters worse, Egypt also showed its hostility to Israel, which was a close ally of the French, by attacking some Israeli shipments through the canal and allowing others to be robbed.

In response, Israel secretly agreed to help the British and French regain control of the canal by attacking Egypt. In 1956, the three countries carried out their plan, and Israel quickly captured all of the Sinai, which is an important desert border buffer for Israel and Egypt. British troops started their drive for Suez City once Israel had control of the Sinai.

U.S. President Dwight Eisenhower, angry at having been left out of the planning, joined the Soviet Union in its fight to stop France and Britain from regaining control of the Suez, as well as Israel from adding to its borders. Israel was forced to give up all territory it had won in exchange for a promise from the United States that it would have freedom to navigate the Canal. This was only the first of many battles to be fought in the Middle East between Israel and its neighbors.

1967 War

The next major battle was instigated by the Arabs when armies of Egypt, Jordan, Syria, Lebanon, and Iraq joined forces to destroy Israel. On May 15, 1967, Egypt began building up its forces on its border with Israel. Syrian troops were ready by May 18 in the Golan Heights. On May 22, Egypt closed the Straits of Tiran to all Israeli shipping and stopped the flow of oil to Israel. Jordan joined the force build-up on May 30, and Iraq joined by June 4. Together the Arabian countries had 465,000 troops with more than 2,800 tanks and 800 aircraft ready to attack Israel.

Israel decided that its only chance to survive was to make a surprise attack on the Arabian forces. On June 5, Israel attacked Egypt. Within just six days, Israel had captured the Sinai, Golan Heights, Gaza Strip, and the West Bank, and unified Jerusalem, which had been divided between the Palestinians and the Jews when Israel was first established. In all, Israel tripled its territory. Most of the captured territory was Palestinian territory, inhabited by more than 750,000 Palestinians who were hostile to Israel's presence in the new territories.

1973 War

The next major war was started by Egypt and Syria in 1973 (with aid from Libya, Sudan, Algeria, Morocco, Saudi Arabia, and Kuwait). They attacked Israel on Yom Kippur, the holiest day of the Jewish year, which fell on October 6 that year. This war drew both superpowers into the game. Russia sided with the Arabs, and the United States took Israel's side. In retaliation for the United States' support of Israel, the Arab oil-producing countries imposed an embargo on oil exports to the United States (as well as Portugal and Holland). The oil embargo wasn't lifted until March of 1974. The Arab countries and OPEC proved their power over oil, but their actions prompted countries dependent on OPEC oil to seek other sources. The United States sought more oil resources in Canada and Mexico, as well as Great Britain, to balance out its imports from the Arab countries. By 1980, OPEC's power was ultimately weakened, but it is still a powerful force in the oil industry today.

Egypt negotiated a peaceful settlement with Israel in the late 1970s and regained control of the Sinai. The rest of the territory gained during the Yom Kippur war is still up for negotiation in the ongoing attempts to find a peaceful solution for the region.

You can read more about the complex conflict in the Middle East in Mitchell Bard's excellent book, *The Complete Idiot's Guide to Middle East Conflict, Second Edition*.

Iran-Iraq War

As the British pulled out of the Middle East, Iran and Iraq started jockeying for power. Control of the waterway between the two countries, Shatt-al-Arab, became a major point of friction. Under British rule, Iraq had a treaty with Iran in which Iraq owned the waterway and had to maintain it, and in exchange, Iran paid fees to use it.

Once British military forces were out of the picture, Iran stopped paying the fees. Iraq retaliated by sending Kurdish dissidents into Iran. Hostilities continued to build between the two until Iraq finally attacked Iran in 1980.

Slick Sayings

The war between Iran and Iraq began in September 1980, and by late 1983 and early 1984, reports of the use of chemical weapons in that conflict began to appear. The United Nations investigated the reports with seven special missions from March 1984 till the end of the war in August 1988. On all occasions, the use of chemical weapons against Iran was confirmed, and by 1986, Iraq was named as the aggressor. Aerial bobs, artillery shells, and ground-to-ground rockets containing chemical agents such as mustard gas or the nerve agents sarin or Tabun were used.

—Dr. Peter Dunn, Commissioner, United Nations Special Commission, New York, in 1995.

By 1986, both sides moved the conflict to the Gulf and started attacking neutral ships in what became known as the "tanker war." More than 110 neutral ships—many of them transporting oil—were either sunk or damaged during that year. In May 1987, the UN Security Council finally stepped in and passed Resolution 598 that called for an end to hostilities. By the beginning of 1988, 18 navies, 10 from the west and 8 from within the region, were patrolling Gulf waters to keep the oil moving and safe from attack. Finally, in August 1988, Iran and Iraq accepted a cease-fire plan.

Casualties were high on both sides of the conflict. Estimates were that 375,000 Iraqis were killed or wounded and possibly more than one million Iranians. Iraq came out of the fight with a massive army of 1 million well-equipped fighters, which was the largest army in the Middle East and second only to Israel in overall power. The Arab neighbors supported Iraq because they preferred the Sunni minority in Iraq to the Shiite majority in Iran.

Iraq also came out of the war owing billions to Arab neighbors, with a huge army to maintain, and an oil industry that needed to be rebuilt to pay for it all. The war tab for Iraq was estimated to be $300 billion.

Before taking on Iran, Iraq's oil industry had been exporting 3.2 million barrels of oil per day. By 1987, with the loss of Gulf oil terminals and war damage to its oil facilities, Iraqi exports were down to only 1.8 million BPD. This all added up to a formula that left Saddam Hussein desperate and in need of a quick solution. His economy was shattered and his people, especially the Shiite majority, were becoming restless. His solution was to attack Kuwait and get control of the oil fields and its port.

Gulf War

Hussein justified his decision to attack Kuwait by charging that Kuwait had illegally been pumping Iraqi oil from their joint fields in Rumalyah. He also contended that a significant portion of Kuwait was actually Iraqi territory—an old charge with little merit.

Misinterpreting signals that he was getting from the Arabs and Americans, Hussein thought he had free reign to take over his tiny neighbor. On August 2, 1990, Saddam Hussein made his move and attacked Kuwait. His force of 120,000 quickly overpowered Kuwait's force of 20,000. About 7,000 of the Kuwaiti military forces made it to Saudi Arabia and helped with the fight to regain their country.

Hussein was mistaken about the wrath his actions would engender from both the United States and his other Arab neighbors. The United States surprised him when it was able quickly to put together a coalition of both Western countries and Arabs. On the same day that Iraq moved into Kuwait, the UN Security Council passed a resolution calling for Iraq to leave Kuwait. A series of UN resolutions were passed imposing economic sanctions on Iraq, which blocked Iraqi imports as well as oil exports.

When it was apparent that Hussein wasn't voluntarily going to pull out his forces, the UN Security Council passed a resolution on November 29, 1990, authorizing the use of force if Hussein did not leave Kuwait voluntarily by January 15, 1991. The war started on January 17, 1991, two days after the UN deadline, and the coalition quickly chased the Iraqis out of Kuwait.

Slick Sayings

I was convinced, as were all our Arab friends and allies, that Hussein would be overthrown once the war ended.

—George Bush, in his memoir, *All the Best, George Bush*

Petro-Facts

By the end of the war on February 27, about 100,000 Iraqi troops were killed, 300,000 wounded, and 60,000 were captured. The U.S. coalition forces lost 148 troops and 458 were wounded (there were also 121 noncombat U.S. troops losses).

The Persian Gulf wasn't a total victory for the Coalition, however. For, as they retreated from Kuwait, the Iraqis set fire to more than 500 Kuwaiti oil wells, which took over a year to quell and caused indescribable environmental damage. In addition, even though the Coalition achieved its aim of removing the Iraqis from Kuwait, Saddam Hussein stayed in power. He would go on to play a cat-and-mouse game with the UN until 2003, when the United States led another invasion to oust him.

The Least You Need to Know

- Many of the Middle-East borders still in place today were drawn up after World War I as part of the spoils of that war.

- The quest for oil in Middle-Eastern countries drove their economies and politics, which in most cases were controlled by foreign influence until the 1950s and 1960s, when they fought for and won independence.

- Saddam Hussein built up a massive army with profits from its oil industry. When it attacked Kuwait, it kicked off the first Persian Gulf War.

15

Terrorism and Oil

In This Chapter

- Osama, Afghanistan, and oil
- Saddam, weapons of mass destruction, and oil
- Rebuilding the Iraqi oil industry
- Revamping worldwide oil control

The September 11, 2001, attacks on the World Trade Center and Pentagon served as a wake-up call in the United States and other Western countries. It was only then that the majority of people realized the extent of the hatred certain fundamentalist Muslim groups, under the umbrella of al Qaeda, had for the West.

The reasons given openly by the United States and its allies for attacking both Afghanistan and Iraq was to rid the world of terrorists and weapons of mass destruction (WMD). There is no question that terrorists were based in both countries, that al Qaeda was making noise about wanting WMD, and that Iraq had a weapons program, at least in the past. Even though all this is true, there is another reason that the United States was determined to assert itself in Afghanistan and Iraq—oil. Both Afghanistan and Iraq are crucial to future oil markets, and leaders in these countries were creating barriers to the development of the oil industry, especially by U.S. oil companies.

In this chapter, we'll trace the oil connections in Afghanistan and Iraq and consider how these connections may have influenced the wars the United States fought in 2001 and 2003.

Focusing on the Middle East and Central Asia

According to the Statistical Review of World Energy, the Middle East and Central Asia (including Afghanistan and several former Soviet republics) are the source of more than 65 percent of the world's oil and natural gas production. The region's reserves contain an estimated 800 billion barrels of crude petroleum plus its equivalent in natural gas. Compare these figures to those of the Americas and Europe, which, combined, have fewer than 160 billion barrels of proven petroleum reserves. Experts expect that by 2050, by which time most of the reserves in the Americas and Europe will have been exploited, the Middle East and Central Asia will control more than 80 percent of the world's oil.

Slick Sayings

> The map of terrorist sanctuaries and targets in the Middle East and Central Asia is also, to an extraordinary degree, a map of the world's principal energy sources in the twenty-first century … It is inevitable that the war against terrorism will be seen by many as a war on behalf of America's Chevron, ExxonMobil, and ARCO; France's TotalFinaElf; British Petroleum; Royal Dutch Shell and other multinational giants, which have hundred of billions of dollars of investments in the region. There is no avoiding such a linkage or the rising tide of anger it will produce in developing nations already convinced they are victims of a conspiratorial collaboration between global capital and U.S. military might … Fueling this resentment in other oil-producing states is the yawning gap between the living standards of the expatriate Western oil workers and a small local elite on one hand, and the vast majority of ordinary citizens on the other.
>
> —Frank Viviano, *SanFranciso Chronicle*, September 2001

When the Bush administration came into power, finding ways to secure oil was one of its first clear missions. Vice President Cheney commissioned the Baker Institute for Public Policy (a think tank set up by the first President Bush's Secretary of State, James Baker) to write a report entitled "Strategic Energy Policy Challenges for the Twenty-First Century." The report was completed in April 2001, and advisors for it included Enron's Kenneth Lay, Shell Director Luis Glusti, BP Regional Vice President John Manzoni, and Chevron Chief Executive David O'Reilly. Sheik Saud Al Nasser Al Sabah, former Kuwait oil minister and fellow of the Baker Institute, also had a hand in the report.

Bush and his spokespeople continue to deny the war was about oil, but recommendations for military action in Iraq were a crucial part of this report, as the following excerpt makes clear:

> Iraq remains a destabilizing influence to U.S. allies in the Middle East, as well as to regional and global order, and to the flow of oil to international markets from the Middle East. Saddam Hussein has also demonstrated a willingness to threaten to use the oil weapon and to use his own export program to manipulate oil markets … The United States should conduct an immediate policy review toward Iraq, including military, energy, economic, and political/diplomatic assessments … Sanctions that are not effective should be phased out and replaced with highly focused and enforced sanctions that target the regime's ability to maintain and acquire weapons of mass destruction … Once an arms-control program is in place, the United States could consider reducing restrictions on oil investments inside Iraq. Like it or not, Iraqi reserves represent a major asset that can quickly add capacity to world oil markets and inject a more competitive tenor to oil trade. However, such a policy will be quite costly as this trade-off will encourage Saddam Hussein to boast of his "victory" against the United States, fuel his ambitions, and potentially strengthen his regime. Once so encouraged and if his access to oil revenues were to be increased by adjustments in oil sanctions, Saddam Hussein could be a greater security threat to U.S. allies in the region if weapons of mass destruction (WMD) sanctions, weapons regimes, and the coalition against him are not strengthened. Still, the maintenance of continued oil sanctions is becoming increasingly difficult to implement. Moreover, Saddam Hussein has many means of gaining revenues, and the sanctions regime helps perpetuate his lock on the country's economy.

After this report was presented to Bush's cabinet, several news reports circulated that there was agreement in the Bush administration that action against Iraq was necessary. One such report appeared in Scotland's *Sunday Herald* on October 6, 2002, which stated that members of Bush's cabinet agreed in April 2001 that "Iraq remains a destabilizing influence to the flow of oil to international markets from the Middle East and U.S. 'military intervention' is necessary."

Why, then, did the United States take so long to invade Iraq? The most likely answer is that the political timing wasn't yet right for U.S. military action. September 11 changed all that. In fact, immediately after the attacks, the United States tried to connect Saddam Hussein to the attacks, but no connection was ever found. Instead the United States was sidetracked into a war on terrorism and an attack on Afghanistan.

Interestingly, Afghanistan also has an oil connection—as a primary future route for oil from the Caspian Sea region and Central Asia. The United States has made numerous attempts to support U.S. oil companies that want to build a pipeline from Central Asia to Pakistan, so that they could avoid transporting oil through both Russia and Iran. Russian and Iranian oil companies have rejected U.S. involvement in their industries and have a stranglehold on the transport of oil through their own territories.

Pipeline Dream in Afghanistan

In the 1990s, Unocal, a California-based global energy resource corporation, dreamed up the idea of running an oil pipeline from Turkmenistan, with its 700 billion cubic meters of natural gas reserves, through Afghanistan to Pakistan, with a possible extension to India. With such a pipeline in place, U.S. companies like Unocal and others would have an alternative transport route, thereby avoiding the need to ship gas through Iran or Russia. Unocal partnered with Saudi Arabia's Delta Oil to propose the construction of the multi-billion dollar pipeline.

Unocal was in competition with an Argentinean oil company Bridas for the pipeline project. Both companies were trying to win the project by bidding up royalties and financing deals, as well as offering infrastructure improvement projects for Afghanistan. World events interrupted the pipeline project, however. In August 1998, U.S. forces attacked Al Qaeda leader Osama bin Laden's terrorist camps in Afghanistan, in retaliation for U.S. embassy attacks in Kenya and Tanzania. In addition, President Bill Clinton broke off diplomatic contact with the *Taliban* in Afghanistan, because they refused to turn Osama bin Laden over to international authorities. Fearing for the safety of its workers, Unocal halted its push for the pipeline project and pulled all of its staff out of Afghanistan in 1998.

Political tensions increased further on October 15, 1999, when the United States and Russia pushed through a UN Security Council Resolution demanding the extradition of Osama bin Ladin and imposed major economic sanctions on Afghanistan. At this point, Bridas put the project on hold because it found business impossible given the political tensions.

When President Bush took office in January 2001, the U.S. diplomatic position toward Afghanistan took an about-face. The Bush administration started negotiating with the Taliban a month after Bush's inauguration, with the hope of stabilizing the political situation in Afghanistan and, you guessed it, reopening the possibility of a pipeline from Central Asia to Pakistan. The administration hoped to get the Taliban to give up Osama bin Laden and make peace with the Northern Alliance; in exchange for its cooperation, the United States offered the Taliban a cut in the billions of dollars in revenue that would be generated by the pipeline.

Drill Bits

The **Taliban** movement was started in Kandahar, Afghanistan, in 1994 by radical Islamic students with considerable financial support from Saudi Arabia. The Taliban captured the capital Kabul in September 1996 and ousted the ruling party. The Taliban were only recognized and supported by three countries—Pakistan, Saudi Arabia, and the United Arab Emirates. While the Taliban were in control of Afghanistan, about 15 percent of the population in the country outwardly opposed their rule. This opposition force was called the **Northern Alliance.**

Negotiations broke down in July 2001. According to newspaper reports, a meeting was supposed to take place in Berlin on July 17, 2001, between the United States, Pakistan, UN representatives, and representatives from the two warring factions in Afghanistan—the Taliban and the *Northern Alliance*. The Taliban never showed up at the meeting. In the book, *Forbidden Truth*, Jean-Charles Brisard and Guillaume Dasquié say they were told by the Pakistani representative Naiz Naik that someone in the American delegation threatened the Taliban by sending them a message that said, "Either you accept our offer of a carpet of gold or we bury you under a carpet of bombs."

Brisard and Dasquié continue:

> Naturally we hesitate to speculate about whether the Taliban and its Al Qaeda supporters might have tried to anticipate a military action against them by launching a devastating and horrendous attack on U.S. soil on September 11, 2001 …. Moreover, given the nature of the September attacks, on the surface it appears that many months, if not years, of planning went into them. Nevertheless, we know that the Taliban was under the influence or control of bin Laden, that he and his organization were more than just guests living under Taliban control. And at the beginning of August 2001, the Taliban and its terrorist allies knew their days were numbered … Was the statement made to the Pakistanis understood as a signal by them? Did they launch a preemptive strike? We have no clear answer to that, but the months from February to August 2001 must be independently investigated, in the same way that such an investigation also needs to focus on to what extent the Bush administration knew (or didn't know), and whether the right steps were taken to avoid this tragedy.

Brisard and Dasquié weren't the only ones making such speculations. News reports indicated that this breakdown in negotiations and threat of a "carpet of bombs" may have led the Taliban to strike first. However, there is no direct evidence of this connection to the attack on September 11, and it was clearly in the planning stages prior to July 17. The bigger question is this: Why was the United States negotiating with the Taliban at all?

Ousting Osama bin Laden and the Taliban

Immediately after the attacks on the World Trade Center and the Pentagon, the United States quickly identified two potential backers of the plot—Saddam Hussein and Osama bin Laden. As noted previously, investigations turned up no connection to Hussein, but investigators quickly found a trail of evidence leading directly to Osama bin Laden and al Qaeda. After a short and unsuccessful diplomatic effort to get the Taliban to release bin Laden, the United States went to war with Afghanistan.

A U.S.-led coalition of forces started bombing Afghanistan on October 7, 2001. By December 7, the Taliban fled from Kandahar, and by December 22, a new U.S.-backed government was in place in Afghanistan. This was only the first step in the new worldwide war on terrorism. Nations throughout the world joined the U.S.-led war on terror and helped to expose the terrorists and find ways to freeze any funds they had to carry out future operations.

Rebuilding Afghanistan and Pipeline Dreams

Once the Taliban and Osama bin Laden were out of the way and a U.S.-backed government was in place in Afghanistan, the dream of building a pipeline got a new lease on life. President Bush wasted no time getting the ball rolling: He appointed Afghan-born Zalmay Khalilzad, a former advisor to Unocal (the company that proposed the pipeline idea in the first place), as special envoy to Afghanistan on December 31, 2001, just nine days after the new government was in place. (Khalilzad is also involved in rebuilding Iraq.)

Khalilzad reports to National Security Advisor Condoleezza Rice (who was a consultant to Central Asia for Chevron before taking the position of Bush's National Security Advisor). About a year after Khalilzad was appointed, Pakistan, Afghanistan, and Turkmenistan signed the framework for an agreement to build a $3.2 billion pipeline. The pipeline eventually will be built as a consortium among the three countries, and gas reserves in Turkmenistan will pass through Pakistan into Afghanistan. The Asian Development Bank is now studying the project and looking for investors, but oil companies are cautious about investing significantly in Afghanistan, until the situation is more secure. Until there is more security in Afghanistan the pipeline will probably still remain a pipedream. Since major oil production in Central Asia and the Caspian Sea region is just getting under way (as explained in Chapter 24), the industry has some time before the pipeline will be needed.

At the time this book was written, 10,000 to 12,000 coalition forces (7,000 to 8,000 from the United States) were still in Afghanistan trying to maintain a fragile peace while searching for Osama bin Laden and the Taliban. Aid workers cannot leave their compound without approval and a heavily armed military escort. Roads, badly in need of repair, are filled with landmines and blocked by bandits. The *Washington Post* reported on April 28, 2003, that "security issues have made it 'almost impossible' for U.S.-backed education officials to work in 24 of the nation's 34 provinces. An International Red Cross worker was stopped along a roadway March 26 and shot 20 times, becoming the first foreign-aid worker killed since the Taliban's fall. Continuing attacks have forced some humanitarian groups to withdraw altogether."

Dancing With Saddam Hussein

Even while the war in Afghanistan was underway, the Bush administration turned its attention to its next big catch—Saddam Hussein. Since pulling out of Kuwait in 1991, Hussein had been playing a cat-and-mouse game with the United Nations over weapons of mass destruction. The UN passed more than 60 resolutions regarding Iraq after the invasion of Kuwait. In addition, the UN sent in teams of experts to identify and remove weapons of mass destruction from Iraq, but Saddam Hussein did all that he could to hamper their efforts. Nonetheless, by 1998 about 95 percent of known WMD were destroyed as well as most of the equipment needed to produce new WMD. Some equipment that had dual purposes was left in place by UN inspectors.

Changing Regimes in Iraq

Although the Clinton administration had considered taking action to remove Saddam from power, it never did, believing that it couldn't get the necessary support to take such actions. President George W. Bush, however, claimed that the Iraqi regime and its alleged weapons of mass destruction (WMD) posed an immediate threat to the United States and the world.

The administration first tried to get UN approval for military action against Iraq. The United States not only failed to get UN support for the attack but also found itself in the center of one of the ugliest political and diplomatic controversies in years, as its relations with key allies, including France, Germany, and Russia—who strongly opposed war with Iraq—became very tense. Claiming that he had run out of diplomatic options, President Bush put together a small coalition of forces to attack Iraq and oust Saddam Hussein.

Some critics of the war in Iraq argued that the war was more about U.S. control of oil than about terrorist threats of weapons of mass destruction. They cite earlier instances in which we knew of Iraq's use of WMD but continued to negotiate with that country as evidence.

> **Slick Sayings** _____
>
> The only acceptable strategy is one that eliminates the possibility that Iraq will be able to use or threaten to use weapons of mass destruction. In the near term, this means a willingness to undertake military action, as diplomacy is clearly failing. In the long term, it means removing Saddam Hussein and his regime from power.
>
> —Letter to President Bill Clinton in 1998 from the Project for the New American Century, whose members include current members of the Bush administration, Donald Rumsfeld, Dick Cheney, and Paul Wolfowitz.

Why Didn't WMD Matter in the 1980s?

U.S. and other international oil companies lost their Iraqi oil interests in Iraq when the Ba'ath party nationalized the oil industry in the 1970s. Since then, U.S. oil interests—and the U.S. government—have worked to get a foothold back in Iraq. One such attempt has been made public only recently, and it gives us a glimpse of the measures the United States will go to get access to oil.

The Institute for Policy studies recently released information about a secret meeting that took place in 1983 between U.S. and Iraqi representatives. According to the report, which is based on recently declassified memos, President Reagan's special Middle-East envoy, Donald Rumsfeld (who is now Secretary of Defense in the Bush Administration and was responsible for coordinating the wars in Afghanistan and Iraq), met with Saddam Hussein and Iraqi Deputy Prime Minister Tariq Aziz on December 20, 1983. They met to discuss a proposal from Bechtel (which won a $100 billion contract from the U.S. State Department for rebuilding Iraq after the war) for a pipeline that would run from Iraq to the Gulf of Aqaba, in Jordan, a major oil transit point.

On the surface, the pipeline meeting isn't really that big of a deal—after all, the United States gets involved in these kinds of negotiations all the time. However, these secret meetings took place during the Iran-Iraq War, _and at a time when the United States knew that Iraq was unleashing biological and chemical weapons of mass destruction against Iranians_. Critics of the United States' actions in Iraq wonder why the U.S. government was so nonchalant about Iraq's WMD in the 1980s—even going so far as to negotiate with Saddam Hussein's regime when they knew that the regime was using weapons of mass destruction. And even after the State Department finally issued a public statement condemning Iraq's use of WMD on March 5, 1984, it continued to secretly support Bechtel's pipeline efforts (Iraq and Jordan rejected the proposal on December 31, 1985).

It appears to many people that access to oil was a far bigger concern to the U.S. government than WMD in the 1980s, and they wonder if that attitude has really changed all that much since then. Certain actions taken by the U.S. military and the Bush administration seem to validate these claims.

Slick Sayings

The men who courted Saddam while he gassed Iranians are now waging war against him, ostensibly because he holds these same weapons of mass destruction. To a man, they now deny that oil has anything to do with the conflict. Yet during the Reagan Administration and in the years leading up to the present conflict, these men shaped and implemented a strategy that has everything to do with securing Iraqi oil exports. All of this documentation suggests that Reagan Administration officials bent many rules to convince Saddam Hussein to open up a pipeline of central interest to the US, from Iraq to Jordan.

—Jim Vallette, lead author of the Institute for Policy Studies report, "Crude Vision: How Oil Interests Obscured US Government Focus On Chemical Weapons Use by Saddam Hussein" (www.ips-dc.org/crudevision/crude_vision.pdf).

Where Are the WMD?

You'd think that if the search for WMD was the primary reason for attacking Iraq, then the U.S. government would have planned the search for these weapons as well as it planned the war itself. However, as of this writing, no WMD have been found. In fact, the *Los Angeles Times* reported on April 27, 2003, that, "Disorganization, delays, and faulty intelligence have hampered the Pentagon-led search for Saddam Hussein's suspected weapons of mass destruction, causing growing concern about one of the most sensitive and secretive operations in postwar Iraq, according to U.S. officials and outside experts familiar with the effort." David Kay, a former UN weapons inspector, told the *Times*, "My impression is this has been a very low priority so far, and they've put very little effort into it."

Before the war, the Bush administration said that Iraq had vast stockpiles of anthrax material, botullinum toxin, mustard gas, sarin and VX nerve agents, plus 30,000 munitions, ballistic missiles, and mobile biological laboratories. As of the end of April, none of these had been found. Instead, the *Los Angeles Times* reported that "scores of Iraqi military sites, industrial complexes, and offices were stripped of valuable documents, equipment, and electronic data before U.S. forces or the exploitation teams reached them."

Protect the Oil at All Costs

While there is some question about whether the United States, in the war on Iraq, acted quickly enough to locate and secure weapons of mass destruction, there is no doubt that the United States acted quickly to protect the oil fields and the oil ministry. The first visible attack of Iraq was on March 19, 2003, when the U.S. military struck a sight where it suspected Hussein and his sons were staying. The next action was a mad dash to secure the southern Iraqi oil fields. And the only Iraqi ministry that was completely untouched by looting and destruction in Baghdad was the oil ministry, which was heavily guarded by U.S. troops almost immediately upon entering the city.

While the oil ministry was heavily guarded, the key buildings of the State Oil Marketing Organization (SOMO) were left to the looters. SOMO is the organization that managed the sale of oil under UN-imposed economic sanctions. Abdul Jalil Hammadi, who was in charge of crude oil sales at SOMO, told *The New York Times* on April 28, 2003, "No one tried to stop [the looting]. Americans have not contacted us; the ministry had not contacted us." The Bush administration has determined that sales mechanism is no longer needed with Hussein gone. The new oil ministry—designed with considerable input on the part of the United States—will take over that role.

 Petro-Facts

Bechtel won the largest of the early Iraq reconstruction contracts with an initial value of $34.6 million and a potential total of $680 million to repair the war-damaged infrastructure of Iraq. Some estimates are that the contract could eventually be worth up to $100 billion. The contract includes almost all major reconstruction projects in Iraq including seaports, airports, water, electric power plants, roads, railroads, schools, hospitals, and irrigation system. Former Reagan Secretary of State George Schulz, who introduced President Bush to Condoleezza Rice, sits on the board of Bechtel. Riley Bechtel, the company's chief executive, is on the President's export council and John Sheehan, a Bechtel senior vice president, is on the Pentagon's advisory board. Bechtel contributed $1.3 million to political campaigns in the last election; 59 percent of that money went to Republicans.

Iraq's Oil Partners Before the War

So far we've seen that, in the not-too-distant past, the members of U.S. government, including Secretary of Defense Donald Rumsfeld, have been willing to disregard Iraq's use of WMD when oil or access to oil was at stake. We've also seen that U.S. efforts to find WMD have, as of this writing, failed. Finally, we've seen that the U.S.

military wasted no time in securing the oil fields in Southern Iraq and the Iraqi oil ministry in Baghdad, leaving all other government ministries unsecured and thereby vulnerable to devastating looting. It seems as if the people who have argued that this war is, at least in part, about oil have a pretty good case on their hands. Their argument gets even stronger when we consider the negotiations that were taking place in Iraq before the United States attacked the country.

Based on a recent report in *The Wall Street Journal*, several non-U.S.-based companies had contracts with Iraq to quickly exploit its oil reserves if UN sanctions were lifted. Russian oil company LUKoil had the oldest of these contracts, which was signed in 1997. Other contract holders include Chinese National Petroleum and French TotalFinaElf. However, now that the United States has invaded Iraq, all such contracts appear to be in question. On May 23, 2003, Thamir Ghadhban, the U.S. appointed head of Iraqi oil interests, announced that all such contracts were being reevaluated and new contracts would be announced soon.

The Iraqi oil industry was also in talks with oil companies from Italy, Spain, South Korea, the United Kingdom, Malaysia, Canada, Pakistan, Turkey, Vietnam, and Indonesia. U.S. companies, some of the biggest oil companies in the world, were completely left out of the loop.

Interestingly, France, Russia, and China— who all stood to win big oil contracts if UN sanctions were lifted—led the efforts in the UN against the planned U.S. action against Iraq. Many of the other countries that were in negotiations with Saddam refused to support the U.S. action as well. So even if oil wasn't the sole reason these countries didn't support U.S. action against Iraq, it's hard to believe that it didn't play some role in the decision.

 **Slick Sayings**

Iraq possesses huge reserves of oil and gas—reserves I'd love Chevron to have access to.
—Chevron CEO Kenneth T. Derr in a speech to the Commonwealth Club of San Francisco on November 5, 1998

Redesigning the Oil Industry in U.S. Image

Now that the United States occupies Iraq, the Bush administration controls the redesign of Iraq's oil industry and is resisting any UN intervention in the matter. UN economic sanctions were lifted so that Iraq can start exporting more oil, and the United States will control an oil fund for the Iraqi people, which will be monitored by the World Bank and the UN. Countries that opposed the war wanted more UN involvement in the oil profits and rebuilding of the oil industry, as well as reconstruction plans for the rest of Iraq, but the United States put off this discussion for at least a year. The UN does have a representative in Iraq, but he's an expert in human rights, not oil.

According to a report in *The Wall Street Journal* on April 25, 2003, the Bush administration is planning to structure the new Iraqi oil industry just like a U.S. corporation, with a board of directors overseeing major strategic and investment decisions, while a chief executive officer runs the company. Philip J. Carroll, former chief executive of Shell Oil (the U.S. arm of Royal Dutch/Shell Group), is chairman of an advisory committee for the board. The United States initially planned to get Iraqi oil back up to the pre-war production levels of 2.5 to 3 million BPD by the end of 2003, but reports in both *The New York Times* and *The Wall Street Journal* on June 10, 2003 indicated that production likely will come back on line much more slowly.

Experts expect oil production levels to eventually reach 6 million BPD, possibly in five to six years. This production level would place Iraq in the number-two position in oil production in the world—just behind Saudi Arabia's Aramco state oil company, which was developed by Chevron and Texaco (see Chapter 14).

Realigning U.S. Power in the Region

There's no question that the United States will have a tremendous amount of influence on the future of the Iraqi oil industry. An even greater impact of the U.S. action may be its new influence in the region now that it controls Iraqi oil and can manipulate Iraqi politics. Even after the United States leaves Iraq, governmental structures will be filled, at least initially, with people supportive of the United States.

Slick Sayings

It is certainly plausible to think that a democratic, well-run, transparent Iraqi government, the kind that the U.S. would like to see put in place, could be a very dynamic leader in the region, and it may want an equal share of the spoils with the Saudis.

—Phillip Ellis, Boston Consulting Group, *Washington Post* on April 27, 2003

OPEC is feeling the heat of a potential new, democratic Iraq that might decide to flex its muscle and increase its oil output. And this at a time when non-OPEC oil exporters, especially Russia, are already challenging OPEC's control of the world's blood. OPEC wants to maintain oil prices between $22 and $28 per barrel, but Iraq's major new oil exports could drive this price much lower.

Iraq's political and economic futures are a big question mark, as security problems and protests continue to hamper U.S. efforts to rebuild Iraq in its image. The only thing certain about Iraq's future is that its oil will continue to be a major prize for whoever gets to control it.

The Least You Need to Know

- Critics of the war in Iraq argue that the United States wants control of the Iraqi oil industry.

- The Bush administration was negotiating an oil pipeline with the Taliban before the attacks on the World Trade Center and Iraq. That pipeline deal is now in the works.

- Iraq's use of weapons of mass destruction didn't deter members of the United States government, including Donald Rumsfeld, from negotiating a pipeline deal with Iraq in the 1980s.

- The United States is using its new influence in Iraq to redesign Iraq's oil industry and is putting people friendly to the United States and its oil companies in charge.

- As the second-largest oil exporter, Iraq could dramatically recast the entire worldwide oil industry.

Part 4

Clogging the Bloodlines: Policy, Politics, and Greed

If it's true that everything has a price, then what about your senator's or congressperson's vote or even the President's policy decisions? Some people argue that when it comes to setting the nation's energy policy, the price of the politician's vote or the president's decision can be paid with black gold. That might be a particularly cynical view to take, but you might just agree with us after you read the following chapters.

We explain how oil politics turn on a debate between energy conservationists, who argue for a reduction on our reliance on oil, and proponents of exploration, who believe that we need to continue to increase oil production to maintain a robust economy. These decisions are largely influenced by Washington, D.C., politicians. And where there are politicians, there are oil-industry lobbyists with their wallets wide open.

Chapter 16

Conservation Versus Exploration

In This Chapter

- ◆ Making the most of the oil we have
- ◆ The politics of exploring for more oil
- ◆ How energy policies impact conservation and exploration

Folks don't usually care whether it's petroleum, hydrogen, water, or chewing gum that fuels their cars, heats (or cools) their homes, and is used to manufacture the consumer goods that they buy. They simply want their cars to run, their homes to be comfortable, and their shelves overflowing with stuff. Oh, one more thing: They don't want to pay very much for any of these creature comforts.

Today, oil is the source of energy that satisfies most of these needs and desires. However, the world's oil supplies are finite, and the known sources of oil are dwindling at an astonishing rate. Experts estimate that by 2013 the world will use at least 20 percent more oil than it does today, which means that today's global consumption rate of 77 million BPD will increase to 90 million BPD. Older wells will reach a point where they are no longer economical to produce and will have to be replaced with new wells. The oil industry will constantly have to explore for new oil and gas resources.

This situation forces us to make difficult decisions and answer some tough questions regarding our current and future use of energy. One of those questions is this: Must we continue to search for new sources of petroleum to satisfy the needs and desires of the world's consumers, or is there another way?

As with almost every social or political problem, the solution probably falls somewhere in the middle. And as with every other issue that is tainted by oil, the solutions are almost always riddled with controversy.

Understanding the Problem

The battle lines over our future sources of energy have been drawn between a group of people who call themselves conservationists and leaders of the oil and gas industry, who believe exploration is the answer.

People on both sides of the debate agree that the world needs a dependable source of energy to satisfy humans' needs and desires, and both acknowledge that our current known reserves are dwindling. However, they differ on the following key issues:

 ◆ How much time and money we should devote to searching for new sources of oil

 ◆ How much we should try to reduce the amount of oil we consume by curbing our needs and desires for it

 ◆ How much emphasis we should give to getting more energy efficiency out of oil by creating new technologies

 ◆ How much emphasis we should give to developing alternative sources of energy, such as wind and solar power (for more on alternative sources of energy, see Chapter 22)

 Petro-Facts _____

American geophysicist, M. King Hubbert, predicted in 1956 that U.S. oil production would peak in the 1970s. At the time, many people laughed at his prediction. They aren't laughing anymore, because U.S. oil production actually did peak in 1970 or 1971 at 9.5 million barrels per day. In 2002, U.S. oil production was down to just 3.5 million barrels per day.

Using Hubbert's analytical methods, the Association for the Study of Peak Oil (ASPO) predicts the drop off for the world will begin in 2010.

The Conservation Argument: Less Is More

First, let's look more closely at the conservation argument, which essentially says that if you find ways to use less oil (and other nonrenewable sources of energy) now, ultimately you will have more resources that can be used for a longer period of time.

Oil, coal, and natural gas are the three primary sources of energy from nonrenewable resources, which means that once they are used up they can't be replaced. Right now these sources of power are responsible for about 90 percent of the world's energy needs. Renewable sources, such as wind, solar, and water, are examples of potential energy resources that are replaceable.

Energy conservationists believe that we should use fewer nonrenewable resources and increase our use of renewable resources. They argue that we can achieve this by using a two-pronged approach:

◆ Improve fuel efficiency by developing and making available more efficient engines, appliances, tires, and so on

◆ Utilize alternative sources of energy by shifting from a reliance on nonrenewable resources such as oil and coal to renewable resources such as wind, water, and solar power

We'll look more closely at both of these approaches in Chapter 22.

Personal Virtue or Public Mandate?

In a previous chapter, we included a quote by Vice President Dick Cheney in which he said that conservation is a "sign of personal virtue, but it is not a sufficient basis for a sound, comprehensive energy policy." However, there are plenty of folks who think conservation is—or at least should be—more than just an issue of "personal virtue." As a matter of fact, they believe that leaving it up to individuals to engage in energy conservation on a personal level—however virtuous—is tantamount to dismissing conservation as an energy policy. Conservationists argue that energy conservation can really only be effective on a widespread basis when it is adopted as an essential component of governmental energy policy.

Conservationists believe there are a number of ways world governments can help to encourage greater energy conservation. These efforts primarily fall into two categories: incentives and regulations.

Slick Sayings

Behavior is how you express your values in practice ... For example, we should be encouraging consumers to use our products more efficiently. Why? Because we're in this for the long haul. If we want our products to continue accelerating economic growth, conservation will help keep energy plentiful and affordable.

Conservation indeed makes a difference. Over the last 20 years, global improvements in energy efficiency were so significant that it's as if the world "discovered" an extra 20 million barrels of oil a day. With global energy demand expected to grow significantly, we'll need all the energy we can get.

—David J. O'Reilly, Chairman and CEO, Chevron Texaco Corporation, at the Institute of Petroleum conference, London, February 2003.

More Incentives, More Regulations: The Carrot and the Stick

If the United States government wants to consider the recommendations of the conservationists, what steps should it take to encourage U.S. consumers and the oil industry to change their behavior? We all know that one of the best ways to get people to change their habits is to make it worthwhile financially. Congress knows that incentives for people's pocketbooks might make them think twice about conservation. These incentives can take the form of tax breaks or tax credits, subsidies to help offset the costs of producing existing technologies, and research money to encourage the development of new technologies.

Petro-Facts

In an effort to reduce oil consumption, Congress has dangled a big carrot in front of new-car buyers. Anyone who buys a hybrid vehicle qualifies for a $2,000 tax deduction. This Clean-Fuel Vehicle deduction has been approved for original purchasers of qualifying cars, including the Toyota Prius, Honda Insight, and Honda Civic Hybrid.

Congress also knows that restrictions and regulations combined with incentives can sometimes be even more effective. So conservationists argue that in addition to encouraging people to be more conservative with their use of fossil fuels, the government should regulate fuel-efficiency standards.

The Exploration Argument: More Is Better

You're probably not going to find anybody on the exploration side of the conservation-vs.-exploration debate who argues against the benefits of conservation; it's just that they don't view conservation as a realistic short-term solution to the world's energy needs. Cheney probably summed up that side of the debate as best as anyone could when he dismissed conservation as a "personal virtue."

Instead, proponents of exploration believe that we must make the search for new sources of oil and gas a priority, opening up previously closed locations to oil exploration, and developing new technology to aid in that search.

More Incentives, Fewer Regulations: Two Carrots, No Stick

We've already pointed out that energy conservationists are in favor of incentives and regulations to encourage increased energy efficiency and the transition to alternative sources of energy. Proponents of exploration also believe in the value of incentives; it's just that they believe that those incentives should be used to encourage the exploration and development of new oil fields and technology for more efficient extraction of that oil. As for regulations, the oil industry is usually in favor of less restrictive regulations, particularly environmental regulations, which they believe often unnecessarily discourage the development of potentially valuable tracts of oil.

The industry would like to see three key areas of tax legislation changed:

- **Heavy Oil Production Credit**. A Heavy Oil Production Credit would give the oil companies an incentive to produce a type of oil called "heavy crude oil." According to the American Petroleum Institute (API), 11 percent of U.S. production is heavy crude oil, but the potential is much greater. The API claims that the United States has 100 billion barrels of known heavy oil reserves.

  However, heavy crude oil is more difficult and expensive to extract and refine than other types of oil. Also a smaller volume of high-value petroleum products can be refined from a barrel of heavy crude oil. The oil industry says that heavy oil is not economical to produce, but that a tax credit would make it so.

> **Slick Sayings**
>
> While most countries encourage energy development, certain U.S. tax provisions and restrictive land access policies place substantial limits on exploration and production of oil and natural gas in this country.
>
> —From American Petroleum Institute's "National Energy Policy: The Role of U.S. Tax Law"

- **Enhanced Oil Recovery Credit**. The API says only one third of a well's oil can be extracted using primary oil recovery methods. Technology exists to get more oil out of the ground, but the expense makes it uneconomical to use the technology without a tax incentive. The Federal government already provides tax credits for the use of certain kinds of alternative extraction techniques through its Enhanced Oil Recovery Credit, but the API wants the government to expand that credit to offset the costs of more expensive drilling techniques such as horizontal drilling.

Petro-Facts _____

Much of what the industry wants in tax changes has been incorporated into the Bush administration's energy plan (see Chapter 18), which was winding its way through Congress when this book was being written. Only time will tell if the industry gets its way.

◆ **Taxation of Foreign Source Income.** The API says the oil companies face the potential of double taxation by having to pay taxes on income from foreign sources of oil to both the United States and the countries in which they operate. The API believes that U.S. tax rules discourage foreign exploration and development projects and need to be changed.

Conservationists often disagree with such incentives. They argue that the oil industry is a mature one and doesn't need these types of government subsidies or tax breaks.

How Much Is Left, and Where Is It?

The most recent U.S. Geological Survey (USGS) in 1995 estimated that the United States had 112.3 billion barrels of undiscovered, technically recoverable oil and 1,074 trillion cubic feet of natural gas. The Minerals Management Service (MMS), which manages offshore resources, estimated in 2000 that 75 billion barrels of oil and 362 trillion cubic feet of natural gas can be found in the coastal areas of the United States. The American Petroleum Institute says that in 2000, the "industry drilled over 28,000 wells—8,200 oil wells, 16,200 gas wells, and 3,700 unsuccessful 'dry holes'—searching for additional sources of oil and gas in the United States. Despite this rapid pace of drilling, the industry likely did little more than replace what was produced and make up for the closure of old wells that had reached the end of their useful life."

Petro-Facts _____

The oil industry currently spends more than $150 billion annually seeking new reserves of oil and gas.

The API also reports that the 1995 data from the U.S. Geological Survey and the Minerals Management Service show that 69 percent of remaining undiscovered oil resources and 51 percent of remaining undiscovered gas resources are located on government lands. The API and other groups who support oil exploration want restrictions lifted that hamper exploration on these lands. We'll explore this issue in depth in Chapter 18.

Making Their Voices Heard

So how do the oil industry and energy conservationists get their voices heard in Washington? Often through representatives called lobbyists, who donate money and use their influence to get the ears of key policy makers. In the next chapter, we'll take a closer look at just how influential oil lobbyists can be.

The Least You Need to Know

- Energy conservationists argue that we should use fewer nonrenewable resources by increasing the energy efficiency of our machines and turning to renewable sources of power.

- Proponents of oil exploration believe that to meet the world's demand for oil, we must continue to discover and develop new oil fields.

- The federal government, through incentives and regulations, can influence how we handle our dwindling supply of oil.

Lobbying for Oil

In This Chapter

◆ The power of the oil lobby in the U.S. and abroad

◆ Lobbyists, money, influence, and power

◆ How petrodollars affect the U.S. economy

It's no secret that money donated to political coffers helps to drive political decisions in the United States. And although donations to political campaigns might not be the way that money gets into the hands of political leaders in all countries with a major oil stake—in some countries it's kickbacks or bribes—lobbying by the oil companies is a major factor in just about every country that uses or produces oil.

Let's take a look at how the oil lobby and something called petrodollars impact political decision-making in the United States and abroad.

Concentrating Its Power Base

Even after the breakup of Standard Oil, oil companies remained a major force in U.S. politics. And as our country's dependence on oil for defense, transportation, manufacturing, and other industries increased, so did the power of the oil industry.

The industry maintains its power by making sizeable campaign donations each election cycle. In fact, during the past 10 years alone, the oil and gas industry has donated more than $150 million to political campaigns, according to the Center for Responsive Politics. These figures are based on reports to the Federal Election Commission. Only three industries gave more. (The top contributors were lawyers and law firms, who gave a total of $470.8 million, health professionals, who gave $231.2 million, and the insurance industry, which gave $198.9 million over the last 10 years.)

More than 50 organizations represent oil and oil-related industries in the United States. When issues critical to the industry, such as changes in environmental protection laws, taxes, or import regulations, are before Congress, lobbyists from all the organizations swarm like bees in the halls of Congress. The most powerful and effective lobbyists are frequently former members of the House and Senate, as they are able to gain access to areas of Congress that are off limits to most other lobbyists.

In exchange for giving funds, lobbyists expect access both to the congressmen and their staff. Most members know they need these campaign donations to survive, so they are willing to at least meet with their major supporters. While it is illegal to trade money for votes, access to Congress is not illegal, and it's often enough to convince a congressional member or his or her staff to support a particular position.

Petro-Facts

It's not unusual for a lobbyist to provide the draft of an amendment to legislation or even a complete bill to a member who has been friendly to the corporation or association in the past.

In addition to direct congressional contact by paid lobbyists, lobbying groups also contact supporters in as many congressional districts as they can. When congressmen hear from their constituents on a particular issue, they are more likely to throw their support on the side of the issue that represents the predominant position of their district.

Petro-Facts

In 1994, when George W. Bush was campaigning to become governor of Texas, oil companies donated millions of dollars to his campaign. Once he was elected, he signed into law tax breaks for state energy producers. Then in 1997, Governor Bush made changes to the state pollution regulations that were highly favorable to the oil industry. In regulations drafted by Marathon Oil and Mobil executives, power plants that were built before 1971 were not required to comply with state pollution laws. Instead, executives designed a voluntary pollution reduction program, with no punishments for companies that didn't comply. A study published by the Environmental Defense Fund six months after the change in regulations showed that only 3 of the 26 companies involved in the voluntary program actually cut their emissions.

Leading the Oil Lobby

The American Petroleum Institute (API) is the guerrilla of the oil lobby, and several smaller organizations are linked to the Institute. In fact, more than 170 companies are listed as members of the API. You can find a list of companies by clicking on "Links and Resources" at the API website (http://api-ec.api.org/frontpage.cfm). You'll also find a list of all the key oil and gas organizations linked to API.

We won't go through the list of oil-industry organizations in the United States here. Instead, as we discuss the issues, we'll explain the connections between the lobbyists and the government. For instance, in upcoming chapters you'll see how the oil industry benefits from access to politicians when it comes to the design of energy policy (Chapter 18) and federal oil leasing policy (Chapter 19). It also uses its lobbying power to attempt to control oil pricing (Chapter 20) and change environmental regulations (Chapter 18).

OPEC, the Oil Giant

The United States isn't the only country that has influential oil organizations. The most powerful of these foreign organizations, of course, is OPEC (Organization of Petroleum Exporting Countries). Today, OPEC's membership includes Algeria, Indonesia, Iran, Iraq, Kuwait, Libya, Nigeria, Qatar, Saudi Arabia, the United Arab Emirates, and Venezuela. Combined, these nations supply about 40 percent of the world's oil output.

Drill Bits

OPEC, or the Organization of Petroleum Exporting Countries, was formed in 1960 by Iran, Iraq, Kuwait, Saudi Arabia, and Venezuela. OPEC states that its objective is to "coordinate and unify petroleum policies among Member Countries, in order to secure fair and stable prices for petroleum producers; an efficient economic and regular supply of petroleum to consuming nations; and a fair return on capital to those investing in the industry." OPEC carries out this objective by attempting to control the oil output of its member countries. For example, OPEC's oil embargo of 1973 caused major disruptions in worldwide oil supply.

Lobbyists Abroad

In each country that has an oil industry, you'll find an oil-lobbying organization. In Canada, the Canadian Association of Petroleum Producers (www.capp.ca) has an

$8 million budget to support its activities. British Petroleum is the guerrilla when it comes to oil politics in Britain, but other smaller companies make loud noises especially when North Sea oil is involved.

Russia's oil lobby isn't quite as strong. In fact, in a March 2003 meeting with Russian oil companies, Russian Prime Minister Mikhail Kasyanov told the companies that any existent and future oil pipelines will be owned and controlled by the state. Some think that Kasyanov may challenge Russian President Vladimir Putin in the 2004 Russian Presidential election.

It's All About Money—Petrodollars, That Is

Oil isn't the only thing fueling oil politics. Oil money, so-called petrodollars, is another major factor.

Since World War II, the U.S. dollar has been the only currency that OPEC will accept in exchange for oil. OPEC countries then typically deposit their dollars in U.S. banks or other banks. These dollars are nicknamed "petrodollars." This policy encourages non-OPEC countries to maintain a strong U.S. trading partnership so that they have access to U.S. dollars to buy, you guessed, it oil! When the United States wants to buy oil, it can just print the money it needs. However, every other country must buy U.S. dollars in order to trade for oil. Obviously, the United States has a great advantage.

The oil market's dependence on U.S. dollars helps the United States manage its trade deficits. Since the United States is the largest oil consumer, if it needed to buy another country's currency in order to purchase all the oil it wanted, the trade deficits would be even more out of balance.

Slick Sayings

One of the major things the Saudis have historically done, in part out of friendship with the United States, is to insist that oil continues to be priced in dollars. Therefore the U.S. Treasury can print money and buy oil, which is an advantage no other country has. With the emergence of other currencies and with strains in the relationship, I wonder whether there will be, as there have been in the past, people in Saudi Arabia who raise the question of why they should be so kind to the United States.

—Former U.S. Ambassador to Saudi Arabia quoted in a story in Britain's newspaper, *The Guardian*

Estimates are that $3 trillion in circulation in the world economy are directly tied to petrodollars. Others estimate that two thirds of world trade is dominated by the U.S.

dollar. When the dollar drops in value, the value of oil for these oil producing nations drops in comparison to other world currency. Both the United States and the oil producing nations depend on a strong dollar.

Many countries are beginning to think that there should be more than one currency that can be used to buy oil. Iraq led the charge to shift from holding oil reserve profits in dollars to euros when it decided to convert its reserves into euros (the new currency of the European Union) in 2000. While as a member of OPEC, Iraq had to sell its oil in exchange for dollars, it converted the dollars into euros after the sale.

Iran followed Iraq's lead and now holds more than half of its petrodollar reserves in euros according to the newspaper *Iran Financial News* on August 25, 2002. *Business Week* reported on February 17, 2003, that Russia's Central Bank gradually shifted to euros over the past year and by the beginning of 2003 had doubled its euro holdings by selling off U.S. dollars. *Business Week* reported that 20 percent of Russia's petrodollar reserves is in euros. Germany and France have both discussed the possibility of using euros to buy Russian oil, according to the British newspaper, *The Guardian*. The newspaper also reports that Iranian and Russian parliaments have discussed "adopting the euro for oil sales."

Slick Sayings

World trade is now a game in which the U.S. produces dollars and the rest of the world produces things that dollars can buy. The world's interlinked economies no longer trade to capture a comparative advantage; they compete in exports to capture needed dollars to service dollar-denominated foreign debts and to accumulate dollar reserves to sustain the exchange value of their domestic currencies .... This creates a built-in support for a strong dollar that in turn forces the world's central banks to acquire and hold more dollar reserves, making it stronger. This phenomenon is known as dollar hegemony, which is created by the geopolitically constructed peculiarity that critical commodities, most notably oil, are denominated in dollars. Everyone accepts dollars because dollars can buy oil. The recycling of petro-dollars is the price the U.S. has extracted from oil-producing countries for U.S. tolerance of the oil-exporting cartel since 1973.

—Henry Liu, in an April 11, 2002, *Asian Times* article

When you consider the countries that took a strong stance against the U.S. war with Iraq at the United Nations, the list of countries considering a shift to euros looks remarkably similar to the countries that opposed the U.S. position on Iraq. Some people have even gone so far as to speculate that Iraq's conversion of petrodollars to euros was the primary reason that the United States went to war against that country.

However, no matter what the reasons for the Iraqi war really were, now that the United States is in control of the Iraqi oil industry, it will insist that countries buy Iraqi oil with the U.S. dollar and will hold oil profit reserves in dollars. This will help to offset any shift by other nations to place their reserves in euros or other currencies.

In the next chapter, we'll look at how the United States sets energy policy in order to supply its oil and other energy needs.

The Least You Need to Know

◆ The oil industry donates tens of millions of dollars to political campaigns each year, in the hopes of influencing politicians.

◆ The American Petroleum Institute (API) is the leading American oil industry lobbyist.

◆ Powerful oil industry lobbying organizations also exist in other countries with large oil industries.

◆ Petrodollars, which are reserve funds from oil profits, are a major force in world-wide currency.

Chapter 18

The Politics of Energy

In This Chapter

- ◆ The importance of energy policy
- ◆ Controversies surrounding Cheney's energy task force
- ◆ The Bush energy plan

In the previous chapter, we considered how oil industry lobbyists use money and influence to get the attention of lawmakers in an effort to persuade them to pass legislation and create policies favorable to the oil industry. These laws can range from eased environmental regulations to tax incentives for certain kinds of oil exploration or extraction.

Why should we care about the power of the oil lobby and the number of people with industry connections who have easy access to our political leaders? Because these people can have a tremendous amount of influence on whether energy conservation or oil exploration takes precedence as a national priority. It all boils down to who gets to set the nation's energy policy.

Energy Policy Explained

One of the primary ways that the government determines who wins the conservation-vs.-exploration debate is by establishing an energy policy. An administration's energy policy and proposed budgets can be used as both a carrot and a stick (incentives and regulations) to encourage more fuel efficiency and the development of renewable resources, but the political will must be there to make this happen. Alternatively, energy policy can place an emphasis on exploration by offering incentives to companies that explore for oil, by offering tax breaks, by making public land available for exploration and drilling, and by funding research programs that focus on oil-exploration technologies.

Most energy policies include provisions that encourage both conservation and exploration; however, they usually emphasize one over the other. In the case of the current administration, the emphasis on exploration far outweighs the emphasis on conservation. Of course, the nation's energy policy isn't left up to just the president; once the administration creates the policy, its submits it to both houses of congress for approval. Depending on the balance of power in the houses of congress, the policy will either pass swiftly or will come under heavy criticism. Since the Republicans control both the Executive and Legislative Branch, the Bush policy should end up passing (as of this writing, it hasn't), but there are a small number of Republican environmentalists and conservationists, who are trying to moderate Bush's Energy Plan.

In addition, President Bush has come under severe criticism for the secretive way that he handled the development of his energy policy, and this might just influence some politicians to withhold approval. Before we consider the contents of Bush's energy plan, let's take a closer look the controversy surrounding it.

Oil Policy and Secrecy Don't Mix

President George W. Bush appointed his second in command, Vice President Dick Cheney, to head up the administration's Energy Task Force. The task force was charged with developing the Bush administration's energy plan. Within days of taking office, Cheney started the work of the Energy Task Force, meeting secretly with energy industry executives.

Controversy arose quickly. On April 19, 2001, before the energy plan was even revealed, two House Representatives—Henry Waxman (D-CA), member of the Energy and Commerce Committee and John Dingell (D-MI), former Chairman and ranking minority member of the House Energy and Commerce Committee—called for a U.S. General Accounting Office investigation of the Task Force. Essentially, they wanted to know who the Task Force met with, what they talked about, and the names of the staff who worked on the energy plan.

Citing *executive privilege*, Cheney refused to disclose the requested information. However, what Cheney wouldn't disclose, journalists started to find out for themselves.

They discovered that people who contributed heavily to the Bush campaign were the same people who were being called on by the Energy Task Force to help develop the Bush Energy Plan.

Democratic congressmen, as well as organizations that were left out of the loop during these secret task force meetings (members of congress, environmental groups, alternative energy groups, and several others), have pushed to find out what was discussed and how the energy policy was developed. Let's look at who was invited to the party and who was left out.

Drill Bits

Although not mentioned in the Constitution, presidents invoke the claim of **executive privilege** on the constitutional principle of separation of powers. Presidents believe that this privilege permits them to resist requests for information by the Congressional and Judicial branches.

Who Was Invited and Who Wasn't

The *Los Angeles Times* was the first to expose the connections between Cheney's Task Force and Bush's campaign contributions. The *Times* wrote the following on August 26, 2001:

> Some firms sent emissaries more than once. Enron Corporation, which trades electricity and natural gas, once got three top officials into a private session with Vice President Dick Cheney, who headed the energy task force. Cheney did "a lot of listening," according to a company spokesman.

> Many of the executives at the White House meetings were generous donors to the Republican Party, and some of their key lobbyists were freshly hired from the Bush presidential campaign.

The *Los Angles Times* also reported that there was little input from companies that developed alternative energy sources but that the sole meeting with the alternative-energy folks was the only meeting that was made public. The *Times* said, "After producers of power from the sun, wind, and geothermal heat met with Cheney, officials led the group to the front of the White House and waiting reporters." This meeting was held on May 15, just one day before the energy plan was sent to Bush, which wouldn't have given the Task Force much time to incorporate any of alternative-energy industry's suggestions into the plan. But at least they had a chance to voice their opinions; groups like the Union of Concerned Scientists and the Sierra Club, both of whom have had ideological conflicts with the energy industry, were shut out of the plan altogether, according to the *Times* story.

We still don't know the full extent of energy industry involvement, but we got a better idea when almost a year later, Cheney was forced to release Task Force documents after court cases were filed by the Natural Resources Defense Council and Judicial Watch. (The GAO also had also filed suit, but it lost its case in court and decided not to appeal.)

When the Natural Resources Defense Council (NRDC) finally got its hands on the documents on May 21, 2002, it found that industry contacts outnumbered nonindustry contacts 25 to 1. However, many of the 12,000 pages of documents that the NRDC obtained were almost entirely blank—a lot of information had been deleted by Cheney on the grounds that these were private conversations that fell within the scope of executive privilege and did not have to be released—but they revealed that the task force had 714 direct contacts with energy industry representatives and only 29 contacts with nonindustry representatives.

Slick Sayings

With the impending invasion of Iraq, the very serious matters before the court take on even greater relevance, given that Vice President Cheney was developing our nation's energy policy with industry executives in secret. Perhaps the Cheney Task Force records will help explain why only certain countries seem to be "off limits" in this growing international crisis. The American people deserve straight answers and accountability from their government, not secrecy, closed-door meetings, and cover-ups.

—Judicial Watch Chairman and General Counsel Larry Klayman, in a February 7, 2003, press release after the GAO dropped its suit.

How Much Influence Did Oil Representatives Have?

At the time of this writing, the Natural Resources Defense Council and Judicial Watch were still in court trying to get full release of the documents related to the Energy Task Force. The documents already released give us a brief glimpse of how much power the industry has in the Bush administration. For instance, on March 20, 2001, Jim Ford, of the American Petroleum Institute, sent an e-mail to Bush staff recommending language for a Presidential Executive Order that would require cost-benefit analysis of energy related regulations. He included proposed text for the order with the message. Here is one small segment of that text:

> All federal agencies shall include in any regulatory action that could significantly and adversely affect energy supplies, distribution, or use, a detailed statement on (i) the energy impact of the proposed action, (ii) any adverse energy effects

which cannot be avoided should the proposal be implemented, and (iii) alternatives to the proposed action. Prior to taking such regulatory action, the agency shall consult with, and obtain the concurrence of, the Secretary of Energy. The agencies' actions directed by this Executive Order shall be carried out to the extent permitted by law.

Two months after the White House received Jim Ford's e-mail, President Bush issued Executive Order 13211, requiring government staff to prepare a Statement of Energy Effects whenever new regulations were proposed. The wording of the order is strikingly similar to that provided by Ford:

(a) To the extent permitted by law, agencies shall prepare and submit a Statement of Energy Effects to the Administrator of the Office of Information and Regulatory Affairs, Office of Management and Budget, for these matters identified as significant energy actions.

(b) A Statement of Energy Effects shall consist of a detailed statement by the agency responsible for the significant energy action relating to:

(i) any adverse effects on energy supply, distribution, or use (including a shortfall in supply, price increases, and increased use of foreign supplies) should the proposal be implemented, and

(ii) reasonable alternatives to the action with adverse energy effects and the expected effects of such alternatives on energy supply, distribution, and use.

How many more executive orders and other aspects of the Bush energy plan were written by industry insiders, with little or no input from other groups with interests at stake? We won't know until all of the documents are released, and unless Dick Cheney has a change of heart, this won't be for a long time.

The Bush Energy Plan

When the plan was made public, few people were surprised to learn that it was heavily weighted in favor of the oil industry. However, the extent of the imbalance is really quite striking.

Conservation Suffers a Political Blow

The president reduced funding for research and development in the areas of energy efficiency and renewable energy by $82 million in fiscal year (FY)2003—the FY2002 budget was $640 million, and the FY2003 budget is $558 million. It also killed a program that focused on developing more fuel-efficient cars, instead placing emphasis on developing a fuel-cell vehicle. Finally, the administration cut $34 million from the transportation-sector technology research and development budget, which reduced spending on fuel efficiency and renewable energy research.

Petro-Facts

Just to put the Bush energy efficiency and renewable energy budget cuts into perspective, the total Energy department budget for FY2003 is $21.9 billion. Nuclear weapons programs were *increased by* $433 million. That increase is more than the total amount of money slated for renewable energy.

The Bush administration did propose a slight increase in renewable energy research and development from $386 million in FY2002 to $408 million in FY2003, but this money is tied to the passage of drilling in the Arctic National Wildlife Refuge (ANWR), one of the most controversial parts of the Bush energy plan (see Chapter 23 for more on ANWR).

Victory for the Oil Industry

At the same time that it proposed cuts in programs favored by conservationists, the Bush administration planned to open leases for exploration and drilling on vast onshore and offshore areas around the country, including over 6 million acres in the Gulf of Mexico off the coast of Florida.

In addition, the energy plan included the following oil industry-friendly provisions:

◆ Examine land status and lease stipulation impediments to federal oil and gas leasing and review and modify those where opportunities exist (consistent with the law, good environmental practice, and balanced use of other resources).

◆ Promote enhanced oil and gas recovery from existing wells through new technology.

◆ Improve oil and gas exploration technology through continued partnership with public and private entities.

◆ Use U.S. and international finance agencies to fund increased production of oil and gas in Africa.

Petroleum People

President George W. Bush has put more than 50 oil company executives in critical spots on the White House staff.

His appointments started with Vice President Dick Cheney, who made $36 million dollars as head of the oil giant Halliburton. Condoleezza Rice, the administration's National Security Advisor, was on the board of Chevron before joining Bush's team. Commerce Secretary Don Evans also has deep ties to the oil industry—before being tapped for Secretary, he was chairman of the board, president, and CEO of Tom Brown Inc., an independent oil company, and also served as director of TMBR/Sharp Drilling.

Kenneth Lay, former CEO of scandal-ridden Enron, served on Bush's transition team and helped to pick many Bush appointees. Many people chosen to serve in Bush's administration had Enron connections. Larry Lindsey, the first chief economic advisor, was an Enron advisor. So was Robert Zoelick, who is the nation's top trade negotiator. Thomas White, the first Secretary of the Navy under Bush, was a senior Enron executive.

White House Senior Advisor Karl Rove was a paid political consultant for Enron. Harvey Pitt, the first SEC chairman in the Bush administration, was an attorney with a firm that represented Enron auditor Arthur Andersen. In all, estimates are that about 50 people in the Bush administration had ties to Enron.

Congressional Input

The House quickly passed the administration's version of the Energy Policy Act, which has very few incentives for conservation or alternative energy sources. It also includes drilling in the Alaska National Wildlife Preserve, which the Senate will not accept. The Senate Committee on Energy and Natural Resources passed its version of the Energy Policy Act of 2003 on April 30, 2003, but the bill hadn't come before the full Senate for a vote by the time this book went to press. The current version of the Senate bill includes more incentives and regulations for fuel efficiency. Provisions for energy efficiency include the following:

- Requires a 20 percent improvement to federal energy efficiency in the next 10 years.

- Directs agencies to procure energy-efficient products and improve energy efficiency performance for new federal buildings.

- Authorizes grants for energy-efficient projects in low-income urban and rural communities.

- Authorizes funding for states to establish appliance rebate programs to encourage improved energy efficiency.

- Sets several new energy-efficiency standards for consumer products, including transformers, traffic signals, compact fluorescent lamps, ceiling fans, vending machines, and commercial freezers and refrigerators.

- Improves the energy efficiency of public housing.

In addition, the Senate bill currently includes the following incentives and regulations regarding renewable energy:

- Provides new incentives for the increased development and use of clean and renewable energy. Mandates a federal renewable energy resources assessment to assist in the long-term planning for the expansion of renewable energy production.

- Streamlines the re-licensing of hydroelectric facilities to ensure continued reliability of clean and reliable energy.

- Requires federal agencies to purchase 7.5 percent of their power from renewable energy sources by 2011.

- Encourages exploration and development of geothermal energy (see Chapter 22), including a call for a rulemaking on a new royalty structure that encourages new production.

- Provides grants for turning forest materials from areas at high-risk for fire or disease into biomass energy (see Chapter 22).

The House bill includes some of the same incentives, but not nearly as many. How many of these will survive after the full Senate votes and then negotiates with the House is anybody's guess.

The Least You Need to Know

- An administration's energy policy plays a big role in determining how the nation will try to achieve its energy needs.

- The Bush administration developed its energy plan in secret meetings primarily with the oil industry.

- Two groups, the National Resources Defense Council and Judicial Watch, are trying to get their hands on the secret documents related to the energy task force.

- Proponents of oil exploration and development fared far better than energy conservationists in the Bush energy plan.

19

Federal Oil Leasing Policies

In This Chapter

- ◆ The process of leasing federal land for oil
- ◆ Making sure the government gets its fair share
- ◆ The Indians take the federal government to court
- ◆ Drilling controversies off the coasts of California and Florida

Oil companies make billions of dollars extracting oil from federal lands, and they are supposed to pay the U.S. government for that privilege. However, like most companies and individuals, when it comes to paying the government its fair share, oil companies work hard to minimize the amount of money they actually hand over. Sometimes, they work a little *too* hard. For instance, U.S. Department of Interior's Mineral Management Service (MMS) estimated that the oil industry underpaid oil royalties by some $60 million per year before a new rule went into effect in March 2000.

In this chapter, we'll consider how oil companies go about leasing government lands, how lease owners pay for exploiting oil on those lands, and the political controversies that continue to play out regarding these valuable resources.

Leasing the Land

About 564 million acres of federal lands that fall under the jurisdiction of the Bureau of Land Management (BLM) qualify for oil, gas, and geothermal exploration and exploitation. The Minerals Management Service (MMS) manages leases for these federal lands. Revenues from mineral leases totaled over $6 billion in 2002, and the MMS has collected $127 billion in revenue for the government since 1982.

Any adult citizen of the United States can qualify to hold an oil or gas lease, but in reality most Americans can't afford to be part of the bidding process for the most desirable leases. Each lease stipulates where a company or individual can look for resources and for how long they'll have the right to explore the land. Most leases are for 10 years and can be renewed indefinitely as long as the lease holder is developing the land. Once development begins, the company holding the lease retains rights to the land until the oil, gas, or other mineral reserves are exhausted.

The government requires four types of payments on the land it leases:

♦ **Bonuses.** For leases in areas where there are known or suspected mineral deposits, leases are offered in a competitive bidding process. The winning bidder is the one who offers to pay the largest bonus to win the lease.

♦ **Rents.** The government sets a rent schedule at the time the lease is issued, which is a fixed amount per acre, usually $1.50 per acre per year for the first five years and $2.00 per acre per year for the next five years.

♦ **Minimum Royalties.** This is a payment per acre that the winning bidder must pay until production exceeds the minimum royalty required.

♦ **Royalties.** Once production begins, the company pays a percentage of the value of the mineral produced. This is $12\frac{1}{2}$ percent for most onshore leases and can go as high as $16\frac{2}{3}$ percent for offshore leases.

The highest bidder at a March 2003 auction in New Orleans for oil and gas leases offered $8,216,885 for a tract as part of Lease Sale 185 (each time the MMS announces a lease sale, it gives that sale a number). This lease sale included 4,460 tracts totaling approximately 23.4 million acres off the coasts of Alabama, Louisiana, and Mississippi. MMS received $315,532,229 in high bids from 74 companies on 561 of the tracts during Lease Sale 185.

Once the MMS has a winning bid for a tract of land, the agency evaluates the bid to ensure that it is fair market price for the tract involved.

Once the bid is accepted, the lessee must submit a plan of exploration (POE), which is reviewed to see that it meets all regulatory and lease requirements. If the BLM determines that the activity proposed under the lease could cause serious harm or damage to life (including aquatic life), property, or the marine, coastal, or human environment, the BLM can ask that the project be redesigned.

Once the POE is approved, permits and other approvals are required before drilling can start. If the lease involves offshore drilling, state agencies might get into the act as well. For instance, the Coastal Zone Management Act (CZMA) requires a state review for any federal action that could impact the land and water use of a coastal area. (We'll talk more about state involvement below when we discuss off-shore drilling controversies in California later in this chapter.)

After CZMA approval, oil companies have one more hurdle to jump before drilling can begin. If the POE includes a discharge of pollutants into the ocean, a company must obtain a National Pollutant Discharge Elimi-nation System permit from the Environmental Protection Agency.

Petro-Facts

The Mineral Leasing Act of 1920 and the Mineral Leasing Act for Acquired Lands of 1947 gave the Bureau of Land Management responsibility for oil and gas leasing on BLM land, in national forests, and on other federal lands. The BLM also provides technical assistance to Indian tribes, but does not lease Indian minerals. The Bureau of Indian Affairs (BIA) is responsible for Indian oil and gas leases.

Who Gets the Money?

Revenues collected from federal mineral leases are distributed to various state and fed-eral funds depending on the type of lease, as follows:

Drill Bits

The Land and Water Conservation Fund is adminis-tered by the National Park Service and is used to purchase parks and recreation areas and to plan, acquire, and develop land and water resources for recreational use.

- ◆ **Offshore Lands.** Revenues are depos-ited in the General Fund of the Treasury. Congress determines how much of that money will be put in the *Land and Water Conservation Fund* (LWCF) each year. States receive 27 percent of the rev-enues on land within 3 miles of their seaward boundary.

- ◆ **Public Domain Lands.** States get 50 percent of mineral revenues from any lease within their boundaries. The one exception is Alaska, which gets 90 percent. Forty percent of these revenues are deposited in the Reclamation Fund, which is administered by the Bureau of Reclamation. This fund provides revenues to build, maintain, and operate water and associated power projects on arid and semiarid western lands. Lease revenue provides 40 to 50 percent of the fund's revenues. The remaining 10 percent of revenues go to the General Fund of the Treasury.

- ◆ **Acquired Lands.** Distribution for revenues from leases on acquired lands vary depending on the type of land. Seventy-five percent of the mineral revenues for leases within a national forest or national grassland go into the General Fund of the Treasury. The state where the national forest is located gets the remaining 25 percent. The county where the grassland is located gets the remaining 25 percent. Revenues from lands administered by the U.S. Army Corps of Engineers under the Flood Control Act go primarily to the state—75 percent for the state and 25 percent for the General Treasury.

- ◆ **American Indian Lands.** The BIA administers revenues for the Indian lands. Indian representatives recently won a case in which they proved these revenues were underpaid. We'll discuss this case later in this chapter.

Rowing over Royalties

With billions of dollars at stake each year in oil revenues, oil companies try to squeeze every dollar out of the lease. However, in the past few decades, oil companies got a bit too aggressive in reporting costs, and they underpaid their royalties, sometimes significantly. The underpayment scheme was exposed by some whistleblowers as part of the Project on Government Oversight (POGO), which started investigating oil royalties in 1993. MMS released its investigation in 1999, which concluded that oil companies had underpaid at least $856 million since 1991.

The Justice Department took several major oil companies to court over the underpayment of royalties. The companies ended up settling with the government at various times during the late 1990s for a total of more than $400 million dollars—Shell Oil settled for $110 million, Chevron Corporation for $95 million, Texaco for $43 million, and Mobil for $45 million.

Since the royalty scandal, MMS has developed a new rule for valuing oil to correct the underpayment problems. In the Senate, the oil companies contested the rule over a four-year period. The oil companies' charge was led by Senators Kay Bailey Hutchison (R-Texas) and Peter Domenici (R-NM). When the rules were finally ready to be implemented, the Hutchison amendment stopped the rule change by adding a rider developed by oil industry lobbyists to put a moratorium on the rule. The rider was added to Department of Interior appropriations bills to prevent the rule change from taking affect.

> **Slick Sayings**
>
> As part of the battle to stop the Hutchison amendment, Senator Russ Feingold (D-WI) said the following:
>
> I have no doubt that one of the factors contributing to Congress' inaction on this issue of great importance to American taxpayers is the role of campaign contributions in the political process ... [Campaign contributions totaled] more than $2.9 million just from those four corporations (Chevron, Atlantic Richfield, BP, and Exxon) in the span of only two years. They want the Hutchison amendment to be part of the Interior appropriations bill. As powerful political donors, I am afraid they are likely to get their way.

The Hutchison amendment to stop the implementation of the new rule passed 51 to 47 in September 1999 and stalled its implementation for one year. The rule finally took effect in June 2000, after another attempt to stop or change the rule failed in 2000, thanks to a public outcry led by POGO and others. MMS estimates the change increased royalty revenue by about $67 million per year.

Settling with the Indians

American Indians also got into the battle regarding underpayment of royalties. About 54 million acres of Indian lands that contain valuable minerals such as oil, natural gas, gold, or other valuable substances are leased by the Federal government on behalf of the Indians. The money from these leases is supposed to go into the *Individual Indian Money Trust*, but in 1996, a group of Indians sued the Department of Interior for mismanagement of royalties. They claimed in their suit that this mismanagement cost 300,000 American Indians more than $137 billion.

> **Drill Bits**
>
> The **Individual Indian Money (IIM) Trust** was set up by Congress in 1887 after the government, either forcibly or by treaty, relocated Indian tribes from 90 million acres of their land and gave it to white settlers. About 300,000 American Indians are entitled to royalties from about 54 million acres of land. Payments of these royalties have been sporadic.

After battling this case in court since 1996, Federal District Court Judge Royce Lamberth held Secretary of the Interior Gale Norton in contempt on September 19, 2002, because she hadn't fixed the royalty management problems. Norton blamed the problem on failures in a computer system. She is the third cabinet member to be held in contempt because of problems with the Individual Indian Money Trust funds. President Clinton's Interior Secretary Bruce Babbitt and his Treasury Secretary Robert Rubin also faced contempt charges related to this case just before Clinton left office.

In finding Secretary Norton in contempt, Judge Lamberth said, "The agency has indisputably proven to the Court, Congress, and the individual Indian beneficiaries that it is either unwilling or unable to administer competently the IIM trust. Worse yet, the Department has now undeniably shown that it can no longer be trusted to state accurately the status of its trust-reform efforts. In short, there is no longer any doubt that the Secretary of Interior has been and continues to be an unfit trustee delegate for the United States."

Congress set up a special trustee position to oversee the Interior department's management of the fund in 1994, but the first two trustees were ousted when they tried to reveal how badly the trust was being managed. The Judge found that the Interior Department is still not correcting the problems related to how the royalty money is accounted for and has been committing fraud on the court by failing to disclose correct information and filing false and misleading status reports.

In May 2003, the Interior Department was back in Judge Lamberth's court refuting charges made by a court-appointed investigator that the department is still hiding problems. A trial to determine whether the Interior Department has a workable model to account for money generated from Indian Lands was in progress at the time this book was being written.

Enforcing States' Rights

Issues involving federal oil and gas leases can also end up in court on environmental and state's rights issues. While the federal government has the right to lease its land, if the proposed use for that land is opposed locally, a court case could be filed in state courts to stop the company or person who leased the land from using it. The federal government recently lost just such a case in court when it tried to force California to accept offshore drilling.

Most of the leases involved in the case were first issued 12 to 33 years ago. The 36 tracts are valued at about $1 billion. In 1999, President Clinton's Interior Secretary Bruce Babbitt extended the oil leases for another 10 years. The State of California took the federal government to court in an attempt to halt the development of the coastal leases, citing the desire to protect the region's environment. The case was still in the courts when President Bush took office, and Bush decided to continue the fight for the right to allow offshore drilling. He lost in state court.

In June 2001, U.S. District Judge Caludi Wilken ruled that the MMS failed to comply with the CZMA and that the lease extensions were illegal because there was no study of the environmental consequences of drilling, as required by the National Environmental Policy Act. The Bush administration appealed this decision, and the 9th U.S. Circuit Court of Appeals upheld the lower court ruling in December 2002. In April 2003, the Bush administration announced it would not appeal the case to the Supreme Court.

This issue became a major campaign issue in the 2002 governor's race because the Bush administration decided to buy back leases to stop oil development off the coast of Florida to help the re-election of his brother, Florida Governor Jeb Bush, but would not give California's Democratic Governor Gray Davis the same deal.

The big question now is what will happen to the leases. The companies that hold the leases either want to make use of their lease rights to explore for oil or want their money back. To avoid having to refund the companies, Senators Barbara Boxer (D-CA) and Mary Landrieu (D-LA) have proposed that the California leases be swapped with available leases off Louisiana's coast as a possible solution to the problem.

> **Slick Sayings**
>
> Last fall's decision from the 9th Circuit, which was preceded by a federal District Court decision, sent a clear message that the Bush administration should stop its efforts to undermine the strong commitment of Californians to protect our coast.
>
> —Senator Barbara Boxer (D-CA) after hearing that Bush was not going to take the case to the Supreme Court

The Least You Need to Know

- More than $6 billion dollars were collected in revenues from mineral leases on U.S. government land for oil, gas, and other mineral exploitation.

- Several large oil companies have underpaid royalties on their federal mineral leases. The rules have now been changed to make it more difficult for oil companies to underpay royalties.

- Even after winning a lease, an individual or company must go through an extensive evaluation process before oil exploration can begin.

- American Indians claim that they are owed billions of dollars because the federal government mismanaged royalty payments on their land. The case was still pending when this book was written.

Chapter 20

Playing the Oil Pricing Game

In This Chapter

- ◆ Record profits for the oil industry
- ◆ Reduced competition means higher prices
- ◆ The economics of supply and demand
- ◆ How to fix the problem and why nothing is being done

You've probably noticed that gasoline prices are much more volatile today than they were even as recently as the 1990s. You've also probably noticed the oil companies are reporting record profits. That's not surprising, but you may find the reasons behind it illuminating.

In this chapter, we'll take a look at how gas prices are set and why capacity has a lot to do with this price volatility. In addition, we'll review recommendations for stabilizing prices and consider why nothing is being done about it.

Making Record Profits

In the spring of 2003, as the U.S. economy slipped back into a recession and unemployment continued to edge higher, Shell, Exxon, and Chevron all announced phenomenal profits. Shell reported its largest profit ever.

Exxon said it tripled its profit over the previous year. BP's profits jumped a whopping 132 percent.

Why are oil companies doing so well, while large sectors of the American economy are barely surviving? To answer that question, let's look at how gasoline prices are set.

> **Slick Sayings**
>
> Sudden increases in gasoline prices are costly to the consumer and disrupt our economy because the cost of transportation, which is based on the cost of fuel, affects the cost of all our goods and services. Last year's increases in the price of gasoline helped push the American economy into a recession, and this year's increases are threatening the current recovery.
>
> —Senator Carl Levin (D-Mich) in opening remarks on April 20, 2002, for Senate hearing "Gas Prices: How Are They Really Set?"

The Costs Associated with of a Gallon of Gas

The Department of Energy's Energy Information Administration (EIA) breaks the price of gas into four key areas:

- **Crude Oil**—This accounts for the largest share of gas prices today. In March 2003, crude oil accounted for 45 percent of the retail price.

- **Taxes**—Federal and state taxes constituted 25 percent of the March 2003 price per gallon. Federal excise taxes are 18.4¢ per gallon and state taxes average 20¢ per gallon. In some areas of the country, there are additional county and city taxes. Taxes actually decreased slightly between 1999 and 2003, and their percentage of the gas price pie dropped about 4 percent.

- **Distribution and Marketing**—This accounts for 15 percent. Most gas is shipped to terminals through pipelines near your home and then loaded on trucks that deliver the gas to local gas stations. The price at the pump reflects the costs of moving the product as well as operating the service station. Market factors, including the location of the station, also play a part in determining the price at the pump—which we will discuss later in this chapter. Distribution and marketing have increased slightly less than refinery costs—about 17 percent.

- **Refining**—This also accounts for 15 percent of the price of gas. Refining costs vary by region because different formulations are needed to match weather conditions or meet environmental requirements. Another key factor is refining capacity, which we'll take a closer look at later in this chapter. Refinery costs have contributed significantly to the increasing price of gas.

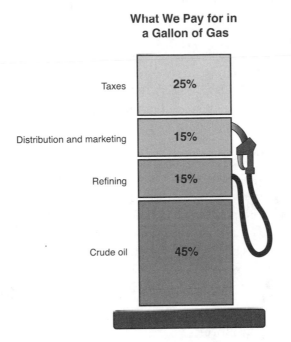

What We Pay for in a Gallon of Gas

Taxes — 25%

Distribution and marketing — 15%

Refining — 15%

Crude oil — 45%

Costs contributing to the price of gasoline in March 2003.

(Source: Department of Energy's Energy Information Administration.)

While crude oil prices and taxes are not directly controlled by the oil companies, the other two components are completely in their control. Controlling supplies to the extent that the oil industry now does is on the edge of violating antitrust laws. Some believe the oil industry has already crossed that line with the control it already has. Remember that the control of oil supplies is the reason Standard Oil was broken up in the early 1900s.

The Government Investigates Gas Pricing Policies

In 2002, the Senate Permanent Committee on Investigations decided to look into how gas prices are set. Senator Carl Levin (D-Mich) chaired the committee, and hearings were held that spring. Committee staff subpoenaed confidential documents from the major oil companies and received 103 boxes with more than 265,000 pages of memos, letters, e-mails, and other papers. These documents provided the committee with an unprecedented view of an industry that has taken actions that some think cross the antitrust line to control capacity and, ultimately, the price of gasoline.

Here are quotes from some of the documents the committee unearthed:

♦ From a November 30, 1995, memo for a Chevron regional meeting:

> A senior energy analyst at the recent API convention warned that if the U.S. Petroleum industry doesn't reduce its refining capacity, it will never see any substantial increase in refining margins, pointing out the recent volatility in refining margins over the past 12 months.

♦ From a Texaco memo dated March 7, 1996:

> As observed over the last few years and as projected well into the future, the most critical factor facing the refining industry on the West Coast is the surplus refining capacity, and the surplus gasoline production capacity. (The same situation exists for the entire U.S. refining industry.) Supply significantly exceeds demand year-round. This results in very poor refinery margins and very poor refinery financial results. Significant events need to occur to assist in reducing supplies and/or increasing demand for gasoline.

♦ From a February 1996 Mobil e-mail regarding the possible restart of the Powerine refinery in California:

> … depending on circumstances, might be worth buying out their production and marketing it ourselves, especially if they start to market below our incremental cost of production.

♦ From a BP Amoco recap of an April 1999 brainstorming session:

> We can influence the niche value (1–3 cents per gallon) but our actions need to be significant (more than 50 million barrels per day) to be sustainable (three years+).

All the ideas that came out of this brainstorming session suggested ways to reduce supply through means such as capacity shutdowns and sending products outside the Midwestern region.

Senator Levin invited the oil companies to testify and answer questions related to the information in the documents. Levin summarized well the oil executive's response to these memos:

> While the oil company executives who testified … said that either their companies didn't adopt the options set forth in their memo to limit supply or that they didn't have any knowledge of the activities discussed in another memo, or that actions described in a memo were against corporate policy, the evidence presented in the Majority Staff Report demonstrated times when refiners acted to limit supply to raise prices.

A BP executive even called some of the ideas presented at the 1999 brainstorming session "outrageous," and he told committee members that the participants were "counseled" and told their behavior was not acceptable. In response, Senator Levin said, "But that doesn't take away from the very key fact that the goal of the BP effort was to increase prices in the Midwest by 1 to 3 cents by restricting supply."

Slick Sayings

… the cause of the price spikes can be attributed clearly to an oil industry that has been allowed to relentlessly and purposefully consolidate more market power in fewer companies. With this increased market power, companies reduce inventories, manipulate supply and orchestrate prices at the gas pump, all at a huge cost to consumers.

—Connecticut Attorney General Richard Blumenthal on May 2, 2002, at the Senate hearings

---

The Power of a Penny

According to the Senate committee's estimates, a 1¢ increase in gas prices generates another $1 billion in revenue for the oil companies. The committee also found that the 35¢ increase in the average annual gasoline price from 1999 to 2000 ($1.16 to $1.51) was matched only one other time in history (gas prices jumped 34¢ at the beginning of the Iran/Iraq war).

Industry Pricing Strategies

While many companies price their products based on the cost to manufacture and sell the product, the price competitors charge for similar products, and what they think the market will bear, the committee found the oil industries took this practice one step further. According to the committee, "Most oil companies and gasoline stations try to keep their prices at a constant price difference with respect to one or more competitors. As a result of these interdependent practices, gasoline prices of oil companies tend to go up and down together."

That's not too surprising. We see that in many consumer products—airline price wars are a good example of this. The key difference is that airline price wars usually start when an airline *lowers* its price, while tight supply of product helps the oil industry to *increase* its prices.

Speedway Bumps

One key example of this practice, which was exposed during the hearings, was what Senator Levin dubbed, "Speedway bumps." This happens almost weekly in the Midwest market. Speedway (a Midwest gas-station chain) bumps up the price on Wednesday or Thursday and others quickly follow. Prices drift back down after the weekend.

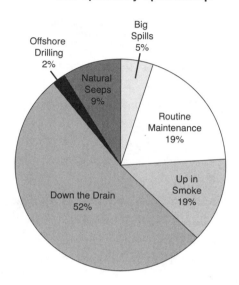

The Speedway Speedbump

Here's a sample of a "Speedway bump" in from April 9 through 16, 2001. You can see how Speedway takes the lead in price increases, while others follow.

(Source: Analysis of OPIS data)

California Attorney General Tom Greene had another name for the practice, "a rockets-and-feathers pricing pattern." Greene testified that this happens most frequently in California if there is a refinery outage. He's watched prices rocket up, but slowly feather back down after the crisis. Greene blames this on the lack of effective competition at the retail level to "push prices down as quickly as [they] rose."

Retail-Back Pricing

Greene also testified about another retail pricing strategy he called, "retail-back pricing." He said, "Prices are being set based on what's happening in the marketplace at the local corner. It's not a question of prices being set by the price of crude oil with a markup. It is what the market makes possible in a local situation."

Committee staff termed this "zone pricing." They found that, "Oil companies use zone pricing to charge different prices for gasoline to different station operators, some of which are in nearby geographic areas, in order to confine price competition to the smallest area possible and to maximize prices and revenue at each retail outlet."

In other words, prices can vary dramatically from neighborhood to neighborhood, and these price differences have nothing to do with the price of crude oil—they are set by the industry to maximize profits.

Dictating Stations' Profit Margins

Committee staff also found that gas prices for many stations owned or leased by the major oil companies were set by the oil companies rather than by the local station dealer or owner. The oil refiners actually set the margin of profit that dealers would be allowed to take. In fact, dealers reported to committee staff that if they tried to raise the price above the one designated by the refiner or wholesaler, then the refiner would raise the price of the gasoline sold to the dealer. Dealers said that their profit margins were controlled by the refiners in this way. Most refiners set a margin price of 7 to 10 cents per gallon over the wholesale price, which is set by tracking prices in a particular zone.

Why Aren't We Doing Anything About These Price-Fixing Practices?

When Levin asked Attorney General Blumenthal about oil-industry efforts to manipulate prices and markets and why action has not been taken to stop it, Blumenthal said:

> ... what we find, at least what I find, is that many of the owners, the franchisees, that is, are very reluctant to come forward because they are very fearful of retaliation;

> ... The degree of fear, that is, the fear factor, simply cannot be overemphasized, and so, no doubt, your staff and you have heard about many of these kinds of abuses, but proving them in court through witnesses who are willing and sufficiently courageous and brave to help us is another challenge.

California Attorney General Tom Greene agreed with Blumenthal:

> I think you are describing, Senator, a very common practice in the industry. One of the sad realities, I think, for lessee dealers is they are increasingly in a form of indentured servitude ... Much of their historic independence has been lost."

Controlling Capacity

You can see from the comments of the Attorney Generals Greene and Blumenthal that the refiners maintain significant control over prices. Let's now take a closer look at why they have this control and how they are using it.

Merger Mania

A wave of oil-industry mergers and refinery shutdowns has significantly reduced refinery capacity. The committee staff found that in 1991, 189 firms owned a total of 324 refineries. In 2001, 65 firms owned a total of 155 refineries. This represents decreases of 65 percent in the number of firms and a 52 percent decrease in the number of refineries.

When one of the authors spoke with committee staff, the staff person reported that the United States in 2003 increased its import of refined fuels from Europe because of this reduction in capacity. Europe, which has been more aggressive about improving fuel efficiency, now has an oversupply of gasoline, which U.S. companies are buying. So instead of decreasing our dependence on foreign sources for the oil products we use—which is a key goal of the Bush energy plan—we are increasing our dependence on yet another part of the global market.

Drill Bits

An **oligopoly** is a market in which there are few sellers. This gives them the ability to affect price and have a strong impact on competitors. In this type of market, there are also significant barriers to entry. For example, the expense of building a refinery is so high it is rare that a new competitor would enter the market.

In fact, after all the mergers, the Federal Trade Commission found that in 28 states the gasoline market was "moderately concentrated" and in 9 states it was "highly concentrated." In fact, in 28 states, four firms control the gasoline markets and their prices, which can be considered a "tight oligopoly." This concentration of oil suppliers is what allows the oil companies to more easily control supply.

Decreased Supply

In the past, the committee found that oil companies maintained inventories for a few week's or month's supply, so it was easy to correct problems if a refinery or pipeline shut down. Today, refineries are operating near maximum capacity and maintaining only a few days' supplies, which means any unexpected cut in production can have a much more dramatic effect on supply and, ultimately, on price.

Before all the oil-industry mergers, refineries ran at about 70 percent of their capacity. Today, the committee staff found that refineries run much closer to full capacity—near 90 percent or above—leaving little room for correcting a supply problem. If a single refinery goes down or a pipeline must be shut down to fix a problem, prices can increase nationwide because there is no refinery that has enough spare capacity to make up for the loss of production.

This gives refiners a great deal of control over how much gasoline they will supply to the market. When supplies are low, prices rise. The committee reported that, "As long as sellers in a market can indirectly affect prices through their supply decisions, it can be expected that sellers will act in their self-interest to manage supply so as to maximize their profits." For example, in California, six refiners own or operate 85 percent of the retail outlets, which sell 90 percent of the gasoline. California has some of the highest and most volatile prices in the country. Part of this is caused by its unique gasoline requirements to protect the state's environment, but evidence revealed in a court case showed that refiners exported product outside the state and limited other companies' ability to import product to the state.

Slick Sayings

We are in a situation now in which concentration has reached the point where it's both in the interest of an individual company to withhold supplies from the marketplace and others will not step in. Now that may be a consequence of oligopolistic coordination .... we now have direct evidence that's exactly what's going on.

—California Attorney General Tom Greene in hearings before the Senate Investigations Committee on May 2, 2002

Kicking Us When We're Down

Studying price fluctuations immediately after the tragedy of September 11, 2001, the committee found that as demand fell because people were traveling less, inventories rose. In response, refineries cut back on production to protect their profit margins. In fact, in some areas of the country, state Attorney Generals reported that prices spiked $1.50 to $2.00 per gallon during the crisis. This cutback in production not only reduced the availability of gasoline and home-heating fuel, but it also took advantage of the American people during a national tragedy.

Filling Reserves

The American people also were finding themselves paying more at the pump due to decisions made by the Bush administration. Since taking office, Bush decided to increase oil reserve supplies. This decision to increase the amount of oil in the Strategic Petroleum Reserve (SPR)—without regard for market prices or crude oil supply—put even more pressure on the market and helped to drive prices even higher, according to a second study released by Sen. Carl Levin on March 5, 2003.

Levin found that the Bush administration, acting against recommendations of professional (nonpolitical appointees) Department of Energy staff, ordered the purchase of crude oil when the prices were at their highest and when supplies were tight. The report concluded that the Bush administration's decision to remove 40 million barrels of crude oil from the marketplace to fill the SPR was a significant factor in the run-up of oil prices to $40 per barrel (the price per barrel was in the high-$20s before the Iraq crisis). This move raised prices on gasoline, home-heating oil, jet fuel, and some diesel fuel, according to the staff report. It also contributed to oil industry profits.

Staff reviewed data over a one-month period in mid-2002 and found that SPR deposits caused a spike in prices that cost consumers between $500 million and $1 billion dollars. During that period, the price of home-heating oil rose by 13 percent, jet fuel rose by 10 percent, and diesel fuel was up by 8 percent. In addition to the hit to consumer's pocketbooks by filling the SPR without regard to price, the Bush administration raised the costs to all taxpayers. Levin's staff estimated that at an SPR fill rate of 100,000 barrels per day, a decision to fill the SPR at $30 per barrel rather than $20 per barrel cost taxpayers an extra $1 million per day.

Levin's staff recommended that for 2003, the Department of Energy should defer filling the SPR until crude oil prices fall and U.S. commercial inventories increase. They also recommended that a cost-benefit analysis be performed to review whether it makes any sense to fill the SPR without regard to price.

Recommending Changes

The following is a brief overview of the recommendations that were sent by Senator Levin to the Federal Trade Commission on June 7, 2002.

Inventories

A shift to producing oil just-in-time has reduced the oil companies' ability to respond to disruptions in oil availability. By making the market more vulnerable to disruption, it is much easier to control supply and ultimately price:

> Most oil companies today have adopted just-in-time inventory practices. Although from each company's perspective these practices may minimize day-to-day operational costs, in the aggregate this has eliminated the refining industry's cushion or "insurance" against price spikes resulting from minor disruptions in the refining, distribution, and marketing system. It also has created a perverse incentive for refiners. The Subcommittee found documents indicating that a number of refiners prefer a market that is vulnerable to disruptions so that they could take advantage of the higher prices that follow any disruption. In reviewing proposed mergers, the FTC [Federal Trade Commission] should carefully examine the potential effects upon the aggregate inventories that would be created as a result of the merger.

Pipeline and Terminal Capacity

The Federal Trade Commission (FTC) must more carefully monitor the impact of pipeline and terminal capacity before any future mergers are permitted within the oil industry. A careful balance of the pipeline and terminal capacity is need to ensure competition:

> In markets in which a dominant player controls the transportation and storage of a product such as gasoline, I urge the FTC to use its available authorities to ensure that this market power is not abused. Similarly, in reviewing proposed mergers, the FTC should ensure that the proposed merger does not create any new barriers to entry into a market through a lack of access to pipelines and terminals.

Moratorium on Mergers

Attorney Generals who testified recommend a moratorium on any additional oil industry mergers until a study can be done on the impact of these mergers on competition and pricing:

> At the Subcommittee's hearing, the Attorneys General from the States of Connecticut and Michigan recommended that a one-year moratorium be placed on all major mergers within highly concentrated markets in the oil industry. The

purpose of the moratorium would be to enable the Congress to consider more effective remedies to the problems arising from increasing concentration and allow the FTC to consider this problem as well.

Parallel Pricing

Standards required to prove collusion related to anti-trust violations need to be adjusted in markets where supplies are highly concentrated. It is far too easy for suppliers in these kinds of markets to track competitors' pricing and mirror any price moves:

> The Subcommittee also received testimony on what the appropriate burden of proof should be in order to establish illegal collusion under the antitrust laws. The Attorneys General testified that the standard currently used by many courts presents too high a hurdle for plaintiffs in antitrust cases to present their evidence to a jury.

> In concentrated markets, juries should be permitted to consider circumstantial evidence in determining whether or not the firms in the market are acting in collusion. In highly concentrated markets, outright conspiracies and collusion between the market participants are totally unnecessary to develop concerted action. When there are few firms in a market, these firms can easily track and follow each other's behavior. In reality, the only way to demonstrate collusion in a concentrated market is through circumstantial evidence.

> We found numerous instances of parallel pricing within the gasoline industry. At certain times in certain markets, all of the major brands went up and down together, and stayed at a constant differential with respect to each other. Although parallel pricing in and of itself does not necessarily indicate collusion, I believe that additional circumstantial evidence should be considered by a jury in determining whether in fact such collusion exists in concentrated markets.

Importance of Independents in Gasoline Markets

The best way to prevent price collusion and preserve competition is to encourage the growth of independent gasoline refiners and dealers. The FTC must act to reduce the decline in independents nationwide by more carefully researching mergers:

> Numerous studies have demonstrated the importance of independent gasoline refiners and dealers in preserving competition in the gasoline wholesale and retail markets. For example, in one of the most rigorous studies to date, which is cited in the Subcommittee's report, Professor [Justine] Hastings [Assistant

Professor of Economics at Dartmouth College] documented how the loss of one independent retail chain in Southern California led to across-the-board price increases at the pump in the areas previously served by the chain. In addition, the Subcommittee's investigation found a number of industry analyses indicating that the greater the presence of non-majors in a specific market, the lower the retail price.

The continuing decline of independents nationwide and in a number of markets presents a significant concern that prices in the affected markets will rise above purely competitive levels. In your reviews of proposed mergers, I urge you to carefully examine the effect of the proposed merger upon the presence of independents in the market. Not only are large retail chains necessary to present effective competition for other large retail chains, but a healthy independent sector is necessary to maintain true price competition.

In 2003, after the Democratic-led sub-committee made its recommendations, the Republicans took control of the Senate. Since then, the Senate has done nothing to change the oil-supply market, and nothing probably will be done until the political winds change direction in Washington or Americans start demanding fair prices at the gas pump.

Petro-Facts

If you'd like to learn more about the subcommittee's investigation and recommendations, you can read the full report at www.senate.gov/~gov_affairs/042902gasreport.htm.

The Least You Need to Know

- Gasoline prices have become more volatile in the past five years. While increases in crude oil are a significant factor, tight supply and reduced refinery capacity also play a major role in the volatility.

- Various pricing schemes are used by oil companies to maximize price and profits.

- Oil industry mergers play a significant role in the increased control over pricing. Some recommend a moratorium on mergers to give Congress and the Federal Trade Commission time to review their impact on prices.

Part 5

Looking to a Bloody Future: Will We Continue to Depend on Oil?

How long will we be able to fulfil our needs and desires with oil? Where will we find more oil? Is our reliance on oil and other fossil fuels permanently damaging our environment? Are there viable alternatives to oil? What role will political entities play in answering these dilemmas? We'll try to answer these and other critical questions in the following chapters.

Chapter 21

Polluting Problems

In This Chapter

- ◆ How oil gets into the environment
- ◆ Natural oil seeps
- ◆ Industrial and consumer pollution
- ◆ Reducing oil pollution

On March 24, 1989, the *Exxon Valdez* ran aground off the coast of Alaska, dumping 10.8 million gallons of oil into Prince William Sound. The media coverage of the spill was extensive. Millions of viewers watched with horror as hundreds of oil-soaked birds died on the shores of Prince William Sound, and volunteers and professional crews tried to clean the shore of thick, black crude oil. Although Prince William Sound suffered a devastating environmental blow and is still recovering today, that spill isn't even one of the top-30-largest oil spills in history.

Major oil spills like the *Exxon Valdez* cause nearly indescribable damage to the environment, but they are not the primary source of oil in the oceans. In fact, according to a 2003 study by the National Academies National Research Council, naturally occurring oil seepage is the number-one way that oil gets into our ocean waters. The Smithsonian Institution disagrees and believes that oil from human use is the primary contributor of oil to the world's oceans. In this chapter, we'll take a closer look at these two viewpoints, review how oil pollutes our environment, and then talk about current means of cleaning up spills and what can be done to prevent them in the future.

Getting to the Ocean

We're going to begin our discussion of oil and pollution with the ocean because that's the crucial link to life on Earth. Although the oil industry might like to think differently, the world's lifeblood is water, not oil. And the only way the world can survive is if we protect our most abundant natural resource. (Of course, clean air is important, too. We'll take a closer look at air pollution and global warming in Chapter 25.)

Most of us don't even think of the impact of oil on our environment until we hear of an oil spill. That's not the only way that oil enters our environment undesirably, but it is the most visible way.

A recent study (sponsored by federal agencies and oil industry organizations) by the National Academies National Research Council concluded that nearly "85 percent of the 29 million gallons of petroleum that enter North American ocean waters each year as a result of human activities come from land-based runoff, polluted rivers, airplanes, and small boats and jet skis, while less than 8 percent comes from tanker or pipeline spills."

The study grouped oils that enter the ocean into the following four categories:

- ◆ **Natural seeps:** Crude oil that seeps in the ocean water from geologic formations beneath the ocean floor.

- ◆ **Petroleum extraction:** The exploration and production of oil. Offshore oil exploration and production sometimes ends up releasing oil into the ocean.

- ◆ **Petroleum transportation:** Refining and transporting of oil sometimes end up accidentally releasing oil into the ocean.

- ◆ **Petroleum consumption:** Use of oil by car owners, boat owners, and non-tank vessels, and runoff from paved urban areas ends up in local rivers and streams, which eventually dump this polluted water into the ocean.

Let's take a look at how oil enters the environment in these four categories and what impacts it has on the environment.

**Sources of Oil in World's Oceans
(from National Research Council)**

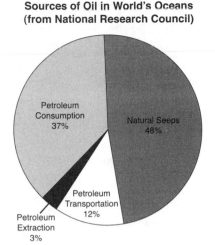

Petroleum
Consumption
37%

Natural Seeps
48%

Petroleum
Transportation
12%

Petroleum
Extraction
3%

Natural seeps and the wastes of petroleum consumers are the primary sources of oil found in the world's oceans, according to the National Academies National Research Council in a report, "Oil in the Sea: Inputs, Fates, and Effects." This chart was developed using data from that report. You can read the report online at the National Academies site (www.nationalacademies.org/nrc/).

Natural Seeps

The largest contributor of oil to the ocean is natural seepage of crude oil from geologic formations below the ocean floor. In fact, the National Research Council estimates that more than 47 million gallons of oil enter the marine environment through natural seepage in North American waters, and 180 million gallons enter the ocean worldwide each year. (As noted previously, researchers at the Smithsonian Institution disagree with these numbers—they believe that the worldwide natural seepage number is 62 million gallons per year.)

Not surprisingly, most of these seeps are in the same place as oil- and gas-extraction activities. The big difference is that natural seeps occur sporadically and at low rates, having a lesser impact on the environment than an oil spill. The National Research Council called for more research about the impact of these seeps, which form a "natural laboratory for understanding crude oil behavior in the marine environment, as well as how marine life responds to the introduction of petroleum." The study found that marine ecosystems near natural seeps have less diversity and consist mainly of bacteria and a few invertebrate species.

The World's Garbage Can

The next-largest category, petroleum consumption, is the source of an average of 25 million gallons of oil in North American waters and 140 million gallons worldwide each year. Most of this consumption occurs on land and ends up in our rivers or streams through runoff in waste- and storm-water systems, eventually finding its way to the ocean. Another source is old, inefficient two-stroke boat engines that release oil into the environment.

Oil from these sources enters the marine environment slowly over time. The National Research Council found there was little documentation of sources in this category, making the estimates uncertain. It recommended that the federal agencies that sponsored the study "develop and implement a system for monitoring the input of petroleum in the marine environment from land-based sources via rivers and storm- and waste-water facilities."

A Smithsonian Institution exhibit, Ocean Planet, estimated much higher numbers for the category of petroleum consumption. The Smithsonian estimated that 363 million gallons of oil enter the oceans from land runoffs and municipal and industrial wastes each year. They also included in this category used engine oil that is not disposed of properly.

Sources of Oil in World's Oceans
(from the Smithsonian Institution's "Ocean Planet" Exhibit)

This chart was developed using the data from "Ocean Planet," a traveling exhibit of the Smithsonian Institution. It estimates that industrial and consumer petroleum consumption contributes far more oil to the oceans than does the NRC study. You can view the exhibit online at seawifs.gsfc.nasa.gov/ ocean_planet.html.

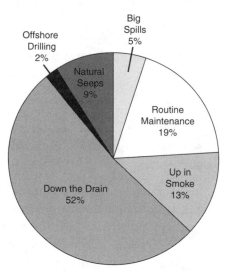

According to the Smithsonian, oil tanker discharges account for 137 million gallons each year. These include cleaning and other ship operations. Air pollution, which is mainly caused by the burning of oil by cars and by industry, accounts for 92 million gallons of oil in the world's waters. Air pollution is created from hydrocarbons being released into the air by the burning of petroleum oil. Rain washes hydrocarbons from the air into the oceans.

If the Smithsonian is right, then consumer and industry use of petroleum significantly dwarfs the impact of natural seeps.

Petro-Facts

These are things you can do to help minimize the amount of oil that enters the environment:

♦ Be careful how you dispose of a waste product that includes oil. Take it to a recycling center. Don't just pour it down the drain.

♦ Be sure you clean up any oil that spills on the ground while you are working on your car or boat. Street gutters and storm-water systems frequently drain into lakes, streams, rivers, and wetlands.

♦ If you have the responsibility at work for disposal of oil products, then be sure to educate your workforce and develop methods for recovering, storing, and disposing of oil and other residues. Even if you don't have control, you may want to point out problems to management.

♦ If you have a motor boat with a two-stroke engine, upgrade to a four-stroke engine.

♦ Look for ways to decrease your personal dependence on oil. This could include buying a more fuel-efficient car, taking public transportation to work, or joining a car pool.

Getting the Oil

Petroleum extraction is a much smaller contributor to the total amount of oil in the world's waters. The National Research Council estimated that 880,000 gallons of petroleum entered North American waters, and 11 million gallons entered oceans worldwide yearly from this source. Smithsonian estimates closely mirrored this with 15 million gallons annually in their "Offshore Drilling" category. While the numbers are small comparatively, the impact can be greater because the entry into the marine environment can occur in large spills. Oil that seeps naturally in slow, chronic releases near production fields doesn't have the potential to cause major, dramatic damage. Another key factor is that petroleum production usually takes place near shore, so coastal areas can be significantly affected.

Drill Bits

Blowouts in the oil industry are a sudden escape of gas or liquid from a well.

Most of the major spills during the extraction process are caused by *blowouts* or surface spills of crude oil from offshore drilling platforms. In fact, the second largest oil spill in history, that of the IXTOC I in Mexico, was the result of a blowout that took place June 3, 1979. By the time it was stopped on March 23, 1980, it is estimated that more than 140 million gallons of oil entered the Bay of Campeche, just 600 miles south of Texas in the Gulf of Mexico. The only oil spill larger than this one was the combined spills deliberately dumped during the 1991 Gulf War.

The second-largest oil spill in the history of the world happened on June 3, 1979, just 600 miles south of Texas in the Bay of Campeche, off Ciudad del Carmen, Mexico. An exploratory well, IXTOC I, blew out and spilled about 140 million gallons of oil before it was brought under control in March 1980.

(Courtesy of the Office of Response and Restoration, National Ocean Service, National Oceanic and Atmospheric Administration)

The industry has made significant technological advances that reduce the risk of spills during petroleum extraction, but aging infrastructures still must be carefully monitored. The National Research Council recommended that federal and state agencies work together to "promote extraction techniques that minimize accidental or intentional releases of petroleum in the environment."

Moving the Oil

Spills from petroleum transportation were estimated at 2.7 million gallons annually in North American waters and 44 million gallons worldwide. These spills include refinery activities as well as transport of oil by tanker and pipeline. Even though the annual numbers are small comparatively, they usually occur in large spills. A spill can occur anywhere in the world that oil tankers travel or anywhere that oil pipelines are located.

While safety improvements have decreased the likelihood of these types of spills, the National Research Council found that the "potential for a large spill is significant, especially in regions without stringent safety procedures and maritime inspection procedures."

The largest tanker spill happened three miles off the coast of Brittany, France, on March 16, 1978, when the *Amoco Cadiz* ran aground because of a failure in its steering mechanism. The vessel dumped all of its cargo, 1,619,048 barrels of oil, into the water. The resulting oil slick was 18 miles wide and 80 miles long, and polluted about 200 miles of the Brittany coastline. Most of the coastline has recovered, but some damage can still be seen today.

Researchers survey the oiled beaches of Prince William Sound after the Exxon Valdez spill.

(Courtesy of the Office of Response and Restoration, National Ocean Service, National Oceanic and Atmospheric Administration)

A more recent oil spill is still threatening the coastlines of Spain, Portugal, and France. The tanker *Prestige* was damaged by a storm off the coast of Spain on November 23, 2002. It was carrying nearly double the amount of oil as the *Exxon Valdez*. The tanker broke apart and sunk to the bottom of the ocean, without immediately spilling additional oil. More than 70,000 tons of oil remain trapped in its cargo hold on the ocean floor and continues to seep out, polluting the coastlines. Initially, holes were patched using a mini-submarine, but at the time this book was written, plans were being made to remove some of the cargo.

Slick Sayings

Significant research has been conducted in recent years—particularly in the wake of the *Exxon Valdez* spill—confirming that large oil spills can be devastating to the marine environment. They kill fish, mammals, birds, and their offspring; destroy plant life; and reduce the food supply for organisms that survive.

—From "Oil in the Sea: Inputs, Fates, and Effects" by the National Research Council

The *Prestige* was a 25-year-old, single-hulled tanker. Today, modern tankers are built with a double hull, which provide greater fortification between the cargo and the ocean. Current international law requires single-hulled tankers built before 1973 to be withdrawn from use by 2007. Those built after 1973 must be withdrawn by 2015.

Exploring the Effects

Areas affected by an oil spill can recover, but it takes many years and sometimes decades. Each situation has a unique set of conditions, so recovery varies greatly.

First, we'll review what happens after a spill. In the ocean, there are actually three things that happen:

1. **Weathering.** Winds, waves, and currents can naturally disperse the oil. How the oil will disperse depends on the type of oil. Light products such as kerosene tend to evaporate and dissipate quickly, while crude oils break up and dissipate more slowly, and usually require a clean-up response. Storms can speed this dispersion.

2. **Spreading.** Once spilled, oil starts spreading quickly across the surface of the water. After a while, depending on winds, wave action, and water turbulence, this slick will break up into narrow bands that parallel the wind direction.

3. **Evaporation.** Lighter components of the oil will evaporate into the atmosphere. How much evaporates depends on the type of oil.

How the coastal areas are affected depends on what kind of marine habitats there are. For instance, the Minerals Management Service performed an extensive study of oil spills on the salt and brackish marshes and mangrove forests in the Gulf of Mexico. This study looked at a 6-million-acre area along the coasts of Louisiana and Texas. The Florida Coast is also dominated by well-developed mangrove forests, and future offshore oil drilling there could have similar effects on the forests.

The study looked at the effects of numerous oil spills in the study area over many years. It concluded that "Oil causes mortality and reduced growth of the dominant plant species in both marsh and mangrove habitats." The amount of the damage depends on the weathering of the oil spill, the types of plants, the frequency of the spills, local conditions, and other biota (for example, fiddler crab burrows can facilitate penetration of oil into the sediment).

> **Slick Sayings**
>
> Oil causes extensive mortality in invertebrate populations, probably affects fish that forage in the systems at high tide, and almost certainly disrupts many important ecological processes that they mediate in mangrove systems. These links have received little attention, and an assessment of the effects of oil on ecological processes needs to be a research priority.
>
> —MMS study, "Managing Oil Spills in Mangrove Ecosystems: Effects, Remediation, Restoration, and Modeling."

Sea Birds

Of all the wildlife that is affected by oil spills, sea birds suffer the biggest blow. They are extremely sensitive to crude oil and its refined products. They spend a lot of time near the surface of the sea and on oil-affected seashores, especially when searching for food. In addition, when birds come in contact with oil or its products, their feathers collapse and matt, changing the feathers' insulation properties. This breakdown in waterproofing and insulation causes hypothermia. Oiled feathers can also reduce a bird's buoyancy, so they sink and drown. They can also be poisoned by attempting to preen themselves or by eating food that has been contaminated.

Marine Mammals

Marine mammals, including sea otters, sea lions, seals, walruses, sea cows, dolphins, porpoises, and whales, are vulnerable to oil spills because of their amphibious habits and their dependence on air. Some think that marine mammals avoid slicks, but whales and seals have been seen swimming and feeding in or near them.

Marine mammals also are subject to hypothermia because of skin changes that result in metabolic shock caused by oil on the skin. They, too, are subject to toxic effects from ingesting oil, plus they can end up with congested lungs and damaged airways. Eye and skin lesions are common from continuous exposure to oil, and decreased body mass is common because of the restricted diet.

An oiled pup on a boulder on the shores of Isla de Lobos, Uruguay, after the 1997 San Jorge spill.

(Photo taken by Tom Loughlin, NOAA. Courtesy of the Office of Response and Restoration, National Ocean Service, National Oceanic and Atmospheric Administration)

Cleaning oiled pups from the San Jorge spill.

(Photo taken by A. Ponce de Leon. Courtesy of the Office of Response and Restoration, National Ocean Service, National Oceanic and Atmospheric Administration)

Little is known about the effects of oil spills on whales. After the *Exxon Valdez* oil spill, people reported the deaths of a number of killer whales, and their numbers declined after the spill. However, some researchers don't believe that there is significant proof of this.

Dolphins stay close to shore and feed on fish and squid. In previous spill areas, some dolphins have avoided the spill while others have not. Dolphins are smooth-skinned, hairless mammals, so oil doesn't tend to stick to their skin. For them, the biggest risk is associated with inhaling oil and its vapors, consuming contaminated food, or not finding enough food.

Going Ashore

So far, we've concentrated on the effects of oil exploration and production on coastal areas. Let's move onto dry ground to see how exploring affects those areas. The National Research Council study, "Cumulative Environmental Effects of Oil and Gas Activities on Alaska's North Slope," a study mandated by Congress and sponsored by the U.S. Environmental Protection Agency, did just that. The North Slope covers an area of 89,000 square miles. Just to put this in perspective, it's slightly larger than the state of Minnesota.

The study found that oil spills on the tundra so far have been small and have had only local impacts. They also found that the damaged areas have recovered.

Changes in animal populations were noted, though. They found that bowhead whales travel a different route for fall migration "to avoid the noise of seismic exploration activities." Some animal populations, such as bears, foxes, ravens, and gulls, have actually increased in numbers because they scavenge for refuse left by the increased number of people. A negative side-effect of this is that these animals feed on the eggs and nestlings of many of the bird species, some of which are on the endangered or threatened lists.

The study did not find a major impact on the Central Arctic caribou herd on the North Slope so far. The only changes observed were to their geographical distribution and some impact on their reproduction success. But they did find that the "spread of industrial activity into additional areas that caribou use for calving and for seeking relief from insects would likely have an adverse affect on their reproductive success; the degree to which the caribou migrations and populations size would be affected cannot be accurately predicted without more specific information about where future oil-production activity would take place."

Impacts to the North Slope tundra have primarily been related to the extensive off-road travel. The study found that "Networks of trails used for seismic exploration have harmed vegetation and caused erosion, and the trails used for seismic exploration degrade the visual experience of local residents and tourists. New technology has lessened—but not totally eliminated—the impact of seismic exploration on the Alaskan slope. The expansion of exploration activities into new areas could further damage the tundra, especially in hilly areas that are difficult to navigate. The roads that have made access to the North Slope easier also have had significant environmental effects."

The study group recommended that further research be conducted to study the environmental effects with a closer look at air pollution and contamination of water and food sources. They also expressed concern about the possible impacts of global warming and how it might affect the exploration and exploitation of oil in the Arctic.

Cleaning Up the Mess

Clean-up operations after an oil spill occurs can take years and cost millions of dollars. Such operations never completely rid an affected area of oil, however. Researchers have developed several methods for cleaning up spills; the techniques they use depend on the characteristics of the spill. We'll just briefly introduce you to the key methods used:

- ◆ **Biological and dispersing agents:** Help break down the oil so that it biodegrades more quickly.

- ◆ **Booms:** Floating barriers to contain the oil.

- ◆ **Skimmers:** Boats with devices that skim up spilled oil from the water.

- ◆ **Sorbents:** Large sponges that absorb the oil.

- ◆ **Gelling agents:** Chemicals that help oil form into rubber-like solids, which makes it easier to remove. These are sometimes called solidifiers.

- ◆ **Vacuum trucks:** Vehicles that collect spilled oil off the beaches or from the water's surface.

In addition, clean-up crews burn freshly spilled oil while it's still on the surface and apply a lot of "elbow grease," using things such as hoses to wash off oil on the beaches, or using rakes, shovels, and bulldozers to pick up oil or move oily sand to where it can be cleaned by waves.

Clean-up workers use heavy machinery and manual removal techniques to clean oil from the beach of San Juan, Puerto Rico, after the Barge Morris J. Berman oil spill in January 1994.

(Courtesy of the Office of Response and Restoration, National Ocean Service, National Oceanic and Atmospheric Administration)

Finally, animal specialists and their volunteers try to save the lives of sea birds and marine mammals.

Who Pays for It?

Who pays for these clean-up operations? An onshore facility owner/operator is limited to pay $350 million per spill unless the government can prove gross negligence, willful misconduct, or a violation of federal regulations. Costs above that limit are paid for by the U.S. Oil Spill Liability Trust Fund, which was established in 1986 as part of the Clean Water Act. This was one of several funds established that year to tax the industry for the cleanup of water pollution.

If the company responsible can prove the spill was the result of an act of God, an act of war, or an act of omission by a third party, that company will not have to pay the costs and damages related to the spill; the Trust will cover those costs instead. In some cases the responsible party is not known, and the Trust also picks up the costs in those situations.

Petro-Facts

After the *Exxon Valdez* spill, the Congress passed the Oil Pollution Act of 1990 to improve the United States' ability to respond to these types of disasters. This act consolidated Federal programs related to oil pollution, including the Oil Spill Liability Trust Fund.

The Oil Spill Liability Trust was funded with a tax of 5¢ per barrel of oil. This tax expired in 1994, but on February 24, 2003, Rep. Lois Capps (D-CA) introduced legislation that would reinstitute the nickel-per-barrel charge for oil transported using single-hulled vessels. Her intent is to create a disincentive for using these older and less-safe tankers and encourage the use of double-hulled tankers. Passage of this bill is unlikely since Capps is a Democrat in a Republican-dominated Congress.

Although there are global agreements regarding compensation after an oil spill, in most cases the individual company responsible for the spill and the nations impacted by the spill bear the brunt of the costs of cleanup. The oil companies seek to minimize their costs and the impacted countries seek to get money from the responsible companies.

Preventing Pollution

Advances in oil-exploration and exploitation technologies have certainly helped to decrease the damage caused by our quest for oil, and new technologies are being developed each year. Improvements are still needed in how we manage storm water, how we treat household sewage and industrial wastewater, and how we collect used oil products. The shift from single-hulled to double-hulled tankers should reduce the number of oil spills from tankers. In addition, we must increase the security of oil pipelines to prevent them from becoming terrorist targets.

Now that we've reviewed all the possible problems related to our oil industry and needs, let's move on to the possible solutions.

The Least You Need to Know

◆ There is some controversy regarding whether natural seepage or human activity is the primary cause of oil entering the world's oceans. It depends upon who you believe—the Smithsonian Institution or a National Research Council, which was funded in part by the oil industry.

◆ While oil spills are a much smaller part of the oil released into the world's oceans, their impact on the environment can be much greater.

◆ Significant improvements in technology and the way oil is transported have greatly reduced the number of spills, but they are still an all-too-common occurrence.

Chapter 22

Fuel Efficiency and Renewable Sources of Energy

In This Chapter

- ◆ Making more efficient use of nonrenewable resources
- ◆ Capturing the wind's energy
- ◆ Solar power's growing popularity
- ◆ Hydroelectricity's benefits
- ◆ Biomass energy catches on
- ◆ How hydrogen fuel cells can power our cars

In Chapter 16, we looked at the fault lines dividing energy conservationists and proponents of exploring for more oil. As we explained, one of the primary areas of disagreement is how much emphasis the government should put on developing alternative sources of energy and on enacting regulations and incentives that increase fuel efficiency.

Energy conservationists are quick to point out that technologies that increase fuel efficiency and that make various types of renewable energy sources more economical are already in existence or are rapidly being developed.

In this chapter, we'll take a closer look at those technologies and see how they can be used to reduce our dependence on oil today and might someday provide power for the world energy grid of the future. Politically, though, those promoting conservation or alternative energy sources don't have the money or the clout that comes with that money to win the kind of support the oil and gas industry has won to support their pet projects.

While the oil and gas industry has bought access to the Bush administration and the Republican-controlled Congress by giving over $150 million in the last 10 years, the alternative energy groups have only been able to afford about $1.7 million in that same time period, with 66 percent of that going to Democrats and 34 percent to Republicans. Instead of increasing funds for research and development in the alternative energy area, we've already pointed out how Bush cut research and development funds in his energy budgets.

Fuel Efficiency

One of the best ways to reduce our dependence on oil is to build more fuel-efficient cars and other types of equipment so we'll use less oil. The more oil we can save by using less, the longer it will last. When it comes to fuel efficiency, less really does equal more!

How Low Can You Go?

Some of our best information about the value of more fuel-efficient cars came about as a result of the 1973 oil embargo. That year, Congress enacted the Corporate Average Fuel Economy Program (CAFE) in an attempt to reduce the use of foreign oil by encouraging the development of fuel-efficient vehicles. Under the program, automobile manufacturers were required to increase the fuel efficiency of passenger cars from an average of 18 miles per gallon (mpg) in 1978 to 27.5 in 1985. Light trucks were supposed to increase their efficiency to 20.7 mpg by 2002.

Petro-Facts

As this book was being written, Congress was considering increasing these standards as part of the new energy package, so keep an eye out for changes.

The National Academy of Sciences (NAS) looked at the effectiveness of CAFE and published a study of the program in 2002. They found that CAFE contributed to increased fuel economy during the first 22 years CAFE was in effect. In fact, NAS found that gasoline consumption would be 2.8 million BPD higher today if the law hadn't been enacted, which represents about 14 percent of today's consumption level. NAS found that light-duty trucks, including SUVs (which are currently categorized as light-duty trucks), pickups, and minivans provide the best opportunity to further reduce fuel consumption.

In addition, the study reported that technologies exist today that could further significantly reduce fuel consumption in 15 years. These technologies are being introduced in Europe and Japan, where the cost of gasoline is higher ($4 to $5 per gallon), so there is a greater financial incentive to cut back on fuel usage. So far, they have not found a major market in the United States, as automobile manufacturers wait for changes in the economy, regulations, and consumer preferences.

New technologies, including engine improvements and hybrid electric vehicles, have the potential to further improve vehicles' fuel economy by 20 to 40 percent. For example, the Toyota Prius, a gas-electric hybrid—it has both an internal-combustion engine and an electric motor—runs at 48 mpg. The car's regenerative braking system recaptures some of the energy lost while coasting, slowing down, or stopping, and stores it in the battery for use by its electric motor.

The NAS study did identify some potential downsides to fuel efficiency. It reported that fuel efficiency has deprived new car owners of some things they value, such as faster acceleration, greater carrying or towing capacity, and reliability, because of the reduction in size and weight of vehicles.

The Natural Resources Defense Council (NRDC) also found that requiring more fuel-efficient tires could play a major role in oil conservation. The NRDC released a report entitled "Responsible Energy Policy for the Twenty-First Century" in March 2001. The report concluded that by raising fuel-economy standards by 60 percent in the United States, automobile oil use could be reduced by 51 billion barrels. Another 5.8 billion barrels could be saved if the U.S. required fuel-efficient replacement tires. The savings is based on improving cars' efficiency to 45 mpg and light trucks' to 34 mpg. Technology that matches these goals has already been developed and is in use in other countries.

Petro-Facts

NRDC believes that U.S. energy policy must rely on the application of technological advances already in place and readily available as a way to reduce consumption. In the short-term, it argues that the United States should reduce its dependence on heavily polluting fuels—oil and coal—and increase reliance on the efficient use of natural gas as a bridge to a longer-term strategy of greater reliance on renewable sources and cleaner technologies. Such an approach will decrease America's dependence on foreign sources of energy in the near- and long-term, protect the environment, provide for America's energy needs, and buffer the economy against short-term swings in the market.

Other Areas Where We Can Improve Efficiency

The NRDC's energy plan for the future covers more than just vehicle efficiency. It also makes the following recommendations:

- Develop improved efficiency standards for appliances and equipment.

- Provide economic incentives to install energy-efficient equipment that is currently available on the market.

- Expand programs to weatherize low-income housing and help low-income citizens pay their energy bills.

- Provide incentives to encourage growth and development in areas that have access to public transportation.

- Provide long-term economic incentives to reward the commercialization of new energy-efficient technologies.

- Encourage research and development of new energy-efficient technologies.

- Offer information and outreach programs to encourage investments in cost-effective energy-efficient measures.

Renewable Energy

Imagine that when you picked up your paper this morning, the front page headline shouted, "New Miracle Fuel Discovered!" Imagine the article went on to say that researchers have located a new source of energy that, unlike oil, coal, or natural gas, is eternally abundant, costs very little to produce once the production facility is built, doesn't produce any pollution, and is available almost everywhere in the world.

Although it sounds like a pretty idealistic daydream, it's closer to reality than a lot of people realize. As a matter of fact, several sources of power already exist that match this description to a tee: wind power, solar power, and hydroelectricity (water power).

Let's consider each in turn.

Capturing the Wind

When you think of wind energy, your first thought may be of picturesque windmills in Holland. However, unless you're Dutch, today you're far more likely to see a wind turbine producing wind energy than an old-fashioned windmill. These giant wind machines can be as tall as a 20-story building, and each one can produce enough electricity to run 200 average U.S. households, as long as there is a good wind source.

Wind turbines harness the power of wind to produce energy. Here's how: Wind turns the blades, and the blades turn a shaft in the turbine that is connected to a generator and, voilà, electricity! (That's the simple version, of course. You'll find a much more technical explanation of how wind turbines generate electricity at the National Wind Technology Center's website: www.nrel.gov/wind/animation.html.)

Turbine installation at the Nine Canyon Wind Project, the largest wind farm to be built in Washington state. It provides, on average, enough electric power to supply over 10,000 households. The project is owned and operated by Energy Northwest to provide a renewable energy resource to participating public utilities.

(Credit: Energy Northwest)

Electric companies build wind "farms" using row after row of huge wind turbines, but home owners are taking power into their own hands by installing small turbines on their land. And in some areas of the world, farmers and local investors cooperatively own and operate small wind projects. They have a series of interconnected wind turbines that distribute wind-generated power over local power lines.

Petro-Facts

Worldwide, more than 31,000 megawatt (MW) hours of wind energy are generated annually in installations today, according to the American and European Wind Energy Associations, with three fourths of that wind power generated in Europe. Germany has the highest total wind capacity with nearly 12,000 MW in operation. The United States is in third place with 4,685 MW. The largest U.S. wind farms are located in California, Minnesota, Iowa, and Wyoming. The World Energy Council expects the worldwide total to be as high as 474,000 MW by 2020.

Just to put this in perspective, 1 MW of electricity is enough to power 750 homes.

Of course, to create energy from wind, you need to have a fairly constant supply of wind. In addition, there must be land available for the wind turbines.

Harnessing the Sun

Solar cells, which convert sunlight into electricity, were first created in the early 1950s. Initially they were developed for the space program to power satellites. Today they are found all over the world, particularly in remote rural areas and developing countries, where there often isn't access to a mainstream energy source.

Two major oil companies have jumped on the solar bandwagon—BP and Shell. BP has invested more than $300 million in solar power over the past five years and expects to have a $1 billion solar business by 2007. BP is concentrating its efforts in the Americas, Europe, Africa, Australia, and the Middle East. Shell is involved in building solar systems in China, India, the Philippines, South Africa, and Sri Lanka.

Two large solar power installations just opened in New Jersey in April 2003. A 500 KW system was installed on the roof of Janssen Pharmaceuticals in Paulsboro, and BP installed a 275 KW system in Titusville. The Titusville installation is on the site of a former petroleum and specialty chemicals storage facility, and was built with the support from the New Jersey Clean Energy Program and the Virginia Alliance for Solar Energy.

Solar cells aren't the only way to take advantage of solar power. Here are some other common techniques:

> **Drill Bits**
>
> **Solar cells,** also called photovoltaic cells, convert sunlight into electricity. Photovoltaics are versatile: They can be used to power tiny objects such as watches and calculators, or can be built as a grid to power large urban areas.

> **Slick Sayings**
>
> This project takes land that has served its purpose for heavy industry in the twentieth century and provides an adaptive reuse with twenty-first-century technology, making clean electricity without a smokestack.
>
> —Paulsboro Mayor John Burzichelli at the opening of the Paulsboro solar facility on Earth Day, April 22, 2003.

- ◆ **Passive solar heating, cooling, and daylighting** is accomplished using buildings designed to incorporate certain features, such as south-facing windows and building materials that absorb and slowly release the heat of the sun. These techniques do not require special machines; instead, they incorporate passive solar architectural designs that can reduce heating bills by as much as 50 percent. These designs can also include natural ventilation for cooling and can reduce lighting costs.

- ◆ **Concentrating solar power** involves technologies that use reflective materials, such as mirrors, that concentrate the sun's energy. This energy is then converted into electricity.

◆ **Solar hot water and space heating and cooling systems** use the sun to heat water or a heat transfer fluid in collectors. These systems can reduce water-heating costs by as much as two thirds. High-temperature solar water heaters can provide hot water and hot-water heat for large commercial and industrial facilities.

Tapping into Water

Water has been tapped as an energy source for more than 2,000 years. In fact, in the United States in 1940, 40 percent of electrical power was generated by hydropower. Today, that percentage is down to about 10 percent, which translates into 77,000 MW of conventional power and 18,000 MW of pumped storage. The Department of Energy thinks that another 30,000 MW could potentially be developed.

Conventional hydropower plants harness the energy from a flowing river, stream, canal system, or reservoir to produce electrical energy. The kinetic energy of the moving water is converted by a turbine to create mechanical energy. This mechanical energy is converted by a generator into electrical energy. Whereas no electricity is required to run conventional hydropower plants, a newer type of facility called a pumped storage plant needs a source of electricity to pump the water, usually through a turbine between a lower reservoir and an upper reservoir. Although pumped storage plants need energy to operate, they offer the big advantage in that they can be rapidly brought online during peak power needs. Hydroelectric plants are operated by federal and state agencies, cities, metropolitan water districts, irrigation companies, and public and independent utilities. Individuals also own small plants at remote sites for their own energy needs, and sometimes even sell the extra power they generate.

Getting Geothermal

Geothermal energy is derived from heat that is contained in the rock and fluid of the earth's crust. The original heat was produced when the earth was formed. In most areas of the country, this heat reaches the surface in a very dispersed state and is unusable, but in some areas there are geothermal resources close enough to the surface that they can be tapped. A geothermal unit amplifies the heat that it draws from the resource and delivers it for use in the home.

Geothermal electricity production began in the United States in 1960. Today there are more than 20 geothermal electric plants in the United States, producing a total of 2,800 MW of clean and reliable energy, which is enough to supply electricity to over 2 million average U.S. homes. Another 23,000 MW potential has been identified in the United States, and there may be as much as five times that amount yet undiscovered. Worldwide geothermal capacity in use today totals 8,000 MW.

Petro-Facts

Geothermal heat pumps use the earth or groundwater as a heat source in winter and as a place to send unwanted heat in summer. About 500,000 geothermal heat pumps are in use in the U.S. today, including one at President George W. Bush's Texas ranch. Geothermal heat pumps have been available since 1948, but they are just starting to catch on.

Geothermal power plants are in operation in California, Hawaii, Nevada, and Utah. The largest geothermal plants in the world are located in the Geysers area of Northern California.

Geothermal energy isn't renewable like solar or wind, but it has a lifetime measured in billions of years. When local sources are tapped, there is a gradual decline in the reservoir, but with proper management, the geothermal reservoir can be used for 100 years or more in most cases. Smaller reservoirs tapped for an individual home may decline over 30 years.

Using Plants for Energy

Even plants can be turned into power! In addition to trees, which have long been used as a source of wood for fires, plants are used in the new alternative-energy source known as biomass. Biomass can include fast-growing trees and grasses, agricultural residues (corn stalks, rice straw, wheat straw, used vegetable oils), and wood waste (sawdust, tree prunings, paper trash, and yard clippings).

Biomass development in the United States is still in its infancy, but it is much more advanced throughout Europe. Finland is the biggest user of biomass energies—it fills more than 27 percent the nation's energy needs with biomass.

Why Aren't Alternative Energy Sources Being Built and Used?

You may be wondering why these sources of energy that are free once a company builds the initial facilities aren't more aggressively developed. This can in part be explained by the fact that the infrastructure in place for most types of energy used today is dependent on nonrenewable sources, such as oil, gas, and coal. Building new facilities costs a lot of money and needs a strong commitment from the government in the form of direct grants or tax incentives to encourage the investment. In addition, companies that produce oil, gas, and coal make money not only through the facilities, but also through the ongoing sales of oil, gas, and coal. Renewable energy won't have that earning potential once the infrastructure is in place, so governments will have to step in to encourage the use of renewable alternatives.

For example, the tax laws related to geothermal energy show how the government is actually discouraging development of alternative energy sources. A study done by the California Energy Commission in 1998 found that tax loads were 1.8 times higher for geothermal energy than for natural gas. For instance, companies can get bigger tax incentives for finding natural gas resources than for maintaining a geothermal facility. This results in less money being spent for research and development of geothermal energy by private companies.

Petro-Facts

Right now the only renewable energy that has a special tax credit is wind, through the Federal Wind-Only Production Tax Credit. This tax credit helps cover the cost of building and running wind energy facilities. Proponents of all types of renewable energy sources are pushing for this tax credit to be available for all forms of renewable energy, plus geothermal.

Revisiting Hydrogen

Hydrogen fuel cells may be the fuel of the future for most types of transportation, but in reality it's an old technology. The original hydrogen fuel cell was invented by Sir William Grove in London in the 1830s, but no one found a practical application for it until the U.S. space program started experimenting with the technology in the 1950s. Fuel cells powered the 1960 Gemini spacecraft and continue to power the space shuttle.

Today, fuel cells are used to produce electricity, similar to the way a battery is used to covert energy into electric power. The key difference is that the cell is fueled using an external fuel source, usually hydrogen gas, so it doesn't need to be recharged as long as there is a constant fuel source. This makes it an excellent choice for use in cars with a hydrogen fuel tank. The fuel cell is fed by a fuel tank and oxygen from the air, which combine to produce energy and warm water.

Drill Bits

Hydrogen is the most abundant element in the universe. The colorless, highly flammable gaseous element is used in the production of synthetic ammonia and methanol, in petroleum refining, and rocket fuels.

The fuel isn't burned during this process, so the fuel cell can operate quietly and virtually pollution free. This energy-conversion method is much more efficient than gasoline, too. The typical automobile engine captures only 15 to 20 percent of the gasoline's chemical energy, while a fuel cell is able to convert almost three times that amount of energy in useable power.

Almost all major automobile companies have fuel-cell projects in the works. Right now fuel cells cost more than conventional power sources, but as the technology catches on, its costs will likely drop.

Some people fear the explosive nature of hydrogen. These fears stem primarily from the Hindenburg disaster of 1937 when hydrogen gas was used to power the zeppelin—a balloon-like airship. People wrongly blame hydrogen for the disaster—the fire was caused by an electrical discharge that ignited the zeppelin's canvas, which was treated with two major components of rocket fuel.

Slick Sayings

From the perspective of safety, storing and transporting hydrogen safely is very similar to handling natural gas or propane, which are currently piped all over the world to industries and homes. A safe hydrogen infrastructure will include a system of detectors to pinpoint leaks, alarms in order to notify of leakage, and a system of cut-off points, all of which will be regularly tested.

Five percent of natural gas is already reformed to produce hydrogen for industrial use in petrochemical production, food processing, microchip manufacture, and for spacecraft fuel. These industries have already resolved the safety issues around the storage and transportation of hydrogen.

—From the website of the Rocky Mountain Institute, a leading nonprofit research institute

Researchers at the College of Engineering at Miami University have performed safety studies on hydrogen-powered vehicles, according to the Rocky Mountain Institute. Tests showed that a fire from a gas-tank leak only raised the temperature inside the car a few degrees—a victim would have to be practically in the flame to get burned. If you have seen pictures of a burned-out car hulk, you know that a gasoline-powered car fire is much more dangerous.

Why Aren't We All Driving Hydrogen Cars?

So why isn't there a mad dash to convert to this new safer, cleaner energy source for cars? Once again, the problem is politics and money. Experts estimate that the initial investment to supply just 2 percent of cars in the United States alone with hydrogen by 2020 is around $20 billion. And until recently, there really wasn't much of a political will to make it happen.

> **Slick Sayings**
>
> The transition to hydrogen will be a long and capital-intensive process. It will need political will and potentially difficult choices to realize the significant benefits of cleaner air, lower greenhouse gas emissions, and a decreased reliance on foreign energy sources. Many of the existing technical and cost hurdles can be overcome with sustained and consistent government support, but even so, governments will still need industry to deliver the huge investment needed for the infrastructure changeover.
>
> —Jeroen van der Veer, President of Royal Dutch Petroleum and Vice-Chairman of the Committee of Managing Directors of Royal Dutch/Shell Group at the Iceland Hydrogen Economy Conference on April 24, 2003

The industry has started putting some demonstration cars on the road. In fact, a hydrogen-refueling station is in operation in California as part of the California Fuel-Cell Partnership, sponsored by BP, Shell, Texaco, Air Products and Chemicals, and Paxair. Tokyo will have a station operating by the end of 2003 with support from Iwatani International Corporation, the Tokyo Metropolitan Government, and Showa Shell Sekiyu KK (the Royal Dutch/Shell Group owns 50 percent of that station).

Although fuel-cell cars are just now coming into their own, local governments have been using fuel cells to power public transportation for a while now. California was the first U.S. state to put a fuel-cell bus on the road in November 2002. The bus was built by ThunderPower, a joint venture of Thor Industries and ISE Research.

Fuel-cell buses are hitting the pavement throughout Europe. Madrid received the first European bus in May of 2003, and another 30 buses are scheduled to be delivered to 10 European cities—including Amsterdam, Barcelona, Hamburg, London, Luxembourg, Porto, Reykjavik, Stockholm, and Stuttgart—within a year. These deliveries are part of a two-year trial program.

Cars and buses aren't the only energy guzzlers that can benefit from fuel cells. Fuel cells also have tremendous commercial potential for commercial buildings. In fact, there are fuel-cell demonstration projects in about 15 countries worldwide including a New York City police station, an Alaskan postal facility, and a Nebraskan credit-card processing system.

The U.S. transportation sector is 95 percent dependent on petroleum today, with transportation consuming 67 percent of the petroleum used in the United States. Getting off this petroleum diet is crucial to stem the growth of imported oil, remove the chokehold that foreign oil exporting countries have over the U.S. economy, and to create a cleaner environment.

Until the world does put more emphasis on developing renewable energy sources, the race for nonrenewable sources will continue. In the next chapter we'll review how energy companies are digging deeper and developing new ways of extracting oil resources.

The Least You Need to Know

♦ Alternative energy sources, some of which have been used for thousands of years, are now becoming more commercially viable as the world looks for renewable, cleaner energy sources.

♦ Wind energy is growing rapidly and is expected to provide 474,000 megawatts of energy by 2020.

♦ Solar energy is catching on around the world with the help of two major oil companies—BP and Shell.

♦ Hydrogen fuel cells may be the primary transportation energy source of the future.

23

Digging Deeper

In This Chapter

- ◆ Revisiting known resources
- ◆ Canadian sand pits
- ◆ Venezuelan syncrude
- ◆ Offshore and deep-sea drilling
- ◆ The Alaskan National Wildlife Reserve

The quest to meet the world's ever-increasing thirst for oil is taking oil companies deeper underwater and into previously ignored areas. Companies are also getting creative in finding ways to extract useable crude from deposits that they once thought were unrecoverable. Extraction costs from these locations far exceed the $2 per barrel it costs to extract, say, Persian Gulf crude, but as the world's oil needs continue to grow, these more expensive sources will become more economically viable, especially as long as a barrel of oil stays above the $20 range.

In this chapter, we'll take a look at projects to extract oil from sites previously thought uneconomical in Canada and Venezuela, and areas considered to be environmentally sensitive or politically unpopular in the United States. We'll also explore how far we can go underwater with the new technologies being developed.

Tapping the Sands

In May 2003, Canada suddenly became the world's number-two source of energy reserves—at least according the U.S. Department of Energy's Energy Information Administration (EIA). In May, the EIA acknowledged the existence of some 175 billion barrels of oil in Canada. These reserves were known to be in existence in Canada since the nineteenth century, but the EIA had ignored them in doing its calculations because the oil sitting in the sands—called *oil sands*—was thought to be too expensive to extract. Canadian oil sands projects are only economically viable when crude oil prices are above $18 to $20 per barrel.

> **Drill Bits**
>
> **Oil sands** are a mixture of bitumen, sand, water, and clay. Each grain of sand is surrounded by a thin envelope of water. Bitumen surrounds the sand and water. The big challenge is to separate this bitumen from the sands and produce synthetic crude.
>
> **Synthetic crude** is a means of processing something that is not pure oil, such as bitumen, into an oil-like substance.

The EIA predicts that Canada's oil sands could produce about 2.2 million barrels of oil per day by 2025 versus the 700,000 per day now being taken from these sands.

Canada is even more optimistic about the oil sands potential. The Canadian Association of Petroleum Producers (CAPP) estimates that the oil sands contain 315 billion barrels of oil. CAPP believes that oil sands production will increase to 1 million barrels per day by the end of 2003 and 1.8 million barrels per day by 2010.

> **Slick Sayings**
>
> Alberta is in a very enviable position to supply its own needs and those of its trading partners over the next 50 to 100 years.
>
> —Murray Smith, Alberta's Minister of Energy

Why the change in attitude? The development of a new technology called steam-assisted gravity drainage (SAGD) extraction made all this possible. Using SAGD technology, two horizontal wells are drilled into the same reservoir, one above the other. Steam is injected into the well on the top. This heats up the surrounding tar-like bitumen and causes it to drain, with the help of gravity, into the lower well.

The cost of SAGD technology is much higher than traditional drilling, but SAGD makes the extraction of oil from the oil sands more economically viable than it had been in the past. Oil companies estimate that this new technology has lowered extraction costs to $4 or $5 per barrel versus $9 to $11 per barrel with the older technologies in use.

Since the development of this technology, investments in oil sands have jumped dramatically. The industry has already spent $10 billion and plans to throw an additional

$15 billion at oil sand production. Major players in oil sands development include Petro-Canada, Shell Canada, Suncor Energy, and Imperial Oil, which is an affiliate of ExxonMobil.

Making Heavy Light

Venezuela's oil industry may soon take a similar jump if technological advances in the extraction and processing of extra-heavy crude and bitumen deposits make this type of oil economically viable. In fact, Venezuela's current known reserves of 100 billion barrels could jump by 170 billions to a whopping 270 billion barrels.

Currently, there are four joint ventures in the works between Venezuela's oil company, Petróleos de Venezuela, S.A., (PdVSA), and foreign companies to create a more usable—and thus more valuable—synthetic crude, called syncrude:

- ◆ Conoco's Petrozuata joint venture with PdVSA is blending Venezuela's extra heavy crude with light crude, and then transporting it by pipeline to a facility for upgrading. This upgrading processes the heavy oil into a higher value synthetic crude oil. Since 1997, Petrozuata has drilled more than 320 wells, and currently produces 120,000 barrels per day.

- ◆ Exxon/Mobil's joint venture with PdVSA started production in 2001. Extra-heavy crude is diluted with naphtha and sent via pipeline to an upgrader complex to process this oil into syncrude. The upgrader processes 120,000 barrels per day of extra heavy crude into approximately 108,000 barrels per day of syn-crude and byproducts—sulfur and petroleum coke. Some of this syncrude is shipped to Louisiana so that it can be refined and sold in U.S. markets.

- ◆ TotalFinaElf and Statoil's joint venture with PdVSA began production in February 2002 and by 2003 was producing 140,000 to 160,000 barrels of oil per day. The extra heavy crude is upgraded in a way similar to Petrozuata.

- ◆ ConocoPhillip's and ChevronTexaco's joint venture with PdVSA started in November 2001 and produced about 30,000 barrels per day in 2003. Peak production of about 190,000 barrels per day is expected after an upgrading facility is completed in 2004.

Venezuela also is experimenting with another product it calls Orimulsion, which is used as boiler fuel. The product is a mixture of 70 percent natural bitumen, 30 percent water, and less than 1 percent emulsifiers to enable the mixture of bitumen and water.

Orimulsion can be used in conventional power plants, and its emissions are similar to that of conventional fuel oil. Bitor, a PdVSA subsidiary, produces 5.2 million metric tons of Orimulsion per year and expects to produce 20 million metric tons by 2006.

Bitor estimates that more than 1.2 trillion barrels of bitumen exist in the Orinoco Belt in Venezuela. Economically recoverable reserves are currently estimated at 267 billion barrels.

Petro-Facts _____

Bitumen is considered a nonoil hydrocarbon, so it can be produced in addition to Venezuela's OPEC crude oil production quota.

Canada, China, Denmark, Guatemala, Italy, Japan, and Lithuania either consume or are considering consuming Orimulsion.

If Venezuela is successful with its experiments, bitumen deposits in other parts of the world may soon be added as potential sources for Orimulsion-like products, which could dramatically alter the world's energy future.

Exploring Ocean Miles

The world's oceans provide some of the biggest potential for finding new sources of oil.

The Technology of Offshore Drilling

Offshore drilling is being carried out off the coasts of all continents except Antarctica. As more and more reserves are found and claimed near the shore, oil companies must go farther off the coast and deeper below the ocean floor to find new resources.

Offshore drilling technology now exists to go down almost 2 miles in water and a total drilling depth of 6.5 miles below the ocean floor.

Petro-Facts _____

The record for the world's deepest well was set by Transocean's *Discoverer Spirit* drill ship, which dug a well in 9,727 feet (just under 2 miles) of water in the Gulf of Mexico for Unocal Corporation in October 2001. Transocean is the largest offshore drilling contractor and works with Shell, Chevron, Texaco, BP, TotalFinaElf and other oil companies. Its high-specification drillships can operate in water depths of up to 10,000 feet with a maximum drill depth of 35,000 feet or more than 6.5 miles under the ocean. Its largest vessel, the *Discoverer Enterprise*, is 835 feet long, which is the equivalent of three U.S. football fields. Crews can number as high as 200 people.

Offshore drilling is one of the most competitive and also riskiest ventures for oil development. In fact, in December 2002, Morningstar (an investment research firm) analyst Paul Larson said, "Transocean has done an excellent job of destroying economic and shareholder value. Over the past decade, it has achieved a return on invested capital above its cost of capital in only one year ... Transocean is not alone in generating subpar returns. Nearly all of its peers make similarly anemic profits, which we take as proof that this is a highly competitive industry."

How Offshore Oil Is Extracted

There are four techniques for drilling offshore, depending on the water's depth. They are as follows:

 ◆ A **fixed platform,** designed for water depths of less than 1,500 feet, is constructed by driving tubular steel piles into the seabed. The deck of the platform provides crew quarters, drilling, and production facilities.

 ◆ **Tension leg platforms** (TLPs) are moored to the ocean floor by high-strength cables, giving the platform vertical and lateral stability. These platforms provide crew quarters, drilling rigs, and production facilities, and can withstand hurricane-force winds and waves.

 ◆ **SPAR drilling and production platforms** are large, cylindrical platforms supported by buoyancy chambers and moored to the seafloor. These platforms can be operated in more than 8,000 feet of water and can be moved easily.

 ◆ **Floating Production Storage and Offloading Systems** (FPSO) are large, tanker-like vessels moored to the ocean floor. FPSO vessels process and store production from nearby offshore wells.

Petro-Facts

Technological improvements have helped to increase the likelihood of finding oil and gas with less exploration. Gone are the days when oil speculators looked for oil seeps on the surface, certain types of rock outcrops, and other surface signs that oil might be below. Today things are much more sophisticated. Satellite imagery and seismic technology enable oil explorers to pinpoint the best locations to drill.

Seismic images are developed by sending shock waves through rock layers (usually by detonating an explosive). These waves are then interpreted using high-speed computer software. The type or density of the rock layers can be determined by reading these waves in order to determine if there are signs of oil and gas deposits.

Three-dimensional seismic images can be generated using high-speed computers to give oil companies an underground picture of oil and gas deposits and help them to plan more effective drilling. Also, new techniques in directional drilling enable oil companies to drill from a site up to 5 miles away.

U.S. Offshore Drilling Operations

Offshore drilling is already a major part of the U.S. oil market and currently accounts for about 25 percent of its oil and gas production. According to assessments by both the USGS and the Minerals Management Services (MMS), the potential for offshore drilling is significant. They estimate that 40 percent of undiscovered U.S. oil resources and 25 percent of natural resources are located offshore. Drilling off the coasts of Alabama, Louisiana, Mississippi, and Texas has been ongoing for years, and the MMS continues to offer leases for further development. Leases for areas off the coast of Florida and California have been more controversial.

The Bush administration had planned to open leases for proposed offshore drilling on over 6 million acres in the Gulf of Mexico off the coast of Florida. The majority of Floridians opposed the sale, however, and even President Bush's brother, Florida Governor Jeb Bush, was against it. Interior Secretary Norton heard the complaints and reduced the lease sale to 1.5 million acres, with most of that acreage off the coast of Alabama rather than the coast of Florida. (Jeb Bush happened to be up for reelection in Florida, and the Bush administration's decision to withdraw the sale was a big help in Jeb's reelection campaign). This smaller leased area netted about $340 million in lease bids from oil companies including Shell, Anadarko Petroleum, Kerr-McGee Oil and Gas, Marathon Oil, and Amerada Hess.

After giving up on Florida, MMS moved on to a different 23.4 million acre offshore tract in the Gulf that abuts Alabama, Louisiana, and Mississippi. Bids from 74 different companies for oil and gas leases netted the government $315 million in bids. Another sale was proposed for August 2003 in the Western Gulf that would include 21.7 million acres off the coasts of Texas and Louisiana.

MMS also manages offshore drilling in the Alaska Outer Continental Shelf. On March 25, 2003, MMS started an 18-month process to seek interest in exploring areas in the Norton Basin (25 million acres) and Chukchi Sea-Hope Basin (about 34 million acres).

Drilling in the Arctic: The ANWR Controversy

As noted in Chapter 18, President Bush made exploration for oil in the Arctic National Wildlife Reserve (ANWR) in Alaska a keystone of his energy plan. This move generated a tremendous amount of controversy, pitting environmental and energy conservationists against the oil industry and the government.

The Senate has already rejected the prospect of drilling for oil in ANWR. Eight Republicans joined 44 Democrats and one Independent to stop the drilling in a vote of 52 to 48.

In voting against the plan, Senator Jeff Bingaman (D-NM) told *The New York Times*, "The solution to our long-term energy problems is not to just open this environmen-

tally sensitive area to drilling. This does not reduce in a significant way our dependence on imported oil." In voting in favor of ANWR drilling, Senator Conrad Burns (R-MT) said to the *Times*, "What's wrong with finding out how much oil we have? It's a land that we can take care of and still use the resources it provides."

 **Slick Sayings**

Secretary of the Interior Gale A. Norton called the proposed drilling area a "flat, white nothingness" that represented the nation's greatest potential for oil.

Petro-Facts

The U.S. Geological Survey concluded that ANWR likely holds about 3.2 billion barrels of economically recoverable oil—less than what the nation uses in six months. Production would be spread over 50 years of the field's lifetime and would likely peak at 150 million barrels per year in 2027—amounting to only 1.5 percent of projected U.S. consumption that year. Given that current U.S. demand for oil—which is more than 7.1 billion barrels per year—is increasing about 2 percent annually, the coastal plain would contribute less than 1 percent of the oil we are projected to consume over the next 50 years.

—From the NRDC's "Energy Policy for the Twenty-first Century"

Is It Really Worth It?

Alaska's politicians are leading proponents of oil exploration in ANWR. Oil provides 80 percent of the state's unrestricted general revenue, which helps the state maintain one of the lowest tax rates in the country. Oil service companies and the Alaskan operations offices of the major oil companies also would like to explore ANWR. They believe the USGS survey underestimates the potential and that two to three times more oil may be there, but these differences relate primarily to the question of economically recoverable versus technically recoverable oil. In other words, there may be more oil there that could be extracted, but the cost of recovery is so high that it wouldn't be economical.

Even the oil that the USGS survey calculates as economically recoverable would need to sell for $22 or more per barrel. Oil prices did rise to over $50 per barrel during the Iran/Iraq war, but they have also dropped as low as $15 per barrel as recently as 1997. In fact, according to *Energy Economics Newsletter*, only 50 percent of the time between 1947 and 1997 have oil prices exceeded $15.26 per barrel. The only times oil prices rose above $22 per barrel were in response to war or conflict in the Middle East. So even if there is more oil there, given these pricing concerns, it might not be economically recoverable.

ANWR and the Environment

Environmentalists ask us not to forget that ANWR is a wildlife refuge. They argue that any large-scale exploration and drilling operations in the area could have a serious impact on the wildlife and wilderness in the region.

Drill Bits

An **environmental impact statement** looks at the impact proposed development or land use activities could have on the environment, including land, water, air, and living organisms. It also reviews any social, cultural, or economic impacts of the proposed land use.

Although drillers are required to file an *environmental impact statement*, environmentalists believe that such documents are often inadequate and do not provide sufficient information about the impacts that oil and gas exploration and development will have on an area.

There are still many hot spots where oil is known or suspected to exist. In the next chapter, we'll review areas of the world the energy companies hope to develop in the future.

The Least You Need to Know

♦ Canada's oil sands, which were discovered in the nineteenth century, are now considered an economically viable source of oil, raising Canada's known oil reserves by at least 175 billion barrels.

♦ Venezuela is experimenting with extra-heavy crude and bitumen deposits, which could boost its economically viable reserves by 170 billion barrels.

♦ Deep-water drilling is now possible in a water depth of almost 2 miles with a maximum drilling depth of 6.5 miles, which increases the potential of offshore-drilling resources.

♦ The United States has been trying to develop more offshore oil reserves on the southern and western coasts. Many citizens protest such new drilling operations.

♦ Drilling in the Alaskan National Wildlife Reserve is a cornerstone of the Bush energy plan, but so far politicians have prevented the administration from following through on these plans.

Global Hot Spots

In This Chapter

- ◆ Exploring for oil in Russia
- ◆ Fighting over the Caspian Sea
- ◆ African oil politics
- ◆ South American crude

As we've discussed, oil exploration and exploitation was the basis for many wars and civil strife. The future for oil doesn't look much different. In fact, a June 10, 2003, *Wall Street Journal* article reported the Pentagon is reorganizing the military and sending troops from Germany to areas where it is critical to protect future energy resources.

Many of the areas where troops will be situated match the U.S. Geological Survey's list of locations with a high potential for undiscovered oil in the Persian Gulf, the former Soviet Union, South America, and Africa. The *WSJ* reported troops from Germany would be moved to the Caspian Sea Region, near the Black Sea, and to northern Africa. Troops in the Persian Gulf were moved out of Saudi Arabia and into Kuwait and Qatar. This is in addition to the troops already in Iraq.

Let's take a closer look at the politics of each of these oil-rich areas and their potential for finding and developing new oil sources.

Russia

You may remember that the Baku region of Russia was a primary source for oil, and its oil field was the largest in the world in the early 1900s. Civil strife and political upheaval devastated the Russian oil potential since that time. Since the first Russian revolution, development of the oil industry as a state-run company has been underfunded, and production has plummeted. Today Russia's proven reserves are 77.8 billion barrels, but the U.S. Geological Survey released in 2000 estimates that with continuing development of known fields, the proven reserves could grow to 137.7 billion, and the undiscovered oil potential is likely 170 billion barrels.

In the mid-1990s, Russia again privatized the oil industry and some smart Russian industrialists were able to buy Russian oil companies cheaply. Mikhail Khodorkovsky, a former banker and communist youth leader, is now the richest man in Russia thanks to his purchase of Yukos, Russia's second-largest oil company, from the state. In May 2003, Yukos announced that it was buying out another Russian company, Sibneft, which is the fifth-largest company. The newly merged YukosSibneft production levels are estimated to be 2.4 million barrels per day. Its oil reserves are estimated at 19 billion barrels, which puts the company on a par with Royal Dutch Shell and very close to Russia's largest company, Lukoil, which has 19.3 billion barrels in reserves.

Seeing these numbers, you can understand why there is a mad dash by oil companies to again claim territory in various parts of Russia, but this time they are doing it by trying to get a foothold in the newly formed Russian companies.

Petroleum People

Mikhail Khodorkovsky, who at the age of 39 is Russia's wealthiest businessman, ousted foreign businessmen in order to seize control of Yukos, which was bought from the Russian government in the mid-1990s for $320 million. He's also known for taking on OPEC and ignoring their demands for cutting production, even though Russia, which is not an OPEC member, has cooperated in the past. Politically, he's closely connected to Russian President Vladimir Putin, whose deputy chief of staff used to work with Kohdoskovsky. He even lunched with President Bush and American oil chiefs at a private Houston club to talk about boosting U.S.-Russian energy ties, according to a May 16, 2003, report in *The Wall Street Journal*. There are reports that he plans to leave the oil industry for politics in about five years.

Yukos's rapid growth can be credited with help from several American companies including McKinsey & Co. (a management consulting firm that helped reorganize the company) and two service companies, Halliburton and Schlumberger, that helped to upgrade its operations. In fact, with the help of these American companies, Yukos's production rose 20 percent and Siberneft's rose 28 percent in 2002, while the average growth for the Russian oil industry was 8.8 percent, according to *The New York Times.*

So far, American oil companies have considered Russia too unstable for investments. British oil-giant BP has been the most aggressive of the oil companies in expanding its Russian stake. In February 2003, BP agreed to buy a 50 percent stake in Russia's third-largest oil firm, TNK, for $6.75 billion. The merger was expected to be finalized in a treaty during Putin's state visit to Britain in June 2003. A declaration for energy cooperation also was expected to be signed at that time.

Slick Sayings

Pressure on top oil firms—Shell Group, ExxonMobil and TotalFinaElf—to get in on the world's second-largest oil exporter will prove hard to resist. "I do not think we have seen the last of attempted merger and acquisition activity. There is a herd instinct among the oil majors," said Jonathan Stern, an energy researcher at the Royal Institute of International Affairs in London.

—*Alexander's Gas and Oil Connections,* a trade industry publication, March 6, 2003

Russian oil production topped 7 million barrels per day, which means that it's the number-two oil producer in the world, after Saudi Arabia. The Russian government has set a target of 7.8 million barrels per day within about two years. The U.S. Department of Energy's Energy Information Agency (EIA) believes that this goal will be hard to maintain for long unless Russia spends more than $1 billion per year to develop current fields plus looks for new sources. Experts expect Russian's known fields, which are primarily in West Siberia, will begin experiencing a decline, so new exploration is desperately needed to maintain current production levels.

New exploration is picking up rapidly in the Caspian Sea Region, the Arctic region, East Siberia, and in the Russian Far-East Sakhalin Island. In addition to finding new oil resources, Russia faces another challenge: expanding its ability to export oil out of the country. Most of the oil is transported through pipelines, and most of the pipelines are in a state of disrepair. In addition, the Russian government is in a major power struggle with the oil companies regarding control of the pipelines.

The Russian government controls how much oil can be exported by controlling the nation's pipelines. The government only allows 30 percent of the oil to be exported, while 70 percent must be sold within Russia. While the government wants the oil revenue to help rebuild its economy, it has to balance that with the desire to keep oil prices cheap in Russia. Also, by maintaining control on exports, the Russian government can have more control over how much oil reaches the world market and, ultimately, more control over world prices.

Russian oil companies have offered to build new pipelines, but they want the government to release its grip on production and oil exports. So far, the government has refused to and has stated that it will not consider relinquishing control.

In addition to pipeline problems, finding ways to get the oil out of Russia leads to regional conflicts in almost every direction, especially for exports from the Caspian Sea (which we'll discuss next). Afghanistan is one possible direction, but the area is still too unstable to build a proposed pipeline. A war between Azerbaijan and Armenia closes off that route. Separatists' conflicts in Georgia make that impassable. Russia's war in Chechnya has devastated that region and closed the door to that alternative route.

Caspian Sea

The Caspian Sea has only 10 billion barrels of proven reserves, but some believe that its potential in unexplored areas could be as high as 230 billion barrels of oil. The sea is landlocked by Azerbaijan, Iran, Kazakhstan, Russia, and Turkmenistan. The number-one problem stalling its development is the need to establish a legal status for the Sea. Before the breakup of the Soviet Union in 1991, only two countries shared the rights to the sea, but now the independent states of Kazakhstan, Turkmenistan, and Azerbaijan want to claim a share.

New exploration of the Caspian Sea, which used to have only two countries claiming a piece of the pie, is slowed while the rights of five countries are sorted out.

Most of the oil reserves of Azerbaijan and 30 to 40 of the oil reserves of Kazakhstan and Turkmenistan are offshore in the Caspian Sea. Right now there is no legal convention for who owns what part of the sea. Iranian gunboats challenged BP when it tried to explore an area that Iran claims. Azerbaijan objected when Iran awarded Royal Dutch/Shell rights to conduct seismic surveys in an area Azerbaijan claims. Turkmenistan and Azerbaijan battle over rights to several oil fields that lie in territorial waters.

In April 2002, a summit failed to produce an agreement. Russia, Azerbaijan, and Kazakhstan have agreed to a principle for division, but Iran and Turkmenistan disagree with their plan. Until a broader plan can be signed, several countries are exploring in territories offshore that are generally considered theirs.

Petro-Facts

Russia flexed its muscles after the April 2002 summit to try to settle the Caspian Sea issues. Within hours of leaving the summit, Russian President Vladimir Putin ordered the largest naval exercises in the Caspian Sea's history, which were carried out for two weeks in August 2002. While Russia insisted that this exercise was designed to confront problems of terrorism and poaching, many saw it as a clear show of its military dominance in the area. Iran rejected Russia's proposal that would have left it with only a 20 percent claim to the sea. The Soviet Union and Iran signed bilateral treaties on the Caspian Sea in 1921 and 1940, but neither established seabed boundaries or discussed oil and natural gas exploration.

Three major projects are currently under development in the region—two by Kazakhstan and one signed by Azerbaijan. The one with the greatest potential is an area off the coast of Kazakhstan, which experts believe holds 7 to 9 billion barrels in proven reserves and 38 billion in probable reserves.

A 1994 agreement for a 30-year contract to develop an area off the coast of Azerbaijan by the Azerbaijan International Operating Company has proven reserves of 3 to 5 billion barrels and is the source of almost all of Azerbaijan's increased exports.

In April 1993, Chevron signed the newest deal in the region with Kazakhstan to develop the Tengiz oil field, which has an estimated 6 to 9 billion barrels of recoverable oil. This $20 billion joint venture is expected to reach peak production of 750,000 bpd in 2010.

In addition to the potential for political conflict in the area, another battle brewing over the sea relates to the environmental impacts to the region. This area has faced years of neglect, with discharges and spills from oil and gas drilling polluting the sea. Making matters worse, untreated waste from the Volga river, which is used to export almost half of Russia's wastes, dumps into the Caspian Sea. Thousands of seals have died since 2000, and pollution and over-fishing of the region have caused a dramatic decline in fish stocks. Environmentalists are pushing for improved regional cooperation and technological improvements to prevent further damage.

Once all this is settled, the other key issues will involve exporting the oil out of this land-locked region. About 13 pipelines—including those already existing and planned—will be the primary route for oil out the Caspian Sea.

Persian Gulf

As we've discussed, the Persian Gulf claims two thirds of proven oil reserves, or 685 billion barrels. The 2000 U.S. Geological Survey forecasts growth in this area, identifying an additional 252 billion barrels in newly found reserves in existing fields and 269 billion in yet-to-be-discovered fields.

Saudi Arabia has the largest reserves as well as the largest production levels. The Saudi oil industry exported 7 million barrels a day in 2002, Iran about 2.3 million, United Arab Emirates about 2.1 million, Kuwait about 1.7 million, Iraq about 1.6 million, and Qatar about 800,000. The EIA expects Persian Gulf oil production to top 30 million barrels per day by 2010, which would be an increase of 9 million barrels per day over 2000 production.

Slick Sayings

World oil supplies are not some finite constant sum. Rather, the picture is dynamic and changing. The reserve picture will continue to shift. It's altogether possible that if and when a "new" Iraq sorts out its arrangements and reintegrates into the world economy, new exploration will substantially increase its reserves, once again pushing up the Persian Gulf's share of the total.

—Daniel Yergin, "Persian Gulf Oil: How Important Is it Anyway?", March 21, 2003, in *Weekend Financial Times*

Africa

Africa doesn't offer the same potential as the states of the former Soviet Union or, of course, as the Middle East, but it is still a key source for new oil exploration. In 2000, the U.S. Geological Survey showed that African countries had reserves of 77.4 billion barrels of oil with a potential of an additional 73.5 in possible new reserves in known fields and 124.7 in undiscovered fields.

Nigeria has the largest output in Africa, but its security is poor, with high rates of violent crime including kidnapping and ethnic and religious strife. More than 10,000 Nigerians have died in violence over the past three years. Oil companies operating there periodically must shut down their facilities when protests or fighting break out. However, when all facilities are operating, Nigeria is a leading African oil exporter with 2.3 million barrels of oil per day exported in 2001. Nigeria's estimated proven oil reserves are 24 to 31 billion. Shell and ChevronTexaco are the two primary oil companies involved in Nigeria.

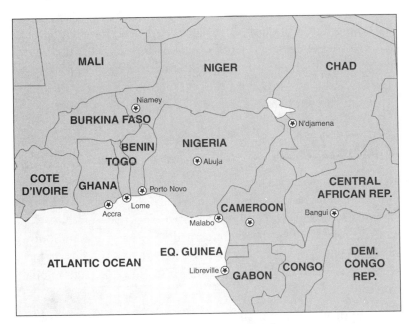

West Africa is the primary region of Africa where oil production and exploration is flourishing. Nigeria is the number-one oil producer.

Angola is the second largest oil producer in West Africa. Most of its oil is located offshore in the Cabinda area, which, like Nigeria, also faces political tensions. Separatists groups periodically kidnap foreign nationals to bring national attention to their political claims for independence. Angola's production is predicted to top 1 million barrels per day in 2003. ChevronTexaco, TotalFinaElf, and Exxon are the major oil companies involved in developing Angola's oil potential.

Gabon is West Africa's third-largest oil producer with total production of 302,000 barrels per day. Gabon is facing output declines and has recently increased its number of exploration contracts.

Libya also has significant known reserves, with 29.5 billion barrels of oil. Libya's oil industry has not been able to grow because of sanctions in place since the 1988 bombing of Pan Am flight 103 over Lockerbie, Scotland. Exxon and Mobil withdrew from Libya in 1982. American oil companies Amerada Hess, Conoco, Grace Petroleum, Marathon, and Occidental withdrew in 1986 when ordered to do so by President Ronald Reagan.

In 2002, Libya exported 1.25 million barrels and is looking to increase that to 2 million barrels per day over the next five years. The UN suspended sanctions when Libya turned over the two bombing suspects, but will not completely remove the sanctions until Libya meets further conditions. Libya is trying to force U.S. companies to either come back to work in the country or relinquish their rights. U.S. sanctions remain in effect and were extended in 2001 for five years. U.S. sanctions forbid companies from making new investments of $20 million or more over a 12-month period in Libya's oil or gas sector. With the United States holding firm on sanctions, European oil companies are jostling for new oil contracts in Libya.

Central and South America

Central and South America don't have anywhere near the potential of the Middle East, but the U.S. Geological Survey estimated that the region has 98.5 billion barrels of proven reserves (confirmed numbers) with an additional 90.75 to be found in known fields (where the existence of oil has been confirmed, but the actual amount of oil in that location hasn't been confirmed). USGS also predicts that 125.3 billion barrels are yet to be discovered (there's some scientific evidence for the existence of oil, but it hasn't been fully investigated).

Venezuela is by far the largest producer in South America, as well as the only member of OPEC in the Americas. It has proven reserves of 77.7 billion barrels plus another 100 to 270 billion barrels of recoverable reserves of extra-heavy crude oil, which may become useable. We talked about extra-heavy crude development in the previous chapter.

In 1975 and 1976, Venezuela nationalized its oil industry, kicked out the major oil companies, and created Petroleos de Venezuela (PdVsA). Today, PdVSA is one of the world's largest oil companies. PdVSA must hold a 51 percent stake in any new exploration or production agreement according to Venezuela law, and the privatization of PdVSA is also banned by Venezuela's constitution.

Venezuela's exploration and production dwindled after nationalization, and Venezuela finally reopened to foreign investment in the 1990s. ChevronTexaco, BP, Norway's Statoil, and France's TotalFinaElf are major players now in Venezuela. ExxonMobil also is negotiating a major development deal.

Workers' strikes in December 2002 to oust Venezuela's President Hugo Chavez shut down Venezuela's oil production. Chavez fired about 1,000 oil company staff in January, and by February its production was back to about two thirds of its pre-strike level. Unrest continued through February with a petition to recall Chavez collecting 3.7 million signatures. A recall referendum was expected in mid–August at the time this book was written.

Other than the giant reserves in Venezuela, the rest of South America has relatively small reserves. Brazil has South America's second-largest reserves with 8.4 billion barrels of oil, and its consumption exceeds its production levels. Ecuador has 4.6 billion barrels of proven reserves, Argentina has 2.9 billion barrels, and Colombia has 1.8 billion barrels.

 Petro-Facts

American lawyers representing a group of 30,000 indigenous people in Ecuador filed a $1 billion lawsuit against ChevronTexaco in May 2003, according to reports in *The New York Times*. The *Times* reported that the group charges that ChevronTexaco dumped more than 4 million gallons a day of toxic wastewater, contaminated with oil, heavy metals, and carcinogens into open pits, estuaries, and rivers from 1971 to 1992. ChevronTexaco denies wrongdoing and says its practices were consistent with the practices of Ecuador's national oil company.

Transporting Chokepoints

Known and future oil reserves are not the only areas that can incite major disagreements. There are several known chokepoints that can quickly cut off oil supplies. Let's take a look at some of key transport hot spots.

Bab el-Mandab

This is a waterway that connects the Red Sea with the Gulf of Aden and the Arabian Sea. If this area is closed off, then oil tankers from the Persian Gulf could be prevented from reaching the Suez Canal and Sumed Pipeline, which means that they would have to be diverted around the Cape of Good Hope at the southern tip of Africa. A terrorist attack in October 2002 off the coast of Yemen damaged an oil tanker. Since then, countries along this route have been on high alert.

Bosporus/Turkish Straits

This waterway divides Asia from Europe and connects the Black Sea with the Mediterranean Sea. This busy waterway hosts 50,000 vessels annually, including 5,500 oil tankers. This is a key proposed route for future Caspian Sea oil. The Black Sea is also the largest outlet for Russian oil exports. Turkey, expressing concern about growing tanker traffic and its environmental threat, has placed some restrictions on oil tankers, banning nighttime transit for ships longer than 200 meters and requiring 48-hour notice in advance for dangerous cargo (including oil). These new regulations have slowed tanker transit by about 3½ days.

Strait of Hormuz

This waterway connects the Persian Gulf with the Gulf of Oman and Arabian Sea. It is considered the world's most important chokepoint. About 13 million barrels of oil pass through this waterway each day destined for Japan, the United States, and Western Europe. If this route were closed off during a Gulf War battle, using another route would increase both time and transportation costs.

Strait of Malacca

This waterway connects the Indian Ocean with the South China Sea and the Pacific Ocean. Approximately 10.3 million barrels of oil per day travel through this chokepoint to Japan, South Korea, China, and other Pacific Rim countries. The October 2002 bombing of a nightclub on the Indonesian island of Bali raised concerns about the risks to this waterway.

Suez Canal and Pipeline

The humanmade canal connects the Red Sea and Gulf of Suez with the Mediterranean Sea. Oil exports, primarily from Saudi Arabia, pass through either the canal or the nearby pipeline destined for Europe and the United States. Closure of this canal would mean that tankers would have to divert around the Cape of Good Hope, which would add time and tie up tanker capacity. The volatile situation in the Middle East makes this a possible target during any battle. The most recent concerns about this chokepoint were expressed before the Iraq war in March 2003.

As the oil companies continue to look for more sources of oil, others are questioning whether we are burning too much now and creating major global problems. In the next chapter, we'll review the arguments surrounding global warming.

The Least You Need to Know

◆ Future oil-exploration potential is based in some of the most unstable parts of the developing world.

◆ Key spots where undiscovered oil may exist include the former states of the Soviet Union, the Middle East, Central and South America, and Africa.

◆ Exploring and exploiting oil isn't the only concern: Key chokepoints in volatile areas also could seriously reduce worldwide oil supplies.

25

Getting Too Warm?

In This Chapter

- ◆ The science of global warming
- ◆ A global agreement on climate change
- ◆ Why the United States won't sign on to the Kyoto Protocol

Is our planet getting too warm? That's the trillion dollar question, which nobody seems to be able to answer conclusively. Although there is certainly evidence indicating a pattern of global warming, the scientific methods for studying the effects are still in their infancy.

Even though the science is inconclusive, the world—or at least most of it—is worried enough about increased temperatures to have taken a strong stand to prevent further global warming. By 2002, most countries signed on to the Kyoto Protocol, a global treaty designed to reduce the threat of global warming.

In a move that angered the rest of the world, the United States refused to sign the Kyoto Protocol—a document that the United States had helped to develop. U.S. government officials don't deny that global warming exists, only that they want to minimize the economic impacts of any new regulations.

In this chapter, we'll consider the science—and the politics—behind global warming.

Scientists Speak Up on Global Warming

The first joint declaration by world scientists that global warming was a problem came at the end of the 1992 UN Framework Convention on Climate Change held in Rio de Janeiro, Brazil. More than 1,600 of the world's senior scientists issued the following warning:

> Human activities inflict harsh and often irreversible damage on the environment and on critical resources. If not checked, many of our current practices put at serious risk the future that we wish for human society and the planet and animal kingdoms.

Scientists believe the global climate temperature will increase somewhere between 2.5 and 10.4 degrees Fahrenheit by 2100. Researchers have already found that global mean surface temperature has increased 1.1 degrees Fahrenheit since the start of the twentieth century, with most of the warming occurring from 1910 to 1945 and since 1976. The 10 warmest years since 1860 have been recorded since 1980. Scientists have also concluded that twentieth-century warming is likely greater than during any century in the past 1,000 years.

The most visible evidence of global warming has been seen in the nonpolar regions of the planet. The Northern Hemisphere sea-ice level has decreased by 10 to 15 inches since the 1950s, and Arctic summer sea-ice thickness has declined about 40 percent in the same period. This has led to a global sea-level rise of between 3.9 and 10 inches. The rate of this rise during the twentieth century is about 10 times higher than the average rate in the last 3,000 years.

What's causing this rise? When we burn wood, coal, or gasoline carbon dioxide (CO_2) is released in to the atmosphere. This gas can't be seen or smelled, but it does get trapped in our atmosphere, which is one of the key causes of global warming. CO_2 is generally considered by scientists to be responsible for about 64 percent of global warming. Burning of oil and/or coal in power plants, industrial facilities and cars are the major sources of these damaging emissions. The rest is caused primarily by the release of other gases including methane (primarily from burning coal), nitrogen oxides (burning fuel), ozone, and chlorofluorocarbons (CFCs) (used in a variety of industrial, commercial, and household products).

Researchers Recommend Change

The Intergovernmental Planet on Climate Change (IPCC) is the international scientific organization charged with monitoring global warming. It reported the following key findings on global warming in a February 19, 2001, report:

- Recent regional climate changes, particularly temperature increases, have already affected physical and biological systems. Examples of these changes include shrinking glaciers, thawing permafrost in the Arctic regions, and earlier break-up of river and lake ice.

- Natural systems such as glaciers, coral reefs, mangroves, tropical forests, polar and alpine ecosystems, and prairie wetlands are vulnerable to climate change, and some will be irreversibly damaged by it.

- Climate change is projected to have adverse impacts on crop yields in most tropical and subtropical regions, water availability and flooding, and human mortality rates. In addition, energy needs will increase because of additional cooling requirements.

- Projected changes in climate could produce more droughts, floods, heat waves, avalanches, and windstorms.

The IPCC also pointed out critical research projects that must be performed to monitor global warming, as well as find ways to increase the planet's ability to adapt to any changes:

- We need to develop a quantitative assessment of sensitivity, adaptive capacity, and vulnerability of natural and human systems to climate change.

- We need a better understanding of the possible events caused by global warming and the thresholds that would trigger such events.

- We need a better understanding of how ecosystems respond to the stress of global warming.

> **Slick Sayings**
>
> Despite the uncertainties, there is general agreement that the observed warming is real and particularly strong within the past 20 years.
>
> —National Academy's National Research Council, "Climate Change Science," released in 2001

- We need to develop basic approaches for adapting to changes as well as studies of the effectiveness, costs, and benefits of any such programs.

- We need better tools to assess risk and the consequences of policy decisions.

- We need better approaches to integrate climate change, its impacts, and adaptation responses into decision-making processes, risk management, and sustainable development initiatives.

- We need to improve long-term monitoring systems to better understand climate-change impacts and other stresses on natural and human systems.

Separating the Myth from the Science

Many myths are circulated by people who don't believe in global warming. For example, some have argued that the winter 2002–2003 record-breaking cold temperatures in the United States is proof against global warming. However, scientists distinguish between daily or seasonal weather patterns and climate. A weather pattern is the state of temperature, moisture, wind, and barometric pressure on a day-to-day basis. Climate describes long-term weather patterns, and is the average temperatures over a much longer period of time. Global warming theory is based on average climate changes, not day-to-day weather changes.

Another major myth is that human activity generates only 4.5 percent of the CO_2 in the environment, while nature is responsible for 95.5 percent, so, therefore, human activity has little impact. While it is true that human activity does account for only this small percentage of CO_2 emissions, even a small increase can have a significant impact a system that was ecologically balanced prior to the human activity. In addition, IPCC has found that since 1750, the atmospheric concentration of CO_2 has increased by 31 percent, which is due mainly to the burning of fossil fuels—oil and coal, primarily—and large-scale deforestation and land-use change.

Now let's look at what has been proposed to get this under control.

Finding Global Agreement

After the 1992 declaration on global warming, little was done by world governments as part of a UN activity to make any voluntary changes in carbon-dioxide emissions. So five years later, in 1997, a second worldwide conference was called to come up with a global solution to fix the problem. That second conference was held in Kyoto, Japan; at that conference, attendees developed the Kyoto Protocol.

The Kyoto Protocol was developed by more than 1,500 scientists including 110 Nobel laureates. In fact, 104 of the 178 living Nobel Prize winners in the sciences signed on to this agreement. This Protocol, which is a type of worldwide treaty to fight global warming, calls for a worldwide reduction of emissions of carbon-based gases by an average of 5.2 percent below 1990 levels by 2012. Different countries agreed to different levels of cuts. The European Union agreed to an 8 percent cut, the U.S. delegation agreed to a 7 percent cut, Russia and the Ukraine agreed to stabilize at the 1990 levels.

Politics of the Kyoto Protocol

However, since participating in the conference and helping to develop the Protocol, the United States has had a change of heart. While President Bill Clinton supported the Protocol, many Republicans in the Senate opposed it (the U.S. constitution gives the Senate the power to support or oppose any treaties). Clinton was not able to garner the necessary support for the treaty, and the United States did not sign it during his administration. One of President Bush's first acts was to announce the United States would not sign the Kyoto Protocol.

The United States, as well as Australia, has expressed concern about the impact that meeting these levels could have on their economies. Both countries have refused to sign on to the protocol. Instead of committing to direct cuts, the United States and Australia want to meet their targets primarily by offsetting their domestic emissions by trading with another country that has a surplus in their targets.

The United States also is concerned about the fines that will be imposed by the treaty if targets are not met. A $30-per-ton figure is circulating as the likely fine, which could cost the United States billions of dollars if it doesn't meet its targets.

Slick Sayings

The least important global environmental issue is potential global warming, and we hope that your negotiators can keep it off the table and out of the spotlight.

—Letter to President Bush regarding the 2002 World Summit on Sustainable Development signed by the Competitive Enterprise Institute, the Committee for a Constructive Tomorrow, the American Enterprise Institute, and the National Center for Policy Analysis (all, by the way, supported by ExxonMobil). President Bush decided not to attend the summit, which was attended by 100 world leaders.

Bush's adamant opposition to the Kyoto treaty might actually have helped it along, however. After the Bush opposition, world opinion was so negative that countries that were wavering signed on, including the countries that are members of European Union, Japan, and Canada.

As of this writing, 104 countries have ratified the Kyoto Protocol including Canada, China, India, Japan, Mexico, New Zealand, South Korea, and the European Union. Australia and the United States are the only countries that have rejected it outright. Russia is the only major country that hasn't yet made a final decision. The protocol hasn't taken effect yet, but it would if Russia decides to follow through with its public pronouncements in 2002 to ratify the Protocol.

Wired News reported in February 2003 that the Bush administration is working hard behind the scenes to prevent Russia from signing on, and is instead encouraging it to join the United States in "alternative plans."

The Path of the Lone Ranger

Although Bush hasn't indicated what these global alternative plans might be, he has introduced the "Clear Skies & Global Climate Change Initiatives" for the United States. Jim Jeffords (I-VT) is leading the charge against this initiative with his own version, called the "Clean Power Plan."

"Clear Skies" Means Dirtier Air

Both plans fall short of the Kyoto Protocol, but Jefford's plan gets a lot closer than Bush's. Currently, clean air rules in the United States fall under the Clean Air Act, which was passed in 1970 and renewed in 1990. The Clean Air Act predates the Kyoto Protocol and doesn't specifically call for CO_2 caps. Here's a chart that compares these three pieces of legislation as they relate to CO_2, mercury, nitrogen oxides, and sulfur dioxides. We've already talked about CO_2. Sulfur dioxides and nitrogen oxides are a major cause of acid rain. Nitrogen oxides are also linked to smog.

Clean Air Legislation

Emissions	Clean Air Act	Clear Skies	Clean Power Act
Carbon Dioxide (CO_2)	Not addressed	No caps	Stabilize emissions to 1990 levels by 2008
Mercury	90% Reduction by 2007	69% Reduction by 2018	90% Reduction by 2008
Nitrogen Oxides	60% Reduction by 2012	67% Reduction by 2018	75% Reduction by 2008
Sulfur Dioxides	80% Reduction by 2010	73% Reduction by 2018	75% Reduction by 2008
Grandfather of Older Plants	Older plants are reviewed on a case-by-case basis through the New Source Review Process	No requirements	Older plants must comply by their thirtieth birthday or within five years of enactment, whichever is longer

As you can see by these numbers, President Bush's plan just about guts the 1970 Clean Air Act and pushes back targets 6 to 11 years, depending on the type of emission. The primary contributor of all these emissions is older power plants, which Bush wants to exempt from the regulations altogether.

> ## Slick Sayings
>
> The administration is currently focused on attempts to avoid implementation of the existing clean air regulations. The administration bill threatens public health by delaying pollution cleanup required by simply enforcing the current law.
>
> —John Kirkwood, president and CEO of the American Lung Association, February 28, 2003, story from the *Environmental News Service*

The Connection Between Air Pollution and Human Health

So what are the health effects of these emissions? The Environmental Protection Agency (EPA) told the Senate Environmental Committee in 2001 that the annual health impact from nitrogen oxides and sulfur dioxides is 10,800 premature deaths and over 1.5 million lost work days. Damage to our environment from acid rain attacks soils and plants, and deposits nitrogen in critical bodies of water.

Eric Schaeffer, head of the EPA's Office of Regulatory Enforcement resigned in protest on February 27, 2002, because of Bush's assault on the Clean Air Act. In his resignation letter he said:

> ... I cannot leave without sharing my frustration about the fate of our enforcement actions against power companies that have violated the Clean Air Act. Between November 1999 and December 2000, EPA filed lawsuits against nine power companies for expanding their plants without obtaining New Source Review permits and the up-to-date pollution controls required by law. The companies named in our lawsuits emit an incredible 5 million tons of sulfur dioxide [Sox] every year (a quarter of the emissions in the entire country) as well as 2 million tons of nitrogen oxide [Nox] ...

> Fifteen months ago, it looked as though our lawsuits were going to shrink these dismal statistics, when EPA publicly announced agreements with Cinergy and Vepco to reduce Sox and Nox emissions by a combined 750,000 tons per year. Settlements already lodged with two other companies—TECO and PSE&G—will eventually take another quarter million tons per year. And that does not count the hundreds of thousands of additional tons that can be obtained from other companies with whom we have been negotiating ...

Slick Sayings

The Clear Skies proposal was written with industry profits in mind, not Americans' need for cleaner air and water. This policy would undermine current environmental law, subject communities to more local pollution, and leave the Northeast to the ravages of acid rain.

—Senator Patrick Leahy in an Earth-Day Press release in April 2002

Yet today, we seem about to snatch defeat from the jaws of victory. We are in the ninth month of a "90-day review" to reexamine the law, and fighting a White House that seems determined to weaken the rules we are trying to enforce. It is hard to know which is worse—the endless delay or the repeated leaks by energy industry lobbyists of draft rule changes that would undermine lawsuits already filed. At their heart, these proposals would turn narrow exemptions into larger loopholes that would allow old "grandfathered" plants to be continually rebuilt (and emissions to increase) without modern pollution controls.

Schaeffer's fears finally were proven when the Bush administration introduced the "Clear Skies" initiative that drops any requirements for the older, grandfathered plants to add modern pollution controls.

The Industry's So-Called Solution

The industry's answer to global warming is to cut problem emissions on a voluntary basis by 18 percent in the next 10 years. This was announced as part of a plan led by U.S. Energy Secretary Spencer Abraham. The plan was developed by a task force he led with major U.S. energy industries. The World Resources Institute (an environmental research and policy institute) looked at the plan and found that it actually would result in a 15 percent increase in the same emissions that are blamed for accelerating global warming.

The States Revolt

Just as we were putting the finishing touches on this book, the news magazine website *Salon* reported that a bipartisan group of Northeastern governors were expected to announce a historic agreement to reduce carbon dioxide emissions from power plants. This agreement would be a major break with the Bush administration policy on global warming.

The agreement could result in mandatory greenhouse-gas emissions caps, which would put the United States closer to complying with the Kyoto Protocol. Republican governors from as many as six states in the Mid-Atlantic and New England regions are expected to sign on, ignoring pressure from the Bush administration, because they say it would benefit the environment as well as the economy in their states, according to the *Salon* report. Four states mentioned as likely signers include New York, Connecticut, Vermont, and New Hampshire. New York Republican Governor George Pataki led the Republican side of this effort.

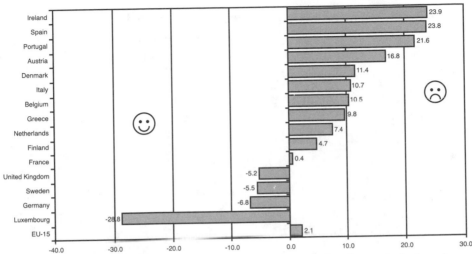

This chart released by the European Environmental Agency shows how few countries have been able to even come close to their emissions targets. On the chart, the "0.0" line is each country's target. Those countries within the segment with a happy "smiley" have exceeded their target, while the countries in the segment with the frowning icon show how far the country is from meeting targets.

Coming to Terms with Kyoto

European countries are already beginning to discover how difficult it will be to meet targets set in the Kyoto Protocol. According to a study released by the European Environmental Agency on May 3, 2003, European Union (EU) emissions have increased for the second year in a row.

As the world looks for solutions to our global warming problem, it is also balancing this with ways to meet our energy needs. Finding acceptable energy solutions and moving away from oil may be the answer to finding the right balance. In our next chapter, we'll do some crystal-ball gazing to look at these questions and review possible solutions.

Petro-Facts

Insurance companies are becoming concerned about the potential risks for companies that aren't doing enough to reduce their emissions. They are concerned about suits that could be filed against companies they insure, should those companies fail to comply with expected government restrictions.

The Least You Need to Know

◆ Global warming is a generally accepted problem. The key controversies surround how serious the problem is and how can it be fixed.

◆ Only two countries have rejected the Kyoto Protocol, which is the globally accepted way of fixing the global warming problem—the United States and Australia. Russia has said it would ratify the Protocol, but is stalling its decision pending a fall 2003 conference in the United States.

◆ The Bush administration is pushing for a plan that is more industry-friendly and actually reduces goals set in the 1970 and 1990 Clean Air Acts.

26

Crystal-Ball Gazing

In This Chapter

◆ The rising demand for oil

◆ Reaching peak production

◆ Looking to alternatives

◆ Facing the facts

Everyone wants to know the answer to the multibillion-dollar question: When will we run out of oil? Just in case you missed it earlier, oil is a non-renewable energy source and there's no question that the wells will run dry at some point in the future. When we'll reach that point, or even if we will reach that point before we find alternative energy sources, is at the center of all discussions regarding the future of oil.

Demanding More Energy

No one doubts that we are going to need more energy. While the developed countries' hunger for energy continues to grow, the developing countries are beginning to look for their fair share. In fact, by 2025, the U.S. Energy Information Administration (EIA) estimates that the developing world will most likely come close to needing the same amount of energy as the developed world. In 2001, developing nations consumed about 64 percent as much oil as the industrialized nations. The EIA expects that number to jump to about 85 percent by 2025.

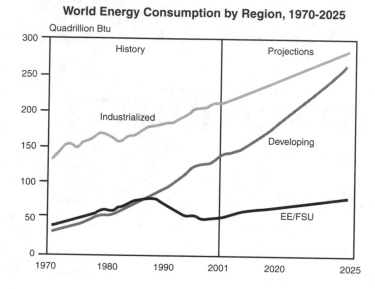

World Energy Consumption by Region, 1970-2025

This chart from the U.S. Energy Information Administration shows that while energy consumption will continue to grow at a gradual pace for the industrialized world, the developing world's consumption will shoot up more dramatically. Eastern European and Former Soviet Union countries' (EE/FSU) consumption will also rise at a gradual pace.

(Sources: History: Energy Information Administration, International Energy Annual 2001, DOE/EIA-0219 [2001] [Washington, D.C., February 2003]. Projections: EIA, System for the Analysis of Global Energy Markets [2003].)

In addition, the EIA expects that oil will retain its predominance in the global mix over the next 24 years, even as new technologies penetrate the market.

Natural gas is projected to be the fastest source of primary energy growth during this period, as industrialized nations shift to natural gas in response to the need for cleaner energy sources to meet the goals of global-warming treaty, the Kyoto Protocol (see Chapter 25). The EIA expects natural-gas consumption to double to 176 trillion cubic feet by 2025. The natural-gas share of total energy consumption is predicted to jump from 23 percent in 2001 to 28 percent by 2025. The consumption of natural gas for electricity generation is projected to jump into majority status of 53 percent by 2025. (Coal, not oil, will be the primary loser in this scenario.)

Even though the technology already exists to create energy from renewable resources such as the sun, wind, and water (see Chapter 22), the EIA doesn't expect renewable energy sources to make a major impact on energy consumption between now and 2025 in the United States. In fact, the EIA estimates an average increase of only about 1.9 percent per year in that period unless there is significant government support to help make renewable energy sources more competitive economically.

However, the EIA does expect the developing world to invest heavily in renewable energy sources. China, India, Malaysia, and Vietnam are constructing or planning large-scale hydroelectric projects. The first electric generating unit for China's 18,200-megawatt Three Gorges Dam project is expected to be installed in 2003. India is set to begin the final phase of building its dam by filling the reservoir for a 2,000 megawatt Tehri dam, and Malaysia awarded the main construction contract for its 2,400-megawatt Bakun dam in 2003 as well.

Petro-Facts

China's electricity demand is expected to triple by 2025.

Petro-Facts

One of reasons that no one can be sure how much oil is actually left in the ground is the politics of reporting oil reserves. Many suspect that OPEC countries pump up their estimated reserves because each country's production quotas are based on the size of their reserves. In fact, in 1988 and 1990, many Middle-Eastern countries increased their reserve totals even though there were no new oil discoveries. According to the major industry trackers, *World Oil* and *Oil and Gas Journal*, global oil reserves jumped 39 percent from 708 billion barrels in 1986 to 983 billion barrels in 1990.

Making Energy Choices

We clearly are at a crossroads, and we need to choose a direction for our energy future. Royal/Dutch Shell has developed two potential scenarios, depending on the choices that we make today. They call the scenario, in which we continue to rely heavily on nonrenewable resources and only develop alternatives as necessity dictates, "Dynamics as Usual." The second scenario, "Spirit of the Coming Age," describes a situation in which we actively pursue alternatives to oil. Let's look at what is predicted to happen within each possibility.

Dynamics as Usual

This world option focuses on a slower shift to clean, secure, and increasingly sustainable energy. In this timeline, Shell predicts that people will follow this path:

2005   Hybrid vehicles proliferate.

2010   World will start the dash for natural gas or renewable energy sources.

2015   Oil-price shocks will trigger a more rapid move toward alternatives.

2020   About 20 percent of the electrical needs in industrialized countries are generated by renewable sources, as well as 10 percent of all global primary energy needs. Growth is then expected to slow as rural communities deny support for more wind-energy farms, and protests arise against development of other major renewable-energy development. Some moves are made to increase nuclear power.

2030   Nuclear power growth stalls, and the final push for the next generation of renewable energy emerges.

2040   Oil scarcity arrives, and biofuels finally start their major expansion.

Spirit of the Coming Age

This scenario predicts a much more rapid shift to revolutionary new energy ideas:

2005   First stationary and vehicular hydrogen fuel cells hit the market and there is high consumer interest.

2010   Fuel-cell distribution innovations help the market to grow rapidly. Renewable energy sources fill niche market needs.

2015   World converges around fuel cells for transport and stationary uses, such as heating homes and running industrial complexes.

2020   Unconventional oil and gas expand in China and India. Fuel cells reach 25 percent of sales in the industrialized world.

2030   Use of hydrogen expands, and renewables are pulled along because of the strong hydrogen expansion.

2040   Hydrogen expands rapidly and becomes the primary energy source of the future.

> **Slick Sayings**
>
> The internal combustion engine will go by the way of the horse. It will be a curiosity to my grandchildren.
>
> —Geoffrey Ballad, founder of Ballard Fuel Cells

Which of the two scenarios do you think is most likely?

Acknowledging the Inevitable

Many wonder when the major oil companies will accept the inevitable. As noted previously, many people question whether it makes sense to spend billions of dollars on more oil exploration, while the world destroys sensitive ecological areas. Instead, they believe that we should shift as quickly as possible to cleaner-burning natural gas and work to develop renewable energy sources more rapidly to rid ourselves of the oil addiction.

The Kyoto Protocol on global warming is certainly helping to turn the tide in the alternative-fuel direction as industrialized nations look for ways to meet their targets for reducing emissions from burning coal and oil. For instance, Denmark expects windmills to provide half of its energy needs by 2030. Wind power dominates Europe's planning, which expects 22 percent of its energy to come from renewables by 2010.

Solar power is also seeing somewhat of a boom, growing at a rate of 26 to 42 percent a year based on research by the Rocky Mountain Institute. Most of this growth is happening in small, new-home projects or in construction of new commercial buildings.

Shell is certainly taking the lead of the oil industry and setting itself up to be able to meet the demands for whichever scenario takes hold. Its two divisions—Shell Renewables and Shell Hydrogen—are being given the necessary corporate resources to support their development.

Most of the other oil major oil companies are giving lip service to the push for renewables and hydrogen, if they mention it at all. In a February 11, 2003, speech, ExxonMobil Chairman and Chief Executive Officer Lee R. Raymond made the following statement:

> We expect conventional fuels will remain the dominant energy source, at least through the mid-century. I would note that we project wind and solar energy will continue to grow rapidly, but only due to government policies and incentives, not market economics. To put this in perspective, solar power can cost somewhere between $100–$250 per barrel of oil equivalent. The intermittent nature of solar energy can bring on additional costs.
>
> Starting from such a low base today, wind and solar are unlikely to exceed a 1 percent share of the world's energy needs by 2020, even with double-digit growth rates. Thus, oil and gas—representing 60 percent of energy supplies today—will remain the dominant energy source until at least the middle of this century.

In Closing

These are just a few examples of the energy choices we'll need to make in the near future. How these questions are answered will determine the paths the countries of the world choose. There is no question that the politics of oil will be a factor in how different countries determine their energy future.

The Least You Need to Know

- ◆ Oil consumption will continue to rise through 2025, with the developing world claiming the largest share of that increase.

- ◆ Oil production is nearing its peak, which could come as early as 2010.

- ◆ The world now has to make the choice of whether to work toward weaning itself from oil dependence or putting its head in the sand and waiting until resources are scarce.

Glossary

asphalt   Also known as pitch or bitumen, is formed naturally when petroleum bubbles to the surface and the gases trapped inside evaporate. In modern times, asphalt is one of the products left behind after crude oil is distilled for various uses.

bitumen   A black, tarry substance that is found in abundant deposits in many places, including the Dead and Caspian Seas.

blowouts   In the oil industry, these are a sudden escape of gas or liquid from a well.

catagenesis   The process that transforms carbon molecules into petroleum.

coal oil   A fuel extracted from coal by heating the coal to just below the burning point and condensing the gas that's emitted. Kerosene has the same chemical makeup, although it's extracted from petroleum.

cogeneration   A group of technologies being developed that enable companies to make use of heat generated from a primary energy source that is currently being wasted. Various new technologies are being developed that enable companies to capture this heat and use it to provide steam or hot water to meet onsite energy needs.

coltan   An ore found in the Congo. Its scientific name is *columbite tantalite*. In its refined form, it becomes a heat-resistant powder that holds a high electrical charge, making it perfect for capacitors in laptops, cell phones, and other electronic devices. Congolese factions battling over coltan deposits have killed several million people since the 1990s.

double-hulled tankers Ships built for transporting oil and other products that have a second hull built inside the outer hull, so that a collision or running aground will, in theory at least, not rupture both hulls and cause a spill. In addition, many double-hulled vessels have two engine rooms, two rudders, and twin propellers, all to make sure the vessel can maneuver should one system become crippled.

fixed platform A type of offshore-drilling platform designed for water depths of less than 1,500 feet, it is constructed by driving tubular steel piles into the seabed. The deck of the platform provides crew quarters, drilling and production facilities.

Floating Production Storage and Offloading Systems (FPSO) Large, tanker-like vessels moored to the ocean floor for use in offshore drilling. FPSO vessels process and store production from nearby offshore wells.

hydrogen The most abundant element in the universe that might in the future replace petroleum as the world's primary energy source. The colorless, highly flammable gaseous element is used in the production of synthetic ammonia and methanol, in petroleum refining, and in rocket fuels.

hydrogenation A key purification process used in both the refining and petrochemical industries.

Individual Indian Money Trust Set up by Congress in 1887 after the government forcibly or by treaty relocated Indian tribes from 90 million acres of their land and gave it to white settlers. About 300,000 American Indians are entitled to royalties from about 54 million acres of land. Payments of these royalties have been sporadic.

kerosene A fuel extracted from petroleum by condensing the vapor that boils off between 300 and 525 degrees Fahrenheit. It has the same chemical makeup as coal oil.

lacustrine Anything having to do with a lake. It is in shallow lakes and basins that tiny critters died to form oil.

Land and Water Conservation Fund A fund administered by the National Park Service and used to purchase parks and recreation areas and to plan, acquire, and develop land and water resources for recreational use. It is funded in part through revenues from federal oil leases.

Metagenesis A geological phase that must be avoided to form oil, because this combination of extreme heat and pressure, with temperatures above 390 degrees Fahrenheit, makes the carbon unstable and converts it not into oil, but into graphite and, eventually, pure carbon.

naphtha A light element of petroleum used to make gasoline. Naphtha also is used in the production of solvents and feedstocks for the petrochemical industry.

National Petroleum Reserve – Alaska A federal oil reserve that was established in the 1923 by the Navy, which began active exploration in 1974. The Naval Petroleum Reserves Production Act of 1976 transferred responsibility for the area to the Department of the Interior. Today the Interior Department's Bureau of Land Management (BLM) manages oil and gas leases for the 23 million acres in the reserve.

oil sands A mixture of bitumen, sand, water, and clay that can be processed into synthetic crude.

oligopoly A market in which there are few sellers. This gives the few existing sellers the ability to affect price and have a strong impact on competitors. In this type of market there are also significant barriers to entry. For example, the expense of building a refinery is so high that it is rare for a new competitor to enter the market.

Organization for Cooperation and Economic Development (OCED) An association formed among the Europeans and Americans in 1961 to maintain the free flow of oil.

Organization of Petroleum Exporting Countries (OPEC) Cartel that was started in 1960 in Baghdad to maintain a high price for oil. Saudi Arabia is the leader of OPEC, which includes Algeria, Indonesia, Iran, Iraq, Kuwait, Libya, Nigeria, Qatar, the United Arab Emirates, and Venezuela.

percussive drilling A petroleum extraction technique that probes the earth for oil by pounding down and digging in. The system was invented by the Chinese around 600 B.C.E. and was in use until the nineteenth century, when the first rotary drills were developed.

reciprocating engine An engine that uses a piston to compress air (or a mixture of air and fuel) until that compressed material is either ignited (like in an automobile engine) or the compressed steam expands (like in Watt's engine). In both cases, the piston is forced down in the cylinder.

retail price The price you pay for a product in the store.

seep oil The term applied to any form of crude oil that seeps to the surface from underground "springs," from eroding rocks rich in hydrocarbons, and from fissures leading to oil deposits.

seismic imaging Technique used by researchers in search of oil. It sends shock waves through rock layers (usually by detonating an explosive). These waves are then interpreted using high-speed computer software. The type or density of the rock layers can be determined by reading these waves in order to determine if there are signs of oil and gas deposits.

solar cells   Also called photovoltaic cells, they convert sunlight into electricity. These were first used in space to power satellites, but today they are used throughout the world to capture the power of the sun. Photovoltaics are versatile. They can be used to power tiny objects such as watches, or can be built as a grid to power large urban areas.

SPAR drilling and production platforms   Large, cylindrical platforms supported by buoyancy chambers and moored to the seafloor are used for offshore drilling. These platforms can be operated in more than 8,000 feet of water and can be moved easily.

stratigraphic trap   Any layer of impenetrable rock that traps oil or natural gas underneath it, acting as a sort of dam and forcing the petroleum to accumulate.

synthetic crude   An oil-like substance that's created from nonpetroleum based products.

tension leg platforms (TLPs)   Platforms that are moored to the ocean floor by high strength cables, giving the platform vertical and lateral stability when drilling oil offshore. These platforms provide crew quarters, drilling rigs, and production facilities and can withstand hurricane-force winds and waves.

wholesale price   The price that the store owner pays to get the product from his or her supplier.

wildcatter   Speculators who mine for minerals or drill oil wells in areas that are not known to be productive. These are the people or companies who take the initial risks to figure out whether an area might hide a potential gold mine or oil rich reservoir.

Further Reading

Government Departments and Agencies

The key agencies involved in issues surrounding oil and politics are listed in the following sections.

Department of Energy

There are numerous key links for the Department of Energy. The main site is at www.energy.gov/.

Energy Information Administration, which collects and reports key energy data, is at www.eia.doe.gov/.

Fossil Energy information is at www.fe.doe.gov/.

Energy Efficiency and Renewable Energy is at www.eere.energy.gov/.

Federal Energy Regulatory Commission (FERC), which is an independent regulatory agency within the Department of Energy, regulates the transmission of oil and gas by pipeline, as well as other energy transmission. You can find out more about FERC at www.ferc.gov/.

National Renewable Energy Laboratory is the primary Department of Energy research facility for renewable and energy efficient resources. You can visit it at www.nrel.gov/.

Information about the U.S. push to develop a hydrogen-powered FreedomCar is at www.eere.energy.gov/hydrogenfuel/.

Department of the Interior

Here are key links for the Department of the Interior:

The main site is www.doi.gov/.

The Bureau of Land Management, which manages 264 million acres of public lands, is at www.blm.gov/nhp/index.htm.

Minerals Management Service, which manages the natural gas, oil, and mineral leasing programs, is at www.mms.gov/.

Environmental Protection Agency

The main site for the Environmental Protection Agency is at www.epa.gov.

The Clear Skies Initiative, which is the Bush administration alternative to the Clean Air Act, is at www.epa.gov/clearskies/.

Cleaner Diesel, which supports and promotes clean diesel engines, is at www.epa.gov/diesel/.

Combined Heat and Power Partnership, which promotes cogeneration, is at www.epa.gov/chp/.

NOAA Office of Response and Restoration

The National Oceanic and Atmospheric Association's Office of Response and Restoration responds to oil and other spills of other hazardous materials. The office also helps emergency planners prepare for potential accidents and manages software, databases, and other tools to help people respond to accidents. You can find out more about its work at http://response.restoration.noaa.gov/.

Oil-Industry Associations

There are hundreds of oil industry sites on the Internet, including one for each of the major oil companies.

American Petroleum Institute

The API, which represents more than 400 member companies, is a great jumping-off point for U.S. oil companies and related industries. The main site is at http://api-ep.api.org/. A wealth of resources and links can be found at http://api-ec.api.org/links/index.cfm?bitmask=001008000000000000. Links to global companies such as BP and Royal Dutch/Shell are also included.

Canadian Association of Petroleum Producers

To find out more about the Canadian oil companies, go to www.capp.ca.

Association for the Study of Peak Oil

ASPO tracks the predicted decline of oil production. Find out more at www.peakoil.net.

Alternative Energy Sources

Here are some key places to find out more about alternative energy resources:

Fuel Cells

California Fuel-Cell Partnership can keep you up-to-date on fuel cell news at http://cafcp.org/index.html. The two key fuel-cell developers are Ballard (www.ballard.com) and UTC Fuel Cells (www.ifc.com).

Environmental Defense

Environmental Defense is a national nonprofit organization that links science, economics, and law to create innovative, equitable, and cost-effective solutions to environmental problems. For example, it is sponsoring an ongoing project with FedEx and Eaton Corporation that involves a low-emission, hybrid electric-powered delivery vehicle. FedEx is currently testing this vehicle for its fleet. You can find out more about Environmental Defense's work at www.environmentaldefense.org/home.cfm.

Rocky Mountain Institute

The Rocky Mountain Institute focuses on energy policy and looks for ways to encourage the shift to alternative energy sources. You can find out more about its research at www.rmi.org/. One of its research projects is a fuel-efficient car called the Hypercar. Find out more at www.hypercar.com.

Solar Energy

Find out more about solar energy at the Solar Electric Power Association at www.solarelectricpower.org/.

Wind Energy

Keep up on wind energy news at www.windustry.org/.

Index

partnership with Shell Transport and Trading Company, 113

Royal Dutch/Shell deal, 113-114

Russian Siberian Tundra, 27

Tundra of North-Central Russia, 25

S

SAGD (steam-assisted gravity drainage) technology, 250

Samuel, Marcus

contract with Rothschilds, 113

Royal Dutch/Shell merger, 114

Shell, 96-97

Shell-Guffy deal, 97

Saudi Arabia, oil concessions, 153-154

sea birds, effects of oil spills on, 231

seep oil

pollution problems (oceans), 225

Titusville, 55-58

Senate Permanent Committee on Investigations, 209

Seneca Oil Company

Drake, Edwin L., 59-60

Townsend, Robert, 58-60

sheep breeding, 49

Shell

Royal Dutch/Shell

deal with Rothschilds, 113-114

Fortune Global 500 rankings, 114

mergers, 114

Samuel, Marcus, 96-97

Shell-Guffy deal, 97

Sherman Anti-Trust Act, 106

Shiite Muslims, 151

shipping oil

Elizabeth Watts, 72-73

hot spots

Bab el-Mandab, 265

Bosporus/Turkish Straits, 266

Strait of Hormuz, 266

Strait of Malacca, 266

Suez Canal and pipeline, 266

spills

Amoco Cadiz, 228

clean-up operations, 234-235

effects of, 230-232

Exxon Valdez, 229

prevention, 235-236

Sinclair Oil, 108

Sinclair, Harry, Teapot Dome scandal, 133-134

sinking wells

moving oil from the ground to the surface, 25

tips, 23-24

Smith, William "Uncle Billy," Titusville, 60-61

Socal, 108

social implications, modern oil-based economy progression

agricultural revolution, 48

middle class, 49-50

sheep breeding, 49

Socony, 107

Sohio, 107

solar power

concentrating solar power, 242

daylighting, 242

hot water and space heating and cooling systems, 243

passive solar heating and cooling, 242

solar cells, 242

SOMO (State Oil Marketing Organization), 170

sources of oil

Afghanistan, 27

Algeria, 28

Bay of Campeche, 26

Caspian Sea region, 26

Central China, 27

development of new oil sources

Africa, 262

Angola, 263

Gabon, 263

Libya, 264

Nigeria, 263

Caspian Sea, 260-262

Central and South America, 264

Persian Gulf, 262

Russia, 258, 260

Gulf of Mexico, 26

Kashmir, 27

Libya, 26

Nigeria, 26

North Sea, 26

North Slope of Alaska, 26

Pakistan, 27

Russian Siberian Tundra, 27

Southern Caspian/Iran region, 27

Texas, 28

Tundra of North-Central Russia, 25

Venezuela, 26

Western Canada, 28

A Little Knowledge Goes a Long Way ...

Check Out These
Best-Selling
COMPLETE IDIOT'S GUIDES

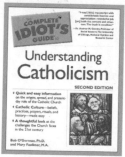

Understanding Catholicism
SECOND EDITION

1-59257-085-2
$18.95

Learning Spanish
THIRD EDITION

0-02-864451-4
$18.95

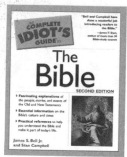

The Bible
SECOND EDITION

0-02-864382-8
$18.95

Feng Shui
SECOND EDITION

0-02-864339-9
$18.95

Playing the Guitar
SECOND EDITION

0-02-864244-9
$21.95 w/CD-ROM

Personal Finance in Your 20s & 30s
SECOND EDITION

0-02-864374-7
$19.95

Creating a Web Page
FIFTH EDITION

0-02-864316-X
$24.95 w/CD-ROM

Digital Photography
THIRD EDITION

0-02-864453-0
$19.95

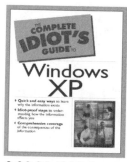

Windows XP

0-02-864232-5
$19.95

More than *400 titles* in *26 different categories*
Available at booksellers everywhere

ALPHA